PLATO'

PLATO'S WORLD
MAN'S PLACE IN THE COSMOS

JOSEPH CROPSEY

THE UNIVERSITY OF CHICAGO PRESS

CHICAGO & LONDON

THE UNIVERSITY OF CHICAGO PRESS, CHICAGO 60637
THE UNIVERSITY OF CHICAGO PRESS, LTD., LONDON

© 1995 by The University of Chicago
All rights reserved. Published 1995
Paperback edition 1997
Printed in the United States of America
04 03 02 01 00 99 98 97   2 3 4 5
ISBN: 0-226-12121-6   (cloth)
ISBN: 0-226-12122-4   (paperback)

Library of Congress Cataloging-in-Publication Data

Cropsey, Joseph.
    Plato's world : man's place in the cosmos / Joseph Cropsey.
        p.   cm.
    Includes bibliographical references and index.
    1. Plato.   2. Socrates   3. Man   4. Plato—Political and social
views.   5. Political science—Philosophy.   I. Title.
B398.C66C76   1995
184—dc20   94-34538
                                                CIP

To L L C

CONTENTS

PREFACE
ix

INTRODUCTION
1

I PROTAGORAS 3

II THEAETETUS 27

III EUTHYPHRO 62

IV SOPHIST 69

V STATESMAN 111

VI APOLOGY OF SOCRATES 145

VII CRITO 166

VIII PHAEDO 175

SELECTIVE INDEX OF NAMES
227

PREFACE

THERE ARE AT LEAST THREE PRINCIPLES ON WHICH THE DIALOGUES of Plato, or some of them, can be arranged to form a general schema. The first to be employed was the ancient grouping of the dialogues in the famous tetralogies according to their perceived subject or other attribute. This principle, no longer popular, produced a result described in detail by Diogenes Laertius (3.57–62). In later times the effort has been made repeatedly and of necessity inconclusively to arrange the dialogues in the order of their composition, perhaps on the basis of perceived differences in the writing style presumed to be characteristic of a younger or older author, such speculation fortified when possible with the more objective information provided by occasional internal references to historical events. It would be more than merely interesting, it would be important, to know the order in which Plato wrote his works, so that one might observe and be instructed by the progress of Plato's understanding. For better or worse, however, the project for establishing the order of composition will continue to generate uncertain results unless records of sufficient antiquity and authority, themselves untainted with conjecture, dispose of the matter.

Under the circumstances it may be considered fortunate that it is possible to know beyond a doubt the sequential order of some of the Platonic dialogues, though surely not of all. Because of things said within the dialogues themselves, it is incontrovertible that the *Republic, Timaeus,* and *Critias* relate discourses that took place in that order and consecutively. Their order is not conjectural. The interpreter is relieved of the task of defining their sequence and is made responsible instead for attempting to understand the three in the light of the unity among them that Plato has made so obtrusively obvious. In the present book, the guiding but not determining fact is that there is an unbroken dramatic sequence, guaranteed by the speeches of Socrates himself, that arranges *Theaetetus, Euthyphro, Cratylus, Sophist, Statesman, Apology of Socrates, Crito,* and *Phaedo* in that order, a sequence that makes of them an evident entity and thus a true hermeneutic object. I have deviated from the indication of Plato by including *Protagoras* and omitting *Cratylus,* the former because of the heavy involvement of a number of the dialogues with the teaching of Protagoras and the latter because the reference of the nature of speech to the existence of the things in themselves raises questions that are sufficiently attended to in the other texts.

The effort to arrange the dialogues in the order of their composition and the project for interpreting them in their dramatic order when such an order is evident can hardly be said to preclude one another. Judgments will differ regarding the feasibility of each enterprise and the usefulness of the products that they respectively generate. In any case, it is more profitable to weigh the product than the method.

I have been unable to benefit from scholarship on the precise subject of this volume because I have not discovered any that bears on my project as a whole, namely, to search for the meaning of the texts that by Plato's explicit indication cohere as a Socratic valedictory.

In this effort, during the many years it has preoccupied me, I have received the generous support of the Earhart Foundation. It is my pleasure to acknowledge with grateful appreciation the unstinted encouragement of the officers and trustees of the Foundation.

I am grateful to Dr. Gayle McKeen for her dedicated assistance, and I wish to thank John Tryneski and Margaret Mahan at the University of Chicago Press for all their help in seeing this work to its present state.

The chapter on *Protagoras* is reprinted with a few revisions by permission of the editors of *Interpretation*, where it appeared in volume 19, number 2 (1991–92).

INTRODUCTION

THIS BOOK IS AN INQUIRY INTO THE CONSEQUENCES OF ONE EVI-
dent fact, namely, that Plato dates *Theaetetus* in the life of Socrates by concluding that dialogue with Socrates' announcement
that he is leaving his companions so that he may go to the place of the
judicial officer of Athens, hence to what proves to be the scene of *Euthyphro*. Thus *Theaetetus,* and therefore the trilogy of which it is the
first element, are set in the period of Socrates' imminent trial. From
this it follows that the trilogy that begins with *Theaetetus* and ends
with the *Statesman* is joined with the trilogy that begins with Socrates'
Apology and ends with his death in *Phaedo*. This study explores the
meaning of these dialogues if they are considered as a dramatic
whole in sequence.

From the opening of *Theaetetus* and through the *Sophist* and
Statesman, Plato involves the meaning of the dialogues with the obtrusively non-Socratic identity of prominent participants, notably
Theodorus and Theaetetus and then the Eleatic Stranger, Protagorean
and Parmenidean respectively. I begin with a chapter on *Protagoras* as
a proemium to *Theaetetus*, wherein the power of the old sophist is felt.
Through the medium of the Protagorean geometers, the persistent
presence of the irrational or incommensurable in the natural world
becomes conspicuous. Then in *Theaetetus* the young interlocutor's attempt to identify knowledge as perception will elicit from Socrates
the revelation that that definition flows from Protagoras's doctrine of
"man the measure," making Protagoras eventually responsible for
the opinion that the corporeal is the true. As will be seen, Socrates will
denounce that opinion in the last hour of his life in a tacit gesture toward his old adversary. When the revisionist Parmenidean Stranger
enters as senior interlocutor in the subsequent dialogues, he will tell a
tale of the cosmos according to which the whole must spin either under the hand of god or according to its natural impetus, the latter being both the reverse of the former and the actual condition of the
world. In the event, neither the flux of Protagoras nor the immotility
of the whole taught by Parmenides teaches mankind how to live well
in the world. Much then transpires to elaborate the predicament of
humanity thrown so largely on its own resources within a nature that,

like Janus, shows two faces, one that shines on the beautiful, noble, and wise and another that countenances cruelty, meanness, and stupidity. As natural as the excellence of Socrates is the hatred and the folly that destroyed him. Pieties of one description or another may recoil from such a judgment on our natural matrix, but the current that runs in these dialogues bears the reader on from the examination of one human resource to the next in the search for the one that will save us without looking to the One in heaven. The geometers and the natural scientists are inadequate; the "wise" according to the measure of the sophists are a manifest failure; the statesmanly guide of our common existence in political society seems to be our last best hope, given what Socrates rightly or wrongly took to be the inevitable fate of one like himself who would allow his caring to govern his doings. So Socrates ends by singing a song of consolation to himself and edification for any who could hear and would listen. He dies as a poet because a philosopher must be a poet, however seldom the poets might have been philosophers.

Socrates' insistence that he is wise in knowing what he does not know is more than seemliness. It is the ground of his character as philosopher. The love of wisdom on the part of a human being who knows that his love must be imperfectly consummated is a love mixed with resignation and sustained by fortitude. The love that draws him on cannot exceed the courage that enables him to look into darkness without seeing defeat, as Socrates looked into death itself without surrendering. In the world that we inhabit, as these dialogues reveal it, philosophic *erōs* without philosophic *thumos* would be, perhaps, sophistry.

In making this inquiry I resolved to begin from the beginning and to take account, almost without exception, only of what appears in the texts. The general plan of the project was set out in a paper entitled "The Dramatic End of Plato's Socrates" presented at the meeting of the American Political Science Association in 1979. The study in its present form has the title *Plato's World* because, as it seems, in these conjoined dialogues Plato has achieved his cosmography.

I

PROTAGORAS

GIVEN THE DIALECTICAL CHARACTER OF THE PLATONIC WRITINGS individually, it is not surprising that the Platonic corpus as a whole consists as largely as it does of engagements with one or another alternative to the understandings of Plato/Socrates. It belongs to the genius of Plato that he constructed a universe out of elements that exist in a condition of mutual (dialectical) tension, in a tacit, however limited, concession to the cosmology of Stress. Expecting always the triumphant Socratic finale, even if in the form of aporia and achieved through never so many baited deferences, we come nevertheless to appreciate the seriousness with which Plato scanned the world of available wisdom—the care that he took to draw from Parmenides, for example, what that thinker kept in reserve against a rigid theory of Ideas; and from Protagoras, that chanticleer sophist, the wisdom that might lie in his version of the adage "virtue is knowledge." Plato's sifting of Protagoras runs through *Protagoras* and *Theaetetus*, the former dialogue addressing the climactic question of the coming to be of good and evil among men, the latter the companion question, What is knowledge? If virtue is knowledge, as Socrates must forever insist, then why is virtue not transmissible just as knowledge is transmissible in the act of teaching? And if virtue cannot be somehow "taught," what becomes of the moral pedagogy by which the best political constitution stands or falls? *Protagoras*, on the bringing of good among men (if not by teaching, then how?), is a spacious portal into the Platonic edifice.

The dialogue is made to begin with an encounter between Socrates and "a friend," a chance meeting that occasions Socrates' recounting a discussion from which he has just departed. Since the dialogue itself, i.e., that very discussion, ended with Socrates remarking that he was already late for some business elsewhere, the fact that he is "now" volunteering to repeat the entire proceedings makes it as clear to us as it needs to be that, if he had indeed any affairs elsewhere, they must have been the opposite of pressing. His approach to Protagoras had been at the instance of another, but the impulse to leave him seems to have been more entirely his own. We may speculate that at the time when Socrates terminated it with the fabrication of another démand on his attention, the conversation had been squeezed dry of further benefit or interest.

As SOCRATES TELLS THE STORY, HE GOES TO PROTAGORAS, WHO IS VISIT-ing Athens, because a self-centered young bumbler named Hippo-crates wishes to attach himself to Protagoras as a pupil and considers that an introduction by Socrates would be helpful in gaining him ad-mission to the Protagorean circle. With a patience that thrives best in fiction, Socrates allows himself to be awakened by Hippocrates so long in advance of dawn that the young man has to feel his way around the bed in order to find a place to seat himself. Declaring to Socrates, of all people, that Protagoras is the only wise man, and that he, Hippocrates, aspires to be wise in the same mode, he gives Socrates an opening for some inquiry into the mercenary ways of the sophists. Of course he cannot do this without referring to the sophists as such and by that name. The revelation to Hippocrates that he will end by standing before the Greeks as a sophist raises a blush on his face that can be seen by the light of the barely breaking dawn. More passes as they make their way toward Protagoras, Socrates alerting the youth to the spiritual perils of trusting himself to poorly under-stood mentors. The wind of disparagement continues to blow against the sophists as the two reach the door of Callias's house, where Protagoras is lodging. Their knock is answered by an emasculated servant whose deprivation inhibits in no way the expression of his contempt for the sophists he takes Socrates and Hippocrates to be. Apparently, and as will soon be confirmed when the conversation de-velops indoors, contempt for the sophists is rife in Greece; and as we have seen at the door, it extends to the lowest of the low. That *Protagoras* acquired the subtitle "Sophists: Accusatory" is under-standable, ultimately misleading though that indication will prove to be. We may well wonder why those virtuosi of rhetoric did not en-gender a better opinion of themselves in the world; whether their ob-loquy is not the unavoidable fate of those whose concern for the truth of their arguments seems subordinated to cleverness or advantage. But it would be well for us to reserve judgment on the sophists, for, as will soon appear, so far as Protagoras is representative of them while being perhaps the best among them, their principles do not seem out-rageous or absurd.

Having gained access to Callias's house, Socrates and Hippocrates come upon a telling scene: Protagoras in ambulatory discourse followed by a coterie of acolytes who form up behind him in twin columns, part before him as he reverses direction, and fall in astern once more, ears straining. The sophists Hippias and Prodicus are described in their respective peculiar postures, enlightening sundry adherents. If there is anything serious about the sophists, Plato will introduce it gradually.

Now it is time for Socrates to proceed with the introduction of the hopeful Hippocrates to Protagoras. Since it is the purpose of Hippocrates to advance himself in Athenian life by deploying what he will learn from Protagoras, the latter is grateful for Socrates' delicacy in leaving it up to him whether he will hear Hippocrates' application in private or before the company: local citizenries do not always take kindly to the interference of a foreigner who claims a power to teach their young the arts of ambition. Evidently, Protagoras is alert to the danger of appearing to corrupt the young, even if the appearance attaches unjustly to an effort to improve them. It is out of vanity, Socrates suspects, that Protagoras now prefers that the proceedings go on before the whole company. In the course of declaring his preference for an open interview, Protagoras makes an important observation on the history of the sophists: they constitute an ancient esoteric order whose members include some of the most famous men of Greece: poets, seers, athletes, musicians, and many more—all of them teachers. Homer and Hesiod themselves, and Simonides, were of the number. All sought to conceal their sophistry. They hoodwinked the vulgar, of course, but could not conceal their purpose from the powerful and worldly. He, Protagoras, alone proclaims his sophistry from the housetops, not claiming for himself any superior honesty but doing so out of an unwillingness to bear the humiliation of being caught in a deception he knows is bound to fail. This admitted calculation deserves the reader's respectful attention; the "consequentialist" principle that underlies it will play an important part in the moral doctrine that Socrates himself will develop later.

What suspect practice is it that Protagoras confesses to perpetrate as a sophist, and in which he by indirection implicates the entire brotherhood? Nothing less than "educating men" (*Protagoras* 317B). Why does this philanthropic impulse generate universal revulsion? Because it is a private usurpation of a public prerogative? Because it is done for gain? Because it is artful, using and communicating a profane sorcery? Every one of these possibilities is disposed of in what follows. Protagoras will argue persuasively that men are endowed but not sufficiently endowed with the arts of sociality, in which they do indeed need further cultivation. He charges no fixed fee for his instruction but permits his pupils to pay him whatever they declare on oath to be the value to them of his teaching. (And why should sophistry not get the benefit of the distinction of the teaching art and the moneymaking art?) Finally, Protagoras has exactly renounced secrecy and displayed himself before the Greeks for what he is. We know where our sympathies and antipathies are supposed to lie, but we are less certain, at the moment, of their ground.

Socrates would like Protagoras to tell Hippocrates what the association the latter is seeking would do for him. The general answer is that it would improve him. Socrates wonders how. Protagoras now, once again, distinguishes himself from the herd of sophists, men who do no better than purvey the usual arts—arithmetic, astronomy, geometry, music—while he, Protagoras, teaches how best to manage one's household and how to be most effective, in speech and deed, in the affairs of the city: in brief, "the political art, and making men good citizens" (Socrates' formulation, 319A). To this claim Socrates enters a famous demurrer: virtue is not teachable. He has seen on many occasions that when the issue is a technical one, the knowledge of *trained* experts is respected in the Assembly, which defers to skillful people who can be trusted to have learned an art. In matters calling for political judgment, however, there is no recognized art in which a man can become an acknowledged expert through technical training, i.e., through undergoing a course of formal instruction, without which he is unqualified to pronounce or advise. In principle, anyone can be wise in the affairs of the city. It is as if Socrates is saying that political judgment is something like a natural gift, had by some and not by others, possessed without being acquired; and a "training" in it would be a transaction presided over by a fraud and practiced on the dim. The likelihood of this is supported by the manifest inability of even those most gifted with political judgment, or other virtues, to impart their endowment to the ones nearest and dearest to them. This is as true in the private realm as in the public. Within the home, Pericles was unable either himself to teach or even to find another who could teach the goodness he valued most to the beings he cherished most. The matter is simply not subject to pedagogy. Plainly stated, this argument traces moral character, and judgment as well, to a source that is not man—perhaps nature, perhaps something else, but in any event a power that conveys gifts to patient humanity. It is to this position that Protagoras must address himself. He will do so through one of Plato's magnificent reconstructions of Protagorean doctrine, beginning at 320C (another is in *Theaetetus* 165E–168C).

Protagoras's response will be guided by his immediate understanding that the unspoken premise of Socrates' antipaideutic etiology of virtue is the proposition that the universe is of a certain kind, made or containing or perhaps ruled by What-Endows. We know that Protagoras understands this because he begins his lengthy statement with a zoogonic myth that traces us all, and therewith the status of our virtues, back to the gods.

There was a time, he says, when gods were but the mortal kind was not. The gods made the animals and then charged Prometheus and Epimetheus, the prospective and the retrospective, to assign them their powers. Epimetheus distributes the powers so that each kind will possess means of preserving itself from annihilation by its natural predators. "Balance" (*epanison*) or "compensation" is the principle at work. Unity permeates and supervenes over aggressive multiplicity. Epimetheus seems to have stumbled on a working model of the One and the Many in the shape of the animal kingdom. It is left to Prometheus to see to the needs of man, whom Epimetheus has somehow overlooked. Prometheus provides for mankind by stealing, on their behalf, fire and the arts from the gods, who apparently would not willingly succor mankind, of whom they had washed their hands from the beginning.

Who, by the way, are Epimetheus and Prometheus, retrospect and prospect? Gods they are not; godlike powers they seem to be. Whose backward-looking and forward-looking powers are they then if not man's himself? In the fable that Plato's Protagoras is spinning, Epimetheus is man's looking around himself, his circumspection, his observing the manner of the coming to be and passing away of the living things, the compensatory balance of consumption and being consumed that constitutes a bestial cycle from which forethought alone can liberate him. What the gods will not bestow on him to this end he will rape them of, and he will never cease to consider how far in this world his well-being must be his own far-seeing care.

Protagoras now speaks of man as sharing in the divine, referring of course to the art and fire obtained from unwilling heaven through a force and a fraud; and by virtue of this participation man became reverent of his own close kin aloft, setting up altars to them and making icons of them. We observe that without the contraband arts the human beings would have been not only unable to honor the mean and myopic Olympians with works of art but also unmoved to do so, since the possession of arts encourages introspective man to see a god within. As Plato fashions this skillful projection of Protagoras, the persistent tendency of the great sophist to link humanity to divinity through *techné* becomes clearer; and if we bear in mind that in the background of the discussion is the ever-present issue of teachability, more exactly the teachability of virtue, we can envision an important victory for Protagoras if he can produce the concurrence of divinity-qua-excellence and teachable art-qua-excellence. His pedagogy would then pass divinity from man to man, perfecting the philanthropy of Prometheus.

Protagoras continues. For all his art and worship, man still lived a solitary and dangerous life. His predators were the beasts, not his fellow human beings, and he found that his preservation depended on his joining together with his fellow men in order to deal with the brutes. According to Protagoras, men had been losing the war (*polemos*) with the beasts because humanity lacked "the political art, a part of which is (the art of) war." Now the remedy of association for defense produced a new disorder: in their novel proximity, the humans replaced the beasts as the source of danger to life, and the primitive society threatened to dissolve in mutual injury because men lacked the "political art." Plato will not imply any criticism of Protagoras as being inconsistent in saying that the political art is at the same time the art of war and the ground of peace. The assimilation of the war-making art to the political condition is in the spirit of Socrates' own thought as set forth at the beginning of the *Timaeus*, where he calls for an account of the exploits of the best city in its most characteristic activity, which is war in speech and deed. That peace is impossible without politics and politics is impossible without war seems to have been as evident to Protagoras as it was to Socrates and as it would later be to Machiavelli and Hobbes.

To avert the self-destruction of our kind, Zeus consents to share political virtue, not political wisdom, with the human beings. Protagoras's Zeus hoards the gifts that make human life tolerable, while the Zeus of the Parmenidean Stranger in the *Statesman* abstracts himself altogether, as will be seen, from the human well-being. On what terms does Protagoras's Zeus consent to the assistance of the human beings to save themselves in civil society? Hermes is to convey to all men, not to some few who would be the experts or artisans of political art, the justice and conscientiousness that are at the core of the political art. The words used are *dikē* and *aidos*, the former with its accompanying meaning of righteousness and the latter a complex amalgam of respect and susceptibility to shame or disgrace. Everyone, in principle, participates in the political virtues; it is as if man is by nature a political animal and perhaps even equipped by nature for life in a democratic polity. Protagoras does not derive from this a formula for defining a regime as best or most natural, and he does immediately make provision for the capital punishment of those who are incapable of sharing in the decencies of common life. It is easy for us to see that if Protagoras had devised a god who had endowed all men with equal political virtue for the sake of human preservation in society, the sophist would have left little enough for himself to do as a teacher of political virtue. Conversely, the justification of a pedagogy in political virtue inevitably implicates the dispensing god in the gross imperfection of the human kind in which such a large residue of room for correction persists. Protagoras's myth is a standing demonstration that the image of a god who is chary of sharing with mankind his wisdom of good and evil is available outside the limits of revelation.

Protagoras considers himself to have explained why the assembled citizens will listen to anyone regardless of his profession if he discourses sensibly on matters governed by political virtue (*politikēs aretēs*) (323A1): the very existence of cities testifies to the distribution of the social disposition among men, in effect to the (almost) universal presence of it in the human kind. The observable practice of mankind is an index to profound truth.

It is obvious to us, and it immediately proves to be at least as obvious to Protagoras, that in making this argument he is a step away from arguing himself out of an honest occupation as a teacher of political virtue. Who would need a human provider where a divine one has gone before? Again, Protagoras takes his demonstration from the common practice of mankind. Whereas we blame no one for his ugliness or deformity, because these are seen to be truly involuntary, we blame injustice because we attribute it to the malefactor himself, and we punish it not to retribute it upon the guilty but to deter a repetition—and to deter is to train. As we are all imbued with sociality, so we all know it to be a thing acquired by learning. All that the reader of this myth need do to purge it of gross contradiction is to eliminate a supposition that the imbuing is the effect of the action of any teacher or imbuer who is not human. We are all sociable because we all teach one another sociability. Of course, some do it better than others. The very best teacher of virtue might be struck by the notion that he does for man what nothing else in the cosmos does. Protagoras will in fact go so far as to claim to be, himself, the best of all men at making others noble and good (328B).

Protagoras claims to have shown Socrates how it comes about that the Athenians in assembly would listen willingly to any man of any occupation if he were to address them on civic matters in a sensible way, and Protagoras can claim to have done so through an argument that turns on the teachability of virtue. Abandoning myth for straight speech (*logos*), he will turn next to Socrates' second point, which is that the good men have so much trouble and so little success when they seek means to have their very own sons made virtuous, a fact that Socrates adduces as evidence that virtue cannot be taught. Protagoras insists that the whole weight of the human environment forms an unremitting pressure on a youngster from the beginning of his life, forming him in the mold of the virtues. His parents, his teachers of music and of gymnastic, and eventually the city itself through its laws are all ceaselessly prompting him to virtue throughout his entire life, by coercion where admonition and persuasion fail. Protagoras does not neglect to consider why the relentless moral pressure of humanity upon itself can fail. Men, whose lives should follow the paradigm of virtue everywhere recommended to them, behave instead according to a model of their very own (326D1). What could explain this willfulness? The same cause that explains why a master flutist's son, taught by his father, need not prove to be a master flutist: the element of natural aptitude. As it were, our greater or lesser inclination to virtue is by nature, but virtue itself is by instruction and habituation. This foreshadowing of Aristotle is presented by Protagoras in the medium of rational discourse rather than myth, as he has declared, and we see the sign of that transition when he renders his final account of the distribution and cultivation of the civil virtues in the language of natural aptitude where previously he had spoken in terms of endowment by gods. Much having been made of a natural aptitude for virtue, as much needs to be made of the equally natural capacity for violence and vice, so commonly attributed to the eminently natural passions. According to this Platonic evocation of Protagoras, the human beings are confronted by the parsimonious neglect of the god and the equivocating neutrality of nature as between good and evil. Under the circumstances, it is understandable that Protagoras would conclude that *man* is the measure of all things, not only of their being and not-being but of the means for giving good the advantage over evil.

We must remind ourselves that it was out of a similar premise, namely, that the virtues are ours by reason of an endowment of some origin, perhaps nature, that Socrates appeared to argue their incommunicability by teaching. So the issue between Socrates and the great sophist may be expressed as this question: The two agreeing that it is hard to know what makes, or how to make, a human being good, and agreeing further that the aptitude for virtue is largely by "endowment," which of them makes the stronger argument—the one who maintains that the virtues are not teachable or the one who argues that they are? It might be well to recall that this long exposition by Protagoras was prompted in large part by Socrates' requiring Protagoras to say in what way his instruction "makes men better." We are in a position to formulate his response thus: Protagoras helps to make his young pupils more sociable, to foster whatever natural inclination they have toward justice and the other virtues that make a man a good associate in the city. In brief, Protagoras makes, or at least aims to make, young men into good citizens, even if ambitious ones. By the end of his life, Socrates' doings as a whole will appear to his fellow citizens as a career of making the young into bad or skeptical citizens. The sophist appears in the honorable light, shed upon him by Plato, of one whose concern it is to civilize the human animal, that amazing being with so much capacity for good and evil, so much in need of his fellows if he is to live a fruitful life and so prone to abuse them if he believes he can do so with impunity. Not for a single moment unmindful of these truths, nor inclined to dispute them, Socrates looks so far beyond them that he could appear to neglect and in the end despise them, and this notwithstanding that he is made the propounder of the true and good city. The engagement between the

11

sophist and the philosopher gives us an occasion for wondering whether in a country like Athens the philosopher must choose between being mocked as a fantast or reviled as a felon.

Now (328D) Socrates begins his rejoinder. Politely but pointedly likening Protagoras's flow of speech to a book in its deafness and muteness in regard to questions, Socrates makes an issue, and not for the last time, of the difference between the presentation of argument in sustained speech and the exchange of questions and answers succinctly put. His reason for introducing this issue must be inferred from what follows, for no reason is given. Socrates declares himself to need clarification on one small point alone: Are all those various virtues to which Protagoras had referred one single thing with many names, or are they rather parts of some one single thing? However the question will be pursued, its bearing on the disjunction of long speeches and short answers seems clear enough: this matter should have been taken up and disposed of early in Protagoras's discourse, and if it had been, the discourse would have taken a different, better direction. Reasoning and speech should not be allowed to proceed without continuous confirmation of the steps being taken, one by one, lest the whole inquiry prove in need of redoing. If this explains the introduction by Socrates of what looks like a cavil about methods, then it serves less to protect him from the blame he would deserve as a petulant quibbler and more to indicate that everything Protagoras had maintained stands or falls by the answer to the crucial question— namely, Is virtue one or many?—which would have been raised near the outset if there had been an opportunity to raise it.

In response, Protagoras maintains that the virtues are parts of virtue, as the facial features are parts of the face. Socrates presses toward the assimilation of the virtues to one another. To make his point, Socrates extracts the admission that there is such a thing as justice itself, holiness (*hosiotēs*) itself, and so forth, and that, for example, justice is itself just. We would be easier in our minds if we could intervene at this point and ask how justice can be just without "participating" in some entity called justice, i.e., without "participating" in itself, whatever that might mean. We suspect that Plato's Parmenides, if he had been present, would have sensed Socrates' injection of the Idea of Justice here and would have reminded him of certain difficulties he once experienced when called on to be precise when speaking of "participation" in an "Idea" (*Parmenides* 131A); but Plato's

Protagoras—and presumably the real Protagoras—is not oriented on the problems of the Ideas. Nor does he object when Socrates, taking high moral ground, asks, "Could holiness be not-just and therefore unjust?" (331A), as if it were impossible for anything (for example a bird) to be "not-just" without being "unjust." It is the Eleatic Stranger, not Protagoras, who is shown by Plato to take up in detail what appears to be the thrust of Socrates' question (*Sophist* 257). Protagoras does balk, however, at the notion that whenever two things have anything in common they must have everything in common and be the same. He goes so far as to say that it is not at all just to speak like that (331E). Should he have taxed Socrates with "injustice"?

Socrates moves off on another tack, which will help to reveal his larger purpose. Having failed to obtain Protagoras's agreement to the unity of the virtues in Virtue, he will now argue the unity of the virtues in Wisdom. His key proposition is that to behave wrongly is to behave unwisely (*Protagoras* 332B). This granted, everything else falls into place: since the violation of every virtue is a folly, each virtue has, and all the virtues together have, one and the same single opposite; and having but one opposite, all the virtues are united through that common opposite, which is folly; and folly itself has but one opposite, which would be called wisdom or, as we now see, virtue. Thus, all the virtues have collapsed into the opposite of their opposite and the virtues are united in wisdom, which is what was to be demonstrated. By this conclusion, the virtues cannot be "parts" of something in which they participate to form a whole, as the eyes, nose, mouth, and ears, each with its peculiar function, are parts of a face. Of course, Protagoras is not entirely pleased.

Summarizing the state of the question (333B), Socrates makes explicit that discretion (*sōphrosynē*) and wisdom are the same, and that justice and holiness are almost (*schedon*) the same. We have no clue to the reason for the "almost," but if we must devise one, it might develop around the thought that nothing can disturb the identity of two virtues except their failure to share fully the same opposite, namely, folly. We would want to hesitate at length before deciding which, as between justice and holiness, by failing to contradict folly, participates in it to whatever microscopic degree. Unable to resolve this sensitive difficulty by ourselves, we go on to note the next step in Socrates' argument, which does appear to bear somewhat on the vexing issue. Socrates inquires whether a man acting unjustly is, in

13

his injustice, being discreet, practicing a moderation (*sōphrosynē*). Protagoras says that he would be ashamed to agree to that, although the multitude among men say it. Understandably, Protagoras does not take advantage of the opportunity to point out how this widespread turpitude increases the need for universal moral instruction of the kind he provides, for by his account the citizen mass is a source of moral instruction for the young and for itself. Socrates simply consents to take the deplorable popular view rather than any belief of Protagoras's as his target. Socrates explains his purposes in proceeding as he does: mostly he wishes to try the argument; concomitantly, though, he himself the questioner and his respondent will also be tried (333C). As it seems, the reader is expected to draw conclusions about Protagoras and Socrates as well as about truth, as the argument unfolds, which it will now do in the direction of clarifying the meaning of something being "good for" as a preparation for clarifying the meaning of "good." The drift of the developing thought is uncovered when Socrates moves rapidly (333D) to connect acting temperately (*sōphronein*) with acting prudently (*phronein*) and advancing thence to prudent injustice, by the practice of which a man might do well, which is a locution for profiting. Now who could deny that the good things are those that are profitable (*ōphelima*) to men? Ergo, it is prudent (i.e., right because prudence is a virtue) to do what is profitable, because to do the profitable means to obtain the things that are good. Protagoras, seeing what he has been inveigled into granting, exhibits an irritability in which Socrates perceives a dislike for further questioning. Desiring nevertheless to push on, he asks in a way meant to be mollifying whether by those profitable things Protagoras means things that are profitable to no one or things that are profitable in no way at all, and whether things like that could be called "good." Lurking in the question is the insinuated answer that virtues, for example intelligent prevision of the Promethean kind, might bring satisfactions not comprehended in the pious dictum that virtue is its own reward. Suspicions greatly aroused, Protagoras reacts with a speech long enough to leave no doubt that he has renounced the passivity of the mere respondent. He vents his view that "good" is a complicated thing, different things are good for different beings under different conditions, and what is good for this part of man may be bad for that, etcetera. Socrates confesses to having such a bad memory that he cannot remember what a paragraph is about by the time the speaker has reached the end of it. Answers must be short. Protagoras's rejoinder to this absurdity is an implicit application of his offending speech: short speeches are to your liking and are good for you; long ones or short ones may suit me better; and who is to say, you or I, what is good (presumably advantageous) for me? Socrates' response shows no sign of recognizing the question of "good" as it is buried in Protagoras's rejoinder. Instead, he lays it down that the conversation will proceed on his terms or not at all since he has no aptitude for long speeches—an assertion belied by his conduct on innumerable occasions, including his Apology, and soon to be belied in the present dialogue itself. What can the reader conclude except that, just as Protagoras had implied, men can contend as their respective "goods" can conflict, and that when they do so, the one who succeeds in facing down his opponent will prevail? That insight, which draws on a wisdom only too widely distributed, informs the action of Socrates, who simply threatens to leave. He has an engagement anyhow and really ought to go right now. (Not only does he not go, once he has got his way, but as we all know, he has time to repeat the whole affair verbatim before attending to his urgent engagement.)

Auditors protest the imminent breakup of the meeting, and take sides. Callias, their host, thinks it would be just if each speaker spoke as he wished. Alcibiades weighs in, aggressively of course, on behalf of Socrates. Critias favors cooperation over aggression. Prodicus contributes a paragraph of hairsplitting and sententiousness. Others, unnamed, expose themselves by approving Prodicus. Hippias spreads himself through a farrago of ruminations on nature and convention, the unmatched wisdom of the present company, and the vulgarity of squabbling, leading through notable byways of orotundity to a proposal that a chairman be appointed to moderate the proceedings. Applauded by all, except Socrates, the suggestion is vetoed by the latter, who does not want Protagoras regulated by someone inferior to that sage and cannot imagine anyone superior to him. The entire scene, which emphasizes an irenic but blurry disposition of the often contentious sophists, must have brought enjoyment to many places in educated Greece of Plato's day. More, though, than a witty pastiche of the foibles of eminent sophists, it illustrates the limits of mutual accommodation, where the parties, differing over "good," clash consequently over what is good *for* each respectively.

Agreement is indeed reached, but it largely favors the preference of Socrates: over Protagoras's great misliking, they will proceed by the method of question and answer, but taking turns. Protagoras will be first to ask, and then Socrates will put the questions, to which Protagoras is bound to answer briefly.

Protagoras's proemium to his questioning (338E) marks the beginning of a long section of the dialogue which at first sight appears to lead the discussion in vagrant directions. The sophist announces that, in his view, the greatest part of a man's education is to be skillful (*deinon*) about poems or poetry. If this is to be believed, then Protagoras's teaching of goodness proceeds through the interpretation of poetic texts like the one in which he hopes now to enmesh Socrates, namely, a piece by Simonides with which Socrates proves to be familiar, perhaps to the disappointment of Protagoras. Protagoras quotes, in effect, that it is hard to become good. Then he quotes Simonides, again in effect, as saying that Pittacus was wrong when he declared that it is hard to be good. The double negative puts Simonides in the position of maintaining both that it is hard to become good and it is not hard to be good. Protagoras prepares to gloat over Socrates from whom he has just extracted praise for the poem so marred by manifest contradiction. After a certain amount of business, Socrates drives home the difference between being and becoming, in general and in its relevance first to the consistency of the poem and then in its bearing on the matter of goodness: it is the becoming good that is hard, not the being. By this point, it has been made clear to us that the introduction by Protagoras of the poetic theme did not constitute a simple derailment of the dialogue qua inquiry into the goodness of the human beings, although it is true that a shift of emphasis has taken place: the teaching or making good of the human beings has at least for the moment given way to their being or becoming good. Whether the obvious relation between the difficulty of making someone good and the difficulty of becoming good will emerge we cannot yet foresee. In any case, Protagoras was apparently mindful enough of the central issue when he projected his assault on Socrates through the medium of poetry, although he seems to have underestimated his interlocutor's education in the epic literature. He surely did not anticipate the ease with which Socrates would humiliate his hermeneutic by proving that the poet had not in fact contradicted himself.

Protagoras is far from ready to admit defeat. Now (340E) he accuses Socrates of making things worse than ever when he denies that it is exceedingly hard to be virtuous. Socrates turns to Prodicus, the accomplished microscopist of meanings, to confirm that "hard," in the dialect of Simonides, meant "bad." Thus the true complaint of Simonides against Pittacus was that Pittacus, in saying that to be good was hard, meant in fact that to be good was bad. This profoundly repulsive sentiment is saved from absolute obloquy by our recollection that good, at least in the understanding of Socrates, runs together with advantage or "good for." Thus to be virtuous or good might arguably be bad if being "good" brought losses and pain, which are not good for any human being although they might be overborne by the virtue that is its own incomparable reward (as Socrates is obliged to maintain in the *Republic*). Socrates is, of course, not disposed to advertise any association of his own with the odious notion he has fobbed off on Pittacus, however much it might resonate with the peculiar "consequentialism" he himself will eventually promote.

Protagoras has his own no-nonsense way of clearing up the problem of the badness of goodness: when Simonides said hard he meant hard, not bad. Far from rejoining that what is hard is, *as such*, bad, Socrates soothes Protagoras by agreeing with him, calling "good is bad" a joke, and supporting him by quoting Simonides' next verse, "Only god might have this privilege," that is, of possessing goodness. Granting that Simonides was not a mischief maker who meant to depreciate the qualities of god, what was his true intention? Socrates volunteers to elucidate, and proceeds to do so in a speech that is many times longer than the one of Protagoras's that had brought him to his feet with the threat to leave. In passing, we wonder if his dedication to the method of crisp exchanges is more a matter of tactics in circumstances than fidelity to some profoundly held heuristic principle. We wonder, in other words, whether he reveals in his doing that what is truly good must chime with a (good) purpose, or be "good *for*" the one who does well. We hesitate to draw a general conclusion that a good end justifies means of various kinds, but a situation dominated by polemic—such as the present one in which Protagoras seeks to outdo Simonides, Simonides seeks to overturn Pittacus, Protagoras and Socrates strive to put one another down, and Sparta is said to master everyone—is a plausible setting for thoughts about prevailing.

Socrates' lecture begins (342A) in a comic vein, and light-years from the subject. Philosophy, he says, is most deeply and widely rooted in Crete and Lacedaemon, where sophists are more plentiful than anywhere else. (This trampling the distinction between philosophy and sophistry can be taken as a sign that he is enjoying himself.) The cunning Dorians, jealous of the wisdom by which they predominate in Greece, conceal their sapience behind a facade of militarism that they decorate with a muscular stupidity widely imitated by dupes elsewhere who dress in the athletic Spartan fashion and sport the cauliflower ears that advertise a vigorous regimen. The Spartans, too successful in their duplicity, see encroachment on the privacy of their communion with their sophists because their city is overrun by foreign mimics. Laws are made to restrict immigrant strangers and to inhibit the travel abroad of their own young. Self-satisfaction is at such a peak that even women are puffed up about their education in Crete and Sparta, and the heights of philosophy reached in the latter city may be discerned by anyone who converses with the simplest denizens and reflects on the wisdom latent in the sententiousness of their speech. In Sparta it is known that verbal parsimony is the index of good education. Spartan peasants fire off maxims like shot from a sling (wrapping the terse in the military). The sages of Greece were patent laconizers who spoke in saws: "Know thyself," "Nothing in excess," and so on. (It is unsettling to consider that "knowledge is virtue" has itself a certain flair to it.) Socrates at last heaves into sight of the subject: Pittacus, an authentic sage, scored a hit with his "Hard to be good," and Simonides sang to make a name for himself by overthrowing Pittacus: "Hard to be good" is wrong; "Becoming good is hard" is the line. How did Simonides argue for his purpose? To show this, Socrates composes a discourse addressed by Simonides to Pittacus (343E). Pittacus having said it is hard to be good, Simonides objects: what is true is that it is hard to *become* good. It is hard but possible to become good; it is not hard but impossible to *be*, i.e., remain, good, except for god—as you yourself, Pittacus, say. And, Pittacus, you say in support of your belief (no man can remain good) that no man can withstand overwhelming mishap that besets him to compromise his virtue. Since you speak of overwhelming mishap, you must be having in mind those men to whom "overwhelming" properly applies, men of such exceptional goodness that if they are to change at all—and their being overwhelmed means the alteration of their state—their change must be to bad. They are balanced on a cusp of virtue, they can only fall, and fall they inevitably must.

What, Pittacus, supports any man in his goodness, such as it is? The answer is, the good man's doing is favored and well done, and a bad man is one whose doing is ill done. These verses are so close to tautology that they demand to be rescued by interpretation. What is this decisive "well-doing?" The answer is "learning" (*mathēsis*). What "well-doing" (*eupragia*) makes a good doctor? Learning or studying the cure of the sick. And what would make a bad doctor? Arguing that only a doctor who is a good doctor could be made a bad doctor, the pertinent ill-doing would be some kind of stripping away (*sterēthēnai*) of knowledge (345B). Attractive as the surmise may be that this entire performance of Socrates' is nothing but a bravura travesty on the sophists performed in their garb, it is yet to be noted that he interjects in the course of his interpretation of the poem certain themes of his own, which he undoubtedly adopts in his own name, such as this present one that goodness is knowledge, and the immediately following one that no one does evil willingly. He brings the matter into order by summarizing Simonides' intent: there is no simply remaining good, but becoming good or bad is indeed possible. Then Socrates turns to a passage of the poem where he must anatomize the text delicately in order to make it come right. Simonides wrote words that could be read either "I praise willingly everyone who does no wickedness" or "I praise everyone who does no wickedness willingly." Socrates says that the poet means the former, he must mean the former, because no one does wickedness willingly. The poet writes that even the gods do not fight against necessity. We are expected, perhaps by Simonides but certainly by Socrates, to conclude that mortals must surely give way to it, and their wicked doings are the sign of their subjection to it. This attribution of our wickedness to overwhelming necessity offers us a balm for which we soon realize we might have to pay heavily: if our vice arises out of a necessity that could appear to exculpate, how can we explain our virtue without compromising either reason (only wickedness, not goodness, is dictated by necessity!) or freedom? The difficulty seems to have occurred to Socrates; the ingenuity with which he addresses it can only be admired. He maintains (345E–346B) on behalf of Simonides that a fine and good man (*kalos kagathos*), a thoroughly decent man, will often contrive his own necessity. If his parents or his country happen to fail him, he will force himself (literally, necessitate himself) to praise and love his own. That is, the real harm they may have done him will not

19

constitute the "necessity" that would lead him into wickedness, but his decency will form an opposing "necessity" that will lead him into goodness and that we would call freedom. Socrates gives an example: Simonides knew that he had often praised and eulogized some tyrant not willingly but under necessity.[1] We presume that Simonides is apologizing for a deed he is not proud of; in other words, he is pointing to the necessity that is exogenous, rather than illustrating the autocompulsion of a decent man requiring himself to swallow his resentment of injury done him by his nearest and to replace it with praise and love.

The wrong that we do we do out of necessity, never willingly; but much that presents itself in such a way that we might excuse ourselves by calling it necessity is not of the overwhelming kind but is rather opposable by a "necessity" that we can generate out of our own decency. This preserves the power of necessity, but when is necessity irresistible and when resistible? Is it a matter of recognition, of knowledge—there is a simply irresistible necessity and it behooves us to acknowledge it? Simonides' behavior toward the tyrants shows us in what way this truism is problematic, for it was not literally impossible for him to defy the tyrants, to blame and not eulogize them. It would have been easy for him to do so. What would have been anything but easy were the consequences. Has Socrates not led us to the conclusion that we denominate an outer pressure a necessity, and we accede to it, when we foresee and reject the consequences of resisting it, while we necessitate ourselves to resist an indecency when, or even because, the anticipated pains of behaving well are acceptable? What must a human being know then if he is to make his way through the thickets of being and becoming good? Is it the absolute nature of Necessity and its modes? Or the good or bad consequences of his actions? How much the Socratic formula that knowledge is virtue has been enriched through Socrates' exposition of the poem suggests to us that his interpretation of the ode was considerably more than a mocking demonstration that he can outdo the sophists at their own game.

To this point, we have been presented with two accounts of man's ascent to or falling away from virtue. One turns on knowledge and is exemplified by the good doctor's *mathēsis* and his forgetting; the

1. Cf. the place of Simonides in Xenophon's *On Tyranny*.

other turns, to begin with, on volition and necessity, but the diremption of necessity between external and internal lets necessity be replaced by considerations of consequences, which is to say, knowledge, such as it is, of the future. What men do "willingly" they do out of that self-imposed necessity that is governed by foresight, the Promethean excellence. A listener who was present with Socrates when this conversation took place and not only at its present repetition (i.e., the reader who has already read to the end of the dialogue and is now reading it for the second time) will know how well the rest of the discourse will agree with this deduction from Socrates' gloss on Simonides.

Socrates would like to resume the exchange with Protagoras, but without further use of texts, even poetic ones, for it is impossible to question them about their meaning,[2] as to which the hermeneuts, inevitably differing, will argue endlessly. Serious people would rely on their own minds and powers, preferring to test the truth and themselves in direct exchange of speech. The reader of such words must pause to wonder whether the author of them is not admonishing him to put down the book he is holding in his hands and to seek out instead some companionable interlocutors with whom, testing one another and the truth about the being and becoming of good, he might profit more than by continuing to speculate on the inscrutable intention of his present author. Something, perhaps our waking to the difference between the attributive speaker of those words and the ostensive recorder of them in writing, keeps us at our reading. At worst, we will have been induced to think.

Protagoras, importuned by all, resigns himself reluctantly to a resumption of the questioning (348C). Socrates opens by flattering him so fulsomely that only a desperate egotist could miss the odor of sarcasm. Then the still lingering question: wisdom, temperance, courage, justice, piety (*hosiotēs*)—are these five words for one thing, or is there some distinct being with its own power that underlies each of these words and distinguishes each from the others? You, Protagoras, answered that the virtues differ from one another, being parts in the sense that the parts of the face are parts of a whole which none of them resembles. Do you still think so? Protagoras continues to believe that the virtues are parts of virtue, but he singles out courage from the

---

2. A repetition of the well-known critique of writing in *Phaedrus*.

rest because people lacking the other four virtues are often very courageous. If we are in doubt about the reason for resurrecting this question after it had apparently been put satisfactorily to rest long before, our uncertainties will now be removed. Socrates' will push forward from the earlier unification of the virtues by their reduction to knowledge to an intimation of the nature of that knowledge—a question that agitates the *Theaetetus*, that other "Protagorean" dialogue, as well as the present one. By the time Socrates has accomplished his purpose, Plato will have integrated the discussion of virtue and its teachability into his conception of the human condition.

The thread of the argument that begins (349D) with Protagoras's distinguishing courage from other virtues is as follows. Virtue and all its parts are very good things, and belong to the possessors of knowledge. The courageous, as distinct from the merely rash, possess a knowledge (e.g., horsemanship) that is in fact a skill or an art. If the courageous are wise and the rash are mad, then the wise are courageous. Protagoras objects (350C et seq.) that the knowledgeable virtuous being better at their function than their ignorant semblables does not translate into the identity of wisdom and virtue: other causes are at work. He declares that courage, the virtue proper, comes to be in men by nature and the good nurturing of souls, whereas its inferior imitation, rashness, comes to be out of art (*technē*, which is a knowledge) or anger or frenzy. To this apt recitation of the sophist's paideutic creed Socrates makes answer by changing the subject. What is "living well" (*eu zēn*) if not living pleasantly and not painfully? Causing Protagoras to react against the implication that pleasure is the good, Plato gives himself the occasion to elaborate the far-reaching hedonism of Socrates, which starts with the innocuous thought that pleasant is good. Even so modest a proposition as that pleasure is better than pain would serve as a beginning.

That Socrates' hedonism is not of the garden variety is indicated by his opening question to Protagoras (352A): How is it with you about knowledge? Is it supreme in governing actions, or is it, as most people think, pushed aside by anger, pleasure, pain, and often by fear? Protagoras is for the hegemony of reason, enabling Socrates then to ask what could be meant by anyone's being overcome by pleasure. Reason rules, yet it does not. How so? Well, everyone would admit that people sometimes seek pleasure in acts that they know to be wicked. Wherein lies the wickedness? Not in the pleasure of the act but in the ill of its consequences, which ill always comes down to pain. Also, what appears to us now as painful, like exertion or surgery, is good in the event, which is pleasant. Nothing is wrong with pleasure except that, or when, it produces a pain greater than itself. Socrates apologizes for being at such length about what look like banalities, but when he says that his entire demonstration turns on this point (354E), we do well to take him at his word. In fact, the structure of the argument as a whole is now virtually in place.

Knowledge is indeed decisive for good, for living well, for justly living by a truth that we cannot escape—namely, that living pleasantly is sweet and good. Why not agree with Protagoras, so far as what he means is that our natural inclinations are the soil in which our virtues grow. But what precisely is the crucial knowledge? It is the knowledge of the relative quantities of present pleasures and pains against the quantities of the future pains and pleasures that might be their respective consequences. The sovereign knowledge, the basis for our doing well, for us human beings the salvation of life, is the art of measure, of measurement, of comparing amounts—the art or knowledge of commensuration (*metrikē*) (356D et seq.).

Socrates says (357B) that they will consider this art or science another time; and so one must. For the present, Socrates is willing to settle the earlier question about the overwhelming of knowledge by pleasure by remarking that it is indeed "ignorance," the defect of knowledge, that leads men into evil: they fail to commensurate the present and the future. They do not willingly choose evil over virtue, they unwittingly choose the lesser pleasure or the greater pain. They do this under the influence of false opinion and being deceived (*epseusthai*) about very important things. To seek evil and avoid good would, if a man were not deluded, be as it seems to contravene human nature (358C–D). Now Socrates can begin his exploitation of the point made by Protagoras long ago, the assertion that courage, a distinguishable part of virtue, can be present when all other virtues are absent—a thought that in turn grew out of Socrates' fascination with the unity or multiplicity of virtue. It will help us greatly to understand the dialogue as a whole if we make explicit the chain of reasonings from beginning to end, not only for the obvious reason but more with a view to seeing the work as an example of successful human prevision, the preparation and setting in place of elements conducing in their order to a culmination foreseen from afar. This might exemplify the only envisioning of a future in which a human being can have perfect confidence. It happens to be a future, in fact the only future, that he alone controls.

Socrates brings up fear (*phobos*) and dread (*deos*): it is anticipation of bad or evil (*kakos*). Will anyone voluntarily pursue the dreadful, which is the same as the evil? What about the man who possesses courage, which Protagoras long ago said is a virtue distinguishable from the others and capable of being present where all the others are absent? The brave man could not possibly seek evil, i.e., the anticipated dreadful, for he is a man of virtue. While the coward and the brave man are alike in facing what they can, it happens, as Protagoras points out, that the brave face death in battle and the cowardly do not. Protagoras's unspoken premise is that death is an evil. Socrates would be caught if it were true that a virtuous man knowingly, not deluded or impressed by false opinion, sought evil. Socrates saves himself by introducing "the noble" (*kalon*). Facing death in war is noble, thus good, thus wittingly choiceworthy. Though the courageous and the cowardly may both know fear, the brave man fears virtuously and the coward basely. According to conclusions reached earlier, this means that the courageous man fears knowingly and the coward ignorantly. Knowingly and ignorantly of what? Of the truly dreadful. What has been proved is that courage, not unlike but exactly like all the virtues, is wisdom. Protagoras resigns from the discussion.

From the sidelines we notice that Socrates' argument depends heavily if not absolutely on the power of the noble, clearly good, to outweigh death, clearly or unclearly bad. Unwelcome thoughts disturb us. What if "noble" translates into civic reputation and the arguments that make death perhaps not an evil have an origin in the good of the city? How much of an evil is a bad reputation when measured against the good of survival? The art or science of comparative quantities, the knowledge of commensuration, saves us only when the quantities to be compared can be known. If the commensuration of quantities that can at least be guessed at poses difficulties, how insuperable must those be when there is no way in the world to estimate that future which must be discounted to the present if men are "knowingly" to commensurate present pleasures and future pains. How is an earthly life of pleasure (very knowable) to be measured against a dreadful future, something that a truly courageous man would rather die than confront, when that future is itself unknowable by us? If it be said that that future is not at all unknowable by us, it has been revealed to us by the poets, Socrates would tell us to be reasonable, to think for ourselves rather than construe the poets or other writers, whose works cannot be subjected to questioning and whose meaning will never come clear through interpretation. If we discover some aspect of the future that must necessarily be forever dark to us, we have in that act reached the outer limit of morally relevant commensuration. We have reached the moral equivalent of *pi*, the symbol of the irrational in the universe. Just in passing, we may note that where something so important to virtue as the status of the deepest future must remain uncertain for us, the fact that virtue is knowledge confirms Protagoras in his view that virtue belongs to the class of teachables but refutes his claim that it is simply teachable. The science of commensuration is teachable, but it fails when it ignores that its objects include the incommensurable. Geometry reconciles itself to the presence of the irrational within its boundaries; sophistry has not seen far enough to do so. Perhaps it is the sophists' confidence in reason, speech, persuasion that distinguishes them from the philosophers, whose claim is only to love wisdom, to prize the wisdom that sheds light on the limits of wisdom, and not to possess, surely not to convey it, on demand. Fair as this judgment on the sophists might be in general, it is incomplete—misleading and unjust—if to it is not added the remark of the Eleatic Stranger in the *Sophist* (268A) that there are sophists who learn to suspect and fear that they do not know what they profess to know.

It would be supreme folly to conclude that if a transcendental basis for virtue has not been certified by the universe, a valid immanent one is unavailable. If living and commodious living and the pursuit of wisdom in peace depend on the flourishing of cities, why disparage as merely conventional the orders and rules that nourish the polities? And why revolt against the science of commensuration because it teaches us not everything, only almost everything? When Socrates injects the noble into the consideration of courage and makes it a counterweight to the dreadfulness of death, he wisely refrains from perturbing the discussion with high-flying reflections on the infusion of the rational universe with particles of incommensurability. Rather, he allows its full weight to the system of rewards and punishments, of scanning present and future, of deeds and their stochastic consequences, of what we might call in the end a rational hedonism in the service of goodness. If it serves goodness, why complain that it is hedonism? Is it thinkable that Socrates was a greater benefactor of the city than the rationalist who claimed to raise the human beings to a higher level of civility than the one on which nature left them?

The two interlocutors prepare to part. Socrates notes the confusion of their positions, he denying that virtue is teachable but proving that it is knowledge, Protagoras insisting that it is teachable but denying that it is knowledge. Aporia reigns and will continue to do so unless we pursue our inquiry to answer the question, What is virtue? While we stumble, we are victims of the heedlessness of Epimetheus, who left us short of resources. I, says Socrates, prefer the Prometheus of the myth. I profit by him, looking ahead (*promēthoumenos*) with a view to my whole life when I am engaged in these things. Has he weighed his philosophizing and his death and made the choice of a courageous man? Is not courage the characteristic philosophic virtue, and spiritedness the indispensable philosophic temper, considering that something about our future, on earth and wherever else, is and must necessarily be dark?

The two men exchange good-natured civilities, and Socrates departs on the wings of a small myth.

II

THEAETETUS

THE DIALOGUE *THEAETETUS* REPORTS A CONVERSATION BETWEEN Socrates and Theaetetus that occurred when the latter was perhaps fifteen years old. The conversation took place in the weeks or months preceding the death of Socrates, as the end of the dialogue makes explicit. It suits Plato's purpose to present the conversation through the reading aloud of a certain reconstruction of it, a reading that takes place decades after the original event. Plato injects an interval of thirty years between the conversation itself and the "present" recitation of it, Theaetetus being "now" as near to his death as Socrates was when the conversation itself took place. The person from whom the dialogue receives its name is, by the device of the interval, presented in both the promising outset and the consummated accomplishment of a distinguished life. The interval and its circumstances are set forth in an introductory scene between Eucleides of Megara and Terpsion, also a Megaran. These two were among the admirers of Socrates who were present at his death.

Eucleides and Terpsion encounter each other in the town square at Megara and begin immediately to discuss Theaetetus, recently borne through Megara toward Athens from the battlefield at Corinth. He is said to be gravely ill and wounded, presumably dying. Evidently stricken in the Corinthian War of 369 B.C., thirty years after his conversation with the indicted Socrates, Theaetetus has fulfilled the promise of his adolescence by achieving distinction as a mathematician, more particularly as an expert of the irrationals and incommensurables. The reputation that he gained in his own time was substantial and is preserved to this day in the accepted attribution to him of the proof of the ninth proposition of Euclid's tenth book.[1] *Elements* 10.9 addresses the relation between the commensurability of two lines and the commensurability of the squares erected on those lines. Thus, for example, two lines may be incommensurable, as are one and the square root of two, while their squares are perfectly commensurable, whereas in other cases the incommensurability of the

---

1. *The Elements*, translated with introduction and commentary by Sir Thomas Heath (Annapolis: St. John's College Press, 1947).

plane figure accords with that of the original lines. The subject to which Theaetetus contributed his demonstration is the preoccupation not only of *Elements* 10 but of much classical philosophy, as is evident from Aristotle's *Physics* and *Metaphysics*. What is at stake is made clear when the perplexity of the irrational numbers and the concept of incommensurability are viewed alongside the possibility of infinite divisibility, concretely the infinite divisibility of body. Atomism in any form, whatever the shape or constitution of the atom or Uncut, is per se the contradiction of the thesis of infinite divisibility in the realm of body. The fact that irrational numbers exist, that there is no conceivable unit so small that it will make the side and the diagonal of the unit square commensurable, signifies the inevitable frustration of the thesis of infinite divisibility in the realm of number at the same time that it shows the impossibility of an absolutely small numerical entity or mathematical atom that would stand as motionless monad. Yet there is no way to inhibit the mind's conception of a diminution that proceeds without end, a conception that is as true in its own dimension as atomism and eternal incommensurability are true in theirs. There is a truth in the unyielding realm where the hard irreducible prevails like the letter in the alphabet,[2] and another truth in the realm of thought alone. The large identification of mathematics with geometry[3] brought this home to the Greek thinkers with particular force, for a line drawn on a piece of paper stands everlastingly as the absolute token of the tension between the continuous and the contiguous, the point as the infinitely vanishing that cannot vanish and the point as the small but changeless element of an indubitable and manifest composite. The point as infinitesimal is a construct of reason alone that pertains to the line never seen; the point as element is a thing of the imagination that pertains to the perceptible line.[4] What the Eleatic Stranger will say to Theaetetus in the *Sophist* (246A–C) and what Socrates will say about Anaxagoras's defection from the hegemony of mind to the independence of body in *Phaedo* (97C et seq.), as well as what is argued in innumerable places regarding the intelligible as against the perceptible, is implicated in the geometrical conundrum

2. Cf. Aristotle *Metaphysics* 1086b22–32.

3. Which Aristotle viewed with reservations: "Philosophy has become mathematics for those of our time, although they claim that it is meant to be taken up for other purposes." *Metaphysics* 992b1.

4. Cf. Aristotle *Metaphysics* 992a20–25.

of the thinkable in its opposition to the empirical, of the Ideas, whatever they may be, in their relation to the concrete. Geometry brings to
a head the issue of the constitution and government of the cosmos: Is
the thinkable the key to the all, or does the empirical whole of nature
prescribe to and limit the bearing of veritable thought as it aspires to
transcendency? Surely the critique of pure reason was not conceived
first in the eighteenth century, although its culmination in the mistrust of metaphysics perhaps was. At any rate, Plato begins the sequence of seven crucial dialogues with one named for a fifteen-year-
old boy because that name bears into consideration a paramount
philosophic question, one soon to be seen in the light of Protagoras's
maxim that man is the measure of all things.

The introductory scene, as has been said, opens with a meeting
of Eucleides and Terpsion in Megara. Their speech discloses that
Theaetetus had been engaged in conversation with Socrates many
years earlier and that Socrates had obliged Eucleides by recounting
the discourse to him. Eucleides then wrote what he could remember
of what Socrates had related to him and thereafter consulted Socrates
freely, in the troubled time while the latter was under indictment, on
points that needed clarification. This is as close as Socrates ever came
to writing a Socratic discourse. It is this written record, authorized as
one might say by Socrates, that will soon be read aloud for the benefit
of Terpsion.

It may be wondered why Plato presents his writing as if it were
the product of a decision by Socrates to designate Eucleides as his
confidant and collaborator-cum-amanuensis. Of Eucleides we do not
know a great deal. We are told that he was a Parmenidean who considered himself a pupil of Socrates'; also that he founded the School of
Megara, allegedly on amalgamated principles of Socratic morality
and a version of Parmenidean metaphysics that consigned plurality,
evil, and unreason to nonentity where Socrates would have found the
cause in unwisdom. His School is reputed to have been a center of
eristic, and to have included one Eubulides, who generated examples
of vulgar sophistry on the level of those ridiculed in *Euthydemus* and
soon to be excoriated in the *Sophist*. In a famous passage, Diogenes
Laertius (3.6) writes of Eucleides and of some other parties known to
us as follows: after the death of Socrates, Plato "attached himself to
Cratylus the Heraclitean, and to Hermogenes of the Parmenidean
philosophy. Then, at the age of twenty-eight, . . . he, together with

some other Socratics, withdrew to Megara to Eucleides. Next he went to Cyrene, to Theodorus the mathematician, and on to Italy to the Pythagoreans Philolaos and Eurytos," and so forth, less to our purpose. Why, we wonder, did Plato frame his work as a transcription by a synthesist who was absent from the conversation but who preserved his report of it as if it were a relic; who, unlike Plato himself, was present at the death of Socrates with Terpsion and others who formed the eclectic crowd of grievers; a man whose name is traditionally connected with the conversion of dialectic to eristic on the short road from Athens to Megara; one to whom Plato himself went for whatever reason as he made his tour of philosophy after Socrates' death. In the worst case, it is Plato's way of suggesting that Socrates was not above criticism in his choice of favorites, an intimation present at the end of *Phaedrus* where Socrates' partiality to Isocrates is prominent. Apart from any question of his eligibility for the particular confidence of Socrates, Eucleides was a Socratic with a Parmenidean allegiance, as Theodorus, soon to make his appearance as the teacher of Theaetetus, was a revisionist Protagorean, and the Eleatic Stranger, the mentor of the *Sophist* and the *Statesman*, a strikingly lapsed Parmenidean with Socratic leanings. Plato has populated the trilogy *Theaetetus-Sophist-Statesman* with persuadable adherents of the distinguished philosophic schools of Greece. The dialectical if tacit agon among them is inaugurated in *Theaetetus,* a discourse that embraces the geometrical irrational and fails in its announced purpose to discover the definition of knowledge. Plato will demonstrate in action the exhausting difficulty of maintaining the critical scrutiny of philosophy by philosophy under the sign of Socrates' insistence on the agnostic virtue of his wisdom. *Theaetetus* is an emphatically Socratic dialogue by reason of the fictitious collaboration of Socrates in the writing of it and the extended characterization of Socrates in his maieutic autobiography (149A–151D); but it is an emphatically Platonic dialogue in its demonstration of philosophy in act. Philosophy is what is common to philosophies, which rise to that dignity by addressing the issues that philosophy recognizes as eternal. In the absence of such a dialogue as would be called "The Philosopher," alluded to by implication early in the *Sophist*, the lacuna might be thought to be filled by *Theaetetus* itself, wherein, as will appear, "the philosopher" is a considerable theme.

The introductory scene draws to a close as Eucleides complies with Terpsion's desire to be made acquainted with the conversation of Socrates and Theaetetus. Eucleides' servant reads the transcription:

Socrates would like Theodorus, a noted geometer from Cyrene, to tell him about any especially promising Athenian youth that he has come across and not to bother mentioning Cyrenians, for Socrates is devoted only to the local type. In putting the question, Socrates refers to geometry as belonging to philosophy, an attribution for which we have prepared ourselves. Theodorus answers without hesitation that there is one boy, as homely as Socrates himself, who stands out for his natural endowment (*pephukota* 144A) above all those he has ever known: intelligent, gentle, and courageous; and again, most "gentle" (*praotatos*—we would perhaps say untroubled) in absorbing and inquiring. Socrates asks not who the boy is but who his father is, as if the boy's heritage, natural or social, would bear on his qualities. Theodorus has forgotten the father's name, evincing a certain abstraction from the mere world that might be thought philosophic; but the question is overridden by the arrival of the boy himself. Socrates recognizes him by sight as the son of the late Euphronius of Sunium, saying of the father that he fit the description Theodorus has just given of the son. Were Socrates to mean by this that nature binds the excellence of the man to that of his father or his son, Socrates must have been oblivious to the difference between himself and his own apparently unremarkable father and sons. Not only does nature not provide the automatic transmission of human goodness by the genetic means dreamed of in the eugenic geometry of the *Republic*, but even the artificial means of inculcating virtue seem to be frustrated by the unteachability of the latter that Socrates has argued in *Protagoras*. This inescapable human problem will come to the surface soon enough in the *Apology*, where the obverse of the melioration of the young, namely, their artificial corruption, will dominate so much of the discourse as is not given over to the popular religion, where the desired edification is not to be found under the tutelage of the gods if both *Euthyphro* and *Sophist* are to be trusted. Nature, the pantheon, and surely sophistry are not to be relied upon. Perhaps philosophy in the rare cases where reason without force suffices, and political rule in the multitude of cases wherein reason requires the support of civil coercion will prove to bring relief with the aid of religion purged of vulgarity. All of this lies ahead.

Socrates knows somewhat more about the father than the excellence of his character, namely, that he was very rich, an observation by which Socrates introduces conventional considerations alongside the natural. By now Plato has made it clear that Socrates does not fit the description of the philosopher that he will furnish later as a man totally lost in his city, indifferent to it and ignorant of all such things as who is related to whom, how influential and how wealthy. Presumably, the reader is expected to find Plato's conception of the philosopher somewhere between the alienated eccentric lost to the actualities of his civil existence and the human being mired in the city as matter for gossip and estranged from it as matter for thought. Theodorus now provides Theaetetus's name and contributes the further fact that the youth's substance seems to have been depleted by his guardians, though the youth is himself exceedingly free with money. His family, resources, and habits with money have now been discussed as if between practiced sophists, but since it is almost unthinkable that Plato would represent Socrates as scheming to recruit a youngster for his wealth or standing, we may rather presume that what follows is a demonstration of the selfless Socrates' disproving in act the charge that he corrupts the young. Yet the discourse of Socrates and Theaetetus opens with an initiative on the part of Socrates that again evokes the odor of sophistry. Socrates informs Theaetetus of Theodorus's opinion that the two of them look alike; but because Theodorus is not a painter, he is not qualified to pronounce on the resemblance of one person to another (although Theodorus had been quite observant and particular in referring to the snub nose and the bulging eyes, and even to their being less conspicuous in the young man than in the old one.) With this minor fatuity and gratuitous disparagement of Theodorus, Socrates installs himself between Theaetetus and his teacher, at the same time enabling himself to proceed to a distinction between judgments about body and judgments in praise of a soul—judgments like that of Theodorus in praise of Theaetetus. It is this judgment on the youth's excellence that Socrates proposes to test by questioning. The discussion begins, and discloses that as a pupil of Theodorus's, Theaetetus learns things that fall under specific branches of knowledge. Does not learning mean becoming wiser about the subject? If so, is knowledge not the same as wisdom? Socrates' admits to his uncertainty about knowledge. What is knowledge? We are being asked to believe that all his life, Socrates was not sure of what knowledge is; yet he will prove adept at refuting every definition of knowledge that is proposed, exhibiting a knowledge of what knowledge is not that would be inexplicable in the absence of a serviceable knowledge of what it is. If his purpose is to engender a serious and tenacious temper of inquiry, restricting himself to the role of the midwife he will claim to be and refraining from instruction, he will be distinguishing himself from the sophist that he might otherwise seem to resemble. But it will be impossible for him to achieve that end without demonstrating in act that there is a knowledge and hence an existence of what in some sense "is-not," that bone of contention generated by Parmenides and soon to be worried in the *Sophist*. What must remain outside our scope for the present is the question whether "what is not knowledge" is necessarily something else that *is*—such as, for example, opinion. Opinion certainly *is*. It happens not to be knowledge. To say that it is knowledge is therefore to fall into the error of believing one thing to be another rather than to maintain the being of a nonentity. These matters will presently be the themes of the conversation.

Agreeing to answer Socrates' questions, Theaetetus proposes that knowledge be defined as geometry, astronomy, harmony, and arithmetic as well as shoemaking and the other arts. This attempt at definition by giving examples of the thing to be defined is rejected by Socrates not only for the formal reason that it consists of a many rather than the unity of "what knowledge itself is" (*epistēmē auto ho ti pot' estin* 146E) but because it is tantamount to saying that knowledge means the knowledge that is within the art of shoemaking. What is to be defined is given as the definition of itself. It would follow that if one does not know what knowledge is, he cannot fully understand shoemaking because, by implication, he does not adequately understand what constitutes it as art. A shoemaker would know how to make shoes, but he would not know shoemaking "itself." It goes without saying that a shoemaker who was told that he did not know shoemaking would plausibly disagree, for if he knows how to make shoes, he knows shoemaking. But to know shoemaking is also to understand the shoemaker's art in the context of a whole in which the meaning of knowing is so problematic that mankind is driven to recognize a wisdom about and above knowing—a wisdom that describes itself as agnostic. From the outset, the reader is allowed to see that the question of what we know is bound up with the question or difficulty of knowing what (or that) we do not know. If philosophy were an art or like an art, those who possessed it would have to know what that knowledge is that constitutes their "art." Is it knowledge of the heavens and the visible universe? Of mathematics? Of the soul? Of the Good? Of Being? Of knowledge? Of art? Or of an impenetrable resistance of the whole that mankind inhabits to being known in its entirety? If philosophy is to surpass the arts and sciences, it must disclose to itself the grounds of its own limitation, above all addressing the question whether that limitation is a merely empirical fact in time or an eternal necessity dictated by the nature of the whole. The irrational and the incommensurable in mathematics, about to enter the dialogue, are the sign that the whole is intractable in itself. Their significance explains why Plato put geometry at the gateway to philosophy, to the subsequent disapproval of Aristotle. We may notice that Hobbes and Spinoza put geometry at the gateway to philosophy with an intention opposite to Plato's, conceiving it as the model of irresistible reason rather than the locus of an anomaly.

Theaetetus takes to heart the urging of Socrates that he come forth with a proper definition rather than with examples. To this end, he reports on a recent geometry lesson in which Theodorus introduced him and his companion, a youth named Socrates, to the irrational numbers by way of a demonstration that there is no finite number that measures the length of the side of a square of area three, or five, or the others up to seventeen, at which point he stopped (147D). Theaetetus and his friend Socrates now recognize that there are two indefinitely large classes of numbers, those having square roots and those that can be formed only by the multiplication together of unequal numbers. Theaetetus considers these two classes to be exhaustive of "all number" (*ton arithmon panta* 147E) although the prime numbers are unaccounted for unless multiplication by one is included as meaningful. Theaetetus goes on to distinguish the sides of squares and the sides of such rectangles as that of area seventeen, whose area cannot be the product of commensurable numbers. This rules out the multiplication by one, but Theaetetus's point here is that there are lines incommensurable in length that form plane figures commensurable in area. As has been said, the participation of Theaetetus in the dialogue introduces the irrational and incommensurable into the project for defining knowledge. The colloquy on numbers serves the immediate purpose of demonstrating that

Theaetetus knows how to gather a manifold within a unity or to make a definition, which is to say that he understands the first demand of rationality. He illustrates this practice of rationality with a proposition on the irrationals. So far as a definition can be the token of a knowledge, Theaetetus has shown that he knows something and that he knows something important of what knowing is. What his exposition implies, but only implies, comes to view when we consider that a rectangle of area "seventeen" is a finite quantity, and the sides forming it are finite lengths; but the existence and relations of those lengths are pervaded by the infinitesimal, the incommensurable, and the irrational, that which can be known about expertly without being in any simple sense fully known. To this point, the elucidation of knowledge has hinted at a realm of the unknowable, a realm of such a being that the one who knows its presence is more knowing than the one who does not. If it were impossible to make intelligible this coexistence of knowing and not-knowing, and the ground thereof in the nature of the whole that is man's setting, it would be impossible to make intelligible Socrates' famous claim, both modest and proud, that his wisdom lies in his knowing that he does not know. How can one characterize the love of wisdom that knows itself to be incapable of consummation without thinking at the same time of the love of that mysterious highest which allows itself to be united in perfect union with its faithful lover?

Now (148CD) Socrates makes a short speech of encouragement to Theaetetus, to hearten him after his insufficient efforts at definition. It is Socrates' purpose here as it is everywhere to teach the *ethos* of philosophy rather than its doctrines: unfailing perseverance that is capable of being strengthened by the goodness of the pursuit rather than defeated by the impossibility of consummating it in a world in which light is spread over darkness. The definition of the morality of philosophy will prove to have an importance that cannot be exaggerated, for it will disclose the moral order for man in a whole in which the gods and nature are indifferent and humanity seems abandoned to lawlessness. The insight, thought to be original with Machiavelli, that man has everything to do for himself in a world where courage and caution are the true salvation, is available in any age and was indeed accessible to the time and mind of Plato, as will be seen more and more amply.

Upon Socrates' urging Theaetetus onward, the youth declares

himself unable to discern the One that would define the many knowl-
edges, although he can get no relief from his caring about the thing.
Socrates responds with an account of himself as a midwife of the
mind's fecundity, one who helps such as Theaetetus, heavy with their
gestating notions, to bring those forth and then to determine whether
what has been born is the product of a true or a false pregnancy. In
brief, Socrates promises to help relieve Theaetetus of the pains of labor, not to deliver him of desirable issue. At one strategic blow, by
asserting a doctrine of the latency of knowledge, Socrates distinguishes philosophy, which elicits, from science and sophistry, which
instruct, and lays a foundation for his defense against the charge that
he corrupts the young: he helps them only to know what they know
and to recognize what they believe themselves to know but do not
know. It is clear that a doctrine of the latency of knowledge is implausible or meaningless until an account has been given of the source of
the latent knowledge. Is it present by anamnesis, the mythical recollection of experience on the part of the immortal soul reincarnated?
Or does it enter by way of such simply terrestrial experience as sense
perception? If there is an intelligible latency of knowledge, must there
not be a parallel latency of error to explain the pedagogical midwifery
as a whole? It is a curiosity of the so-called Socratic method that its
first premise, namely, its superiority over the ubiquitous instinctive
and successful method of teaching by informing, is not explicitly de-
fended. The reader is left to infer that the learner is made more fit for
survival in an unwelcoming terrain if he is given the impression that
he is the parent of the truth he is made to utter by the insinuating skill
of his interrogator. He must of course also be made known to himself
as the parent of his own nonsense.

Socrates is at some length (149A–151D) on his life and doings as a
midwife of the mind, introducing the subject with a show of adher-
ence to the method of interrogation but launching soon into an out-
right monologue (150B–151D), thus demonstrating a certain obvious
limit to the method of interrogation. He claims to be an ancilla (presumably by his method of interrogation) to gestating wisdom, not
himself a repository of it; but he alleges also that some who consorted
with him grew vain with their accomplishment, not understanding
that their progress had been his work more than theirs. They left him
and failed. Aristeides was one of many such. When eventually some
apply for permission to rejoin, his no-saying *daimonion* designates

some for rejection as undeserving, which is to say unpromising or un-teachable, and counsels him to allow the rest to return. It is unclear whether some human beings start with a meager store in their larder of latency or are deficient in their care about bringing it into active presence. Whatever the reason, it is obvious that Socrates makes no claim to possess a method that benefits everyone. In fact, he estimates the fertility of all those who come to him, and turns over to such sages as Prodicus the many prospective progenitors of wind.

Now Theaetetus is heartened to the point of willingness to pro-pose another definition of knowledge: knowledge is nothing other than perception (*aisthēsis*). This innocent promotion of the phenome-nal to the rank of intelligible cannot be expected to find favor with Socrates, who begins his assault on it by pointing out that this is how Protagoras defined knowledge, although in a different formula, namely, "Man is the measure (*metron*) of all things, of the being of the things that are and the non-being of the things that are not." This is shown by Socrates to mean that there is no other criterion of the truth of things, of what they are, than their appearance to each human be-ing to whom they appear, or who "perceives" them. Nothing simply is, nothing is one and unchanging, all is movement, motion, mixing, and becoming (152D). Protagoras the sophist is the arch-sage of flux.

As Socrates elaborates, he reveals, in a doxography that will be greatly enlarged by the Eleatic Stranger in the next day's discussion (*Sophist* 242 et seq.) that all the sages—Protagoras, Heraclitus, Empedocles—and the most eminent poets—of comedy, Epicharmus, and of the tragic, Homer—all, with the sole exception of Parmenides, speak for Becoming, for flux and motion, as the source of all. The broad sympathy between Parmenidean and Socratic philosophy on the primacy of One and Being seems to be the basis of an alliance made uneasy by some failure of accord regarding the Ideas. Eventu-ally, we shall have to face the reasons for that discord.

But is not motion good for the health of body and soul? Socrates must elicit the further meaning of the doctrine of flux, especially with respect to the being or nonbeing of the perceptible qualities of things. Each of our perceptions is the result of the interaction of the move-ment in the perceived and the movement in the percipient: the "white" that we see exists nowhere as the white that we see, only la-tently as the movements of small bodies, in a mode that in no way resembles that of which we are conscious. What could possibly ex-

plain the production of a perception out of the collision or cooperation of two motions on the part of two insensate corporeal structures?
It is not in the interest of Socrates' advocacy to advance this question
to a plausible answer; but as we know from the course of the discussion in the *Sophist* (247D et seq.), a plausible if not conclusive answer
might be found: that revisionist Parmenidean, the Eleatic Stranger,
proposes that the very essence of each thing, its "being," as will be
said, is its power (*dynamis*) to cause and to suffer change. Why not
contemplate the possibility that what Protagoras has discovered is
the ground for discovering the being of the things that indisputably
do become and pass away—their power, through their bodily motion, to become perceptible and to make all things perceptible? It becomes clearer to us that *Theaetetus* has a place in the Platonic project
for examining the schools, for considering the state of the issues addressed by all who could raise a plausible claim to possess a wisdom.

Socrates next obtains Theaetetus' agreement that every perception on the part of every sentient being would be a unique and solip-
sistic event, by implication reducing us all to a comprehensive
incoherence from which we evidently do not suffer—presumably because enough stands still in the world to preserve us from absolute
confusion. This is followed by a complaint against a doctrine that
maintains that six is large in relation to four but small in relation to
twelve, the defect being that six is thought by "them" to *become* bigger
and smaller within the two comparisons. The reader is left to choose
between supposing that the Protagoreans are willful enemies of common sense or that Socrates has taken to quibbling. An explanation of
sorts is forthcoming: Socrates will initiate Theaetetus in the mysteries
of Protagoras's doctrines, implying a difference between vulgar and
refined fluxism. We prepare to learn the difference between the initi-
ated Protagoreans, who admittedly replace all being with motion and
becoming, and the exoteric Protagoreans, who go further and believe
that, if all is motion and becoming, then only what is capable of motion, namely, the perceptible, thus presumably the corporeal, "is."
Socrates offers to unveil the esoteric Protagoreanism, and so doing
will indeed expose the crudeness of the vulgar materialism of which
Protagoras need not have been guilty. We will not be told what there
is about the Inner Doctrine that could justify dissimulation, or even
whether the so-called uninitiated are not simply the hangers-on who
must diminish the thought of such eminences as Protagoras until it

will fit within their narrow intelligence. That there could be Socratic epigoni is not even hinted.

The subtle Protagoreans posit two kinds of motion, one slow and belonging to the sensory, the other rapid and belonging to the perceived. The former has a passive power and the latter an active. Perception takes place as the result of the conjunction of the two motions. Neither active nor passive exists without the other, and all things obey this same necessity: nothing simply is, by itself, changeless and one, rather everything *is* in relation to something else. The resemblance of this construction to the Eleatic Stranger's provisional definition of Being (*Sophist* 247E) is striking. Could ubiquitous motion be the premise of a doctrine of Being as well as of Becoming? The present context, dominated by Socrates, contains nothing that would encourage such a thought, although the Parmenidean Stranger will show that he can explore it, as if to wonder whether some measure might exist between Protagoras and Parmenides.

After the usual renunciation of any claim to knowledge, Socrates begins his attack on the doctrine of universal flux. He makes something turn on the illusions brought on by insanity and somnolence: "perceptions," as he calls them, can be false. How can a dreaming or lunatic man be the measure if his perceptions are false? Protagoras is spared the indignity of being made to explain that even a lunatic, and especially a lunatic, must remain the measure of all things *for him*. Socrates presses on. How do we know that we are not dreaming at the present moment, i.e., that all our "perceptions" are not illusions and untrustworthy? But in what way untrustworthy? "Untrustworthy" implies an objective reality to which our perceptions would correspond correctly or would not, and it is precisely the purpose of the fluxists to reject the presupposition of a reality that obligingly stands still in order to be grasped "correctly," to be intelligible. When Socrates declares (158D) that the problem posed by dreaming is severe because we spend half our time asleep, we begin to suspect that the present argument has something of the provisional about it.

In his next effort, he develops at length the coherence of the doctrine of universal flux and its consequence in total relativism and solipsism, which he represents as vindicating the definition of knowledge as perception (160E). But has the demonstration brought forth a viable birth or a flatulence? Socrates wonders how Protagoras can pretend to the wisdom he must claim in order to assert that every man's opinion is as good as every other man's. Since most men think he is wrong about this, why take him seriously? And incidentally, why pay him for his instruction? The attack sharpens when Socrates opines that according to Protagoras's radical subjectivism, a man's measure is not only no better than a frog's but—a great blasphemy—no worse than a god's. And what place would there be for dialectic and for maieutic inquisition if wisdom evaporated into Everyman's impressions? Theaetetus suddenly and completely renounces his Protagoreanism, as if shocked by its impious implication. Socrates checks him, warning him against being swayed by mass rhetoric and reminding him that if Protagoras were able, he would say that never, in speech or writing, does he touch the question of the being or not-being of the gods (in which he might be no more than merely prudent), and that what the two have been saying about him is unsupported—merely likely (*eikos*).

In what appears to be a concession to the validity of "Protagoras's" rejoinder, Socrates offers to start again (163A et seq.), returning to the question whether knowledge is perception. The ensuing discussion turns on the difference between an active, present perception and the memory of one such. If we can be said to know what we retain in memory, then surely our knowing is not limited to our actual perceiving. Socrates points out that the discussion might not be going so smoothly if someone could speak on Protagoras's behalf, hinting to his companions that they are not contributing much to a fruitful inquiry. He goes on to provoke them further with the absurd argument that if perceiving were knowing, and seeing were a way of perceiving, then someone who covered one eye while looking with the other would be seeing and not seeing at the same time, thus knowing and not knowing simultaneously, which is impossible. Theaetetus makes a feeble protest, but Socrates tramples it. As it now appears, Socrates has been demonstrating the kind of eristic quibbling to which Theaetetus would have been vulnerable if he had told his thought about knowledge to some hair-splitter who displays himself for money. We are hard put to understand why Socrates forbears any explicit reference to sophists. What he does instead is to ask what Protagoras would say on his own behalf, if beset by the pack of charlatans. This is as much as to ask what the Grand Master of the sophists would say in defense of the thesis that knowledge is perception, as distinguished from what the vulgarians of his method would say in criticism of it. It seems that sophistic at its best stands for something concrete and considerable, and at its predatory worst is what we know now as sophistry. Socrates will do justice to the seriousness of Protagoras in a very long speech in which he impersonates Protagoras, commencing with a contemptuous dismissal of Socrates' own anti-Protagorean arguments and a denunciation of his practice on a gullible child. "Protagoras" scorns the verbal trifling that is the mark of the familiar sophist and demands that the truth of his doctrine be stated fairly. The plain truth is that whether one likes it or not, every human being has no choice but to be the measure of things, because it is to himself and only to himself alone that each thing presents itself in its appearance (*phainetai*). This puts no obstacle in the way of distinguishing wisdom from folly and good from bad. It is precisely the mark of wisdom that it induces reform in those to whom the bad things appear so that thereafter good will appear to them. "Protagoras" explains. To a man who is sick, his food tastes bitter and, which is decisive, *is* bitter. It is senseless to try to persuade him that it is not bitter, for the bitterness of it is not a matter of his false opinion. (Perhaps this is all the wisdom in *de gustibus non disputandum est.*) What is called for is not an improvement in the state of his wisdom but a recourse to the wisdom of someone who knows how to repair his body so that *his* food will no longer *be* bitter. What justifies the effort needed to bring about the change in the sick man? The fact that health is the better condition. As the physician works his changes with drugs, so the wise man (*sophistēs*) does with speech. Neither one replaces the false with the true, but only the bad with the good. This is so from the level of the farmer, who imbues sick plants with good and healthy perceptions (*aisthēseis*), to that of the city itself, for which whatever appears good *is* good so long as that is its opinion, and which therefore must be taught to deem good what is good according to some solid criterion. The wise man (*sophistēs*) who can accomplish the meliorative teaching is well worth his pay. It is thus that some are wiser than others at the same time that no one opines falsely. "Protagoras" closes with a strong denunciation of unfair argument, of eristic trickery that denies justice to the opponent. Those who avoid that abuse promote the honesty in their pupils that will lead them to seek philosophy as their cure, to cherish you and to blame their confusions on themselves, while those who are guilty of it, as many are, will make their companions end by hating philosophy rather than seeing the source of their ills in themselves. So now go forward with the question of knowledge and perception without distorting my meaning by appealing to the common, imprecise understanding of common language, i.e., without playing to the crowd.

No one can accuse Socrates of bad faith in his impersonation of Protagoras. Where the representation seems to present problems, as in its references to good, to justice, and to honesty as if they had an identifiable meaning in the mind of all listeners, we have the sense that the difficulty belongs to Protagoras himself. What strikes the reader of this apology for fluxism at its highest is the profound disjunction that it opens between the good and the eternally true: for Protagoras there is indeed a better and a worse, a good and a bad, emphatically a wise and an unwise, but these cannot be referred to a "true" and "false"; and where all is in flux, as it is by nature (157B), a man simply cannot escape being his own measure of "true"—no other exists. We may easily understand Socrates' demand that justice be done to Protagoras's seriousness in light of the conviction they share of man's solitude in the whole. Protagoras has recognized in his own way, with inferences that may be subject to all manner of reservations, what Plato will teach on his own grounds, as will be made explicit in the grand myth of the Age of Zeus in the *Statesman:* the human being bears a burden of autonomy that he must grasp correctly if it is to be his glory rather than his corruption. Protagoras's doctrine will stand or fall by his ability to disclose a standard of good that does not imply a truth dependent on rest and being. The Protagoreanism that Socrates has projected evinces a high but limited confidence in the power of speech and persuasion: there is no way to talk a sick man out of his perception of his food as bitter, nor any man out of any other perception; there are only ways of correcting the "condition" of a man in which his perceptions are formed. In important cases, that improvement of condition is achieved by a therapy of teaching. Socrates' portrayal of Protagoras leaves us wondering whether the latter conceives philosophy itself as a therapeutic instrument, reason as edification, serving "truthfully" a purpose served otherwise by mystery and myth or perhaps by the mere force of law and coercion.

When Socrates resumes his own persona (168D), he responds to "Protagoras's" complaint that it was a mere boy whom Socrates had manipulated with his arguments. Socrates compels Theodorus to participate in what he intends shall be a serious scrutiny of Protagoras's "man the measure," especially in its bearing on the autarky of each man in wisdom, alleged to be Protagorean doctrine but denied to be so by "Protagoras." Socrates' argument can be summarized briefly. The multitude of human beings believe that some men are wiser than others, more skilled and knowing. They think that wisdom is true thought and ignorance is false opinion. If they are right, then Protagoras is refuted by the substance of their opinion, which distinguishes wisdom and its defect. If they are wrong, then Protagoras is refuted by the wrongness of their opinion, which demonstrates the distinction of wisdom and its defect. Moreover, the very fact that Socrates and Theodorus are scrutinizing the wisdom of Protagoras proves that men measure other men's measures to test the wisdom of them. Socrates concludes that Protagoras himself would have to grant that neither a dog nor anyone who just happened along would be the measure of a single thing that the passerby had not studied (171C).

Socrates elicits from "Protagoras" an agreement that men are unequal in wisdom and ignorance, paradoxically deriving support for this view from what everyone thinks (171D). Socrates has persistently made Protagoras the proponent of an ostensible epistemic equality among men as percipient beings, and has refuted Protagoras by showing that the beings whose knowledge he is supposed to be affirming disagree with him. We know that "Protagoras" has flatly denied thinking that men, because their perceptions are not subject to refutation, are therefore not greatly in need of and susceptible to improvement, for that improvement is precisely what he claims to be his very own task and purpose. Still, Socrates resurrects the issue and cites the unequal possession of medical knowledge, for one thing, and of political knowledge, for another. As the immediate sequel indicates, Plato fashions the discourse to move toward the political bearing of Protagoras's "man the measure," with the apparent insinuation that the formula implies the radical equality of men. At 172A Socrates introduces the theme of men's judgments of morality and politics, something that he can do plausibly because such judgments, for example in a popular government, rest on more or less widely distributed wisdom or knowledge. Socrates is willing to allow, if only for the sake of the argument, that the decent, just, and pious, and their opposites, might be purely conventional within each country and not by nature, thus only locally "true," the dictate of the regime that expresses the measure of the men concerned. What cannot be said is that whatever a state legislates, believing it to be advantageous, proves in the event to be so, or to have been wise. It is because this incontrovertible argument implies that "advantage" or gain or material aptitude betokens (an unequally possessed) wisdom and points to the power of consequences to reveal uncontroversial truth that Socrates can turn the argument toward the peculiar unworldliness, clumsiness, or incapacity for "advantage" of some who make claims to wisdom and truth, namely the philosophers, whom he can contrast with the worldly-wise (172D et seq.). He is poised to take up the well-worn ridicule of philosophy as woolgathering inquiry into the subtleties of cloud-cuckoo-land. If he can turn the tables on the worldly-wise and their wisdom, he will have exposed the incontrovertible truth of the advantageous as a vulgar misunderstanding of the good. Protagoras cannot be made responsible for the common opinion of mankind, and he can even less be blamed for recognizing it. What he can be criticized for is the claim and the belief that he can bring a remedy for this natural myopia that, down to our time, revelation has been unable to eliminate and liberalism aims merely to exploit. When Socrates reported that he declined to have further conversation with some of those who had taken leave of him, he was signaling his conviction that philosophy benefits from its contemplation of remote things by abstaining from a fantastic aspiration to perfect the proximate ones.

Socrates had remarked on the growing complexity of the arguments, an observation that leads him to contrast the present company's own large leisure or freedom to pursue the discussion wherever it leads, with the bondage of those people of business whose speech is limited in court by the issue in litigation and to the time allowed. The litigants are slaves not only to the issue and the clock but, perhaps most important, to the master of the decision who might even be the *dēmos* itself. For a youth to be raised in that constricting public environment is to be formed to trickery, to sycophancy, and to reciprocating wrong for wrong (*allēlous antadikein*) (173A). It seems that Socrates is describing certain corrupters of youth—the very institutions of the city and those worldly-wise men who traffic in them, and those who sharpen the forensic skills of the youth so that they may prosper in that realm and atmosphere of "advantage" which is the city, where man comes closest to being indeed the measure by prescribing the good. The mutual antipathy between "the city" and philosophy is tempered on the one side by the resigned accommodation of philosophy to the usefulness or advantage of civic existence. That the resignation need not be fully reciprocated is demonstrated in the forthcoming trial of Socrates.

Socrates would like to go on to make use of the company's scholarly freedom to contrast the ones like themselves, the fortunate free, with the slaves to the common opinion of the city. He begins by proposing to speak about the principal figures among the free, not the paltry triflers in philosophy (173D). Socrates does not immediately name any of those chiefs, but what he goes on to say about them has so much of caricature about it, and clashes so obtrusively at certain points with any description of himself, as to raise a suspicion that the ensuing character of "the philosopher" is not intended to be conclusive. In anatomizing the chief philosophers, Socrates draws them as grotesques, utterly ignorant of the very location of their city's public places, of its laws and its political ways. They know nothing and care nothing about the distinctions of birth and wealth and inheritance that exist among the citizens. We must pause to remind ourselves that at the outset of the dialogue, Socrates not only evinced what looked like a parochial interest in the youth of Athens but inquired particularly about the father of the youngster whom Theodorus was praising; and when the boy was pointed out, Socrates identified his father as Euphronius of Sunium, a well-thought-of man who left great wealth (144C). To say that Socrates was a gossip about town would be going too far; but to say that he did not know the way to the agora would be as absurd as to claim that he was not familiar with the rules of the law courts, of which he had demonstrated a knowledge in the immediately preceding disparagement of the men who frequented those places. If we have a suspicion that something is awry in the developing characterization of the chief philosophers, our suspicion would be strengthened when Socrates says that these beings do not even know that they do not know about the human life around them that is their world (173E). Why would such as us go to such as them to be made wise about life? Socrates grants them their sincerity in despising whatever is not under the earth, above it, or abstracted from it, and he goes on to adduce Thales to exemplify total immersion in philosophy—ridiculed by the worldly, and unconscious not only of

45

what his neighbor is doing but even of whether he is a human being or some beast. Socrates has reported (*Phaedrus* 230A–D) that he has no time for the inquiry into strange beings when he is still unable to know himself, and must look within to learn whether he is a beast more complex and violent than Typhon or a gentler and simpler animal sharing by nature in some divine and tranquil lot. More than that, Socrates proclaims himself a city man who learns not from the trees of the countryside but from the human beings of the city. In his present portrait of the chiefs of philosophy, he goes on to describe their overt contempt for the tokens of distinction that the city honors. That he is not indulging his imagination is suggested by the resemblance of his description to the character and doings of the grossly misanthropic Heraclitus. The result of it all is that the philosophers and the citizens exist in a state of mutual contempt—and unequally armed hostility. We are left wondering why it never occurred to the philosophers who fit Socrates' description that, for the simple trouble of keeping their high-mindedness to themselves for their own blissful contemplation, they could have despised their fellow citizens to their hearts' content and no one the wiser. As for Socrates himself, he could not live an urban life without provoking all classes with his improving interrogations, whose most visible effect was to make him an object of murderous detestation.

It would be easier to consider Socrates' verbal picture of the philosopher as mere caricature if it did not end as seriously it does: were the man who is clever in matters of worldly advantage ever willing to be taken in hand by someone who would lead him to inquire into the nature of the things he admires, and to induce him to try to answer when questioned about them, then the tables would be turned and the scoffers would become ridiculous in the view of the educated and the free. Socrates says nothing to suggest that he or anyone known to him has presided over many or any such conversions.

We have learned that there are regimes of political freedom in which the individuals who attend best to their own advantage are in fact slaves to the polity—to its citizenry and to its "values" or opinions. We will learn immediately (176A) that it must always be so: it is not possible to banish evils from mortal nature and this world, where they move of necessity. Therefore it behooves us to flee this place with greatest speed and get us to god and become godlike, which is to say to become good and wise. Short of consummating this perfection in the presence of God, a man may strive for it by the light of true wisdom, true knowledge of his advantage here in the cities. Every other knowledge is ignorance, although the possessors of it think it the key to being safe in the city. But we must say out the truth, for their not knowing themselves makes them what they are, and they do not know the penalty of their unrighteousness, which is to live basely among the base, here and hereafter.

If Plato had made Socrates say, "They know not what they do"; and "We must preach the word to them, lest they fail to be like God and be lost in this life and the next," he could not have put the matter more succinctly. We are not told why Socrates thought that the truth should be said out rather than cherished quietly, in the city that he described as incorrigibly and contemptibly worldly. We can gather only, by the end of this passage (177C), that some good may come for those men of the world who have the courage to stand and be questioned. We have been brought around from the dogmatic rejection of the political state on the part of the unnamed chiefs of the philosophers to the quiet philanthropy of Socrates, who saw a duty to say out the truth, not in order to save mankind, which he deemed impossible, but to benefit some few. It was perhaps the genius of Socrates to know how to contemn the city without leaving it or becoming estranged from it; to recognize the necessary imperfection of political life without losing sight of its indispensability and its gifts; to value it in spite of its irreconcilability with philosophy, whether that irreconcilability be manifest in persecution or indifference; and never to confuse the abstraction of "the city" with its individual members, of whom a few might be brought to rise through their vaunted cleverness to a justified diffidence, with a glimpse of the nature of things as compensation.

Now (177C) Socrates brings the digression on wisdom in the city to a close and returns to the thread of the argument, which proves in fact to be about wisdom in the city: the polis can indeed declare the "truth" of Good qua justice however it thinks best within its borders, but in no way can it prevent its decisions that are intended to produce the Good qua advantage from being falsified by the future. Whatever names are used, it is advantage that cities aim at in their legislation, whereby Socrates implies a priority of advantage before justice that troublingly reminds of Thrasymachus's formula in the *Republic:* justice is the advantage of the stronger, who legislate. At any rate, it is

47

often true that states miss the mark of advantage that they aim at. Advantage is a thing of the future, which is the region also of legislation. Could Protagoras maintain that man as such is the measure of the future, or is it not the men of special knowledge who are the experts of futurity? At this point, no distinction is made between the art of shaping the future and the art of foretelling it, although Protagoras is said to represent himself as superior to any prophet (*mantis*) in looking ahead (179A). Claiming that the thesis of "man the measure" has been thus far refuted in measured terms (*metriōs*), Socrates concedes that they have not disposed of the possibility that states of feeling (*pathos*) and their associated opinions are incontrovertible truths for an individual, and thus are "knowledge." To get beyond this impasse it will be necessary to recur to the doctrine that universal motion is the ultimate irreducible fact of all being (179D), for that premise is the support of the maxim "man is the measure."

Theodorus takes the lead in denouncing the kinetics from Homer through Heraclitus to his own day, apparently because his geometer's mind is exasperated by their slipperiness in argument (180C). Socrates distinguishes the ancient kinetics, who dissembled their doctrines in myths of flowing waters, and the moderns, who blurt their wisdom everywhere, astonishing the very cobblers, who in their simple way think that that some things are in motion and others are at rest. Socrates contrasts all the kinetics with the dogmatic statics, whose chiefs are Melissus and Parmenides, who identify the motionlessness of the one whole as the sovereign truth of being. Socrates, finding himself caught between those extremes, considers the possibility, so presumptuous on the part of a nobody like himself, that he will have to reject the wisdom of both parties of sages. As for ourselves, we wonder if he does not incline from the outset to the insight of the cobblers, those simple men of everyday life, who see their world as a thing of motion and rest. If Socrates or Plato could deepen this superficial apprehension and trace it to its ground in the being of things, he would have reconciled, in a manner of speaking, the consciousness of the man of the city and the wisdom of philosophy—in such a sense transcending the rift between "the city" and philosophy.

Socrates has agreed (181B) that the doctrines of the kinetics and the statics should be examined. He has no difficulty arriving at the conclusion that if all is in motion, and motion includes not only change of place but change simply, nothing stands still long enough to be nameable with a single unchanging name. Similarly, the very act of perception is what we would call a "process," dependent on change of some kind, perhaps in the organ of perception, from instant to instant, and thus by the same criterion as before unnameable, a nonentity. But if perception disappears into change or flux, and one ought not refer to perceiving any more than to not-perceiving, then it is impossible to define knowledge as perception. Socrates concludes (183A) that the theory of universal flux, by which knowledge is identified with incontrovertible perception, now seems to make every assertion incontrovertibly true—as if anything might be said about anything, for nothing "is" and all is "becoming." Socrates declares himself to have disposed of Protagoras and to have refuted the proposition that every man is the measure of all things and thus at the same time to have refuted the definition of knowledge as perception. Theodorus, who has been Socrates' respondent since the point at which "Protagoras" complained that Socrates was winning easy victories over a mere boy, cannot wait to escape his interrogation and says nothing in defense of his master, Protagoras, although neither Protagoras nor any serious human being would maintain that because everything is in flux, therefore the statement that a dog is a god is incontrovertible. Only the most abandoned eristic who believed that a way can always be found to make the weaker argument the stronger would insist on the position that Socrates is fobbing off on Protagoras rather than on a sophist who might exploit his theorem. If this apparent injustice to Protagoras is meant to remind that the master in philosophy is implicated in the excesses of his epigoni, then Plato is inviting us to think of Eucleides, our present narrator, who proceeded from Socrates to eristic.

Theodorus is happy to see Protagoras finished off, the strain of responding to Socrates apparently exceeding any distress caused by denying his master—a further illumination on the relation of the chiefs and their followers. When Theaetetus finds himself nominated to replace *his* teacher, Theodorus, as interlocutor with Socrates, he takes it on himself to remind his elders that they had promised to scrutinize the statics too, as well as the kinetics. Socrates refuses to comply, giving as his reason his unwillingness to play the buffoon with Melissus and the other statics (183E) or to deal with Parmenides, for whom he has the highest respect, without being confident that he understands the thought of that profound man. No such consideration restrains Socrates' treatment of Protagoras and the twin doctrines of flux and equality implicit in the formula "man the measure." Socrates must reckon with Protagoras as with Parmenides, with the universalization of motion as with the universalization of rest; but the former is more odious to him, the latter closer to the intermediate position that he himself occupies. As the discourse has shown, Socrates' criticism of Protagoreanism is aimed at the political egalitarianism and the epistemological confusion—in brief the disorder—that he accuses it of fostering. Where Protagoras finds the unreason of the whole in ubiquitous flux, Socrates finds it in the irrationality disclosed by geometry. Theodorus, the Protagorean geometer, is too old to be weaned from his confusion. Theaetetus, however, will before our eyes drop his Protagorean definition of knowledge as perception and will spend his life elaborating the mystery of the irrational, a somehow Socratic.

Socrates does not want the question of knowledge to be lost sight of, and he now leads the company back to it rather than take up the vast questions raised by the philosophers of rest. The ensuing section, 184B–186E, is in fact a continuation, this time without buffoonery, of the refutation of the Protagorean definition of knowledge as perception. It differs from the earlier, vulgar one in that it turns on the presence and activity of the soul and the soul's directedness toward the unchanging being, which is a gesture in the direction of Parmenides.

Socrates first establishes that perception comes about by way of and not "by" the several bodily organs of perception. Then there must be some interior thing where or whereby the discrete perceptions, which cannot communicate with one another, can be united and be thought about. Whatever that is, it is not itself an organ of perception. The many senses become one "in some one idea, whether it should be called soul or whatever."[5] One sense cannot notice another, for each of the organs of perception is limited to its own class of objects. Therefore, whatever makes possible our thought about the sensoria, discovering that they are, that they are other to each other but identical each with itself, that each is one but that together they are numbered, and whether they are alike or different, whatever accounts for the thoughts is not perception. Perception does not reveal what the senses have in common, namely their being, that which all things

5. *eis mian tina idean, eite psychēn eite ho ti dei kalein* (184D).

have in common. The multiplicity of all things is brought to unity in their being by the power (*dynamis*) of the soul, which may act through an organ of the body but can act directly by itself, as it does when it conceives being, same and other, as well as the noble and base, and good and bad. It is given to Theaetetus to contribute the observation (186AB) that it is the soul that considers the relation of past and present to the future. This reminder of the discussion of advantage makes the soul the faculty for reasoning about what is by its definition necessarily uncertain. Whether the fate of the soul itself is meant to be included in the future is not indicated. In brief: perception, body, and motion do not account for thought and soul, which are indispensable to our consciousness of being and thus to our possible contact with truth. Being is the basis of truth and truth is the condition for knowledge. Therefore knowledge cannot be perception.

Socrates is in accord with Parmenides in maintaining the confluence of being, truth and good. At the same time, in arguing that knowledge is not perception, he argues that the soul, not any bodily organ, is the power that is at the root of knowledge. But is through some form of doing on the part of the soul that knowledge arises; and the act of the soul must be a kind of change and therefore a kind of motion, a thought that puts Socrates in an agreement with Protagoras. It will be argued in *Sophist* (e.g., 248 et seq.) that if soul knows and being is known, the implication of activity and therewith of change in soul and being will disturb the devotees of the Ideas, presumably because they are made restless by any implication of soul or being in motion. It would seem again that Socrates must find his place between the radical statics and the radical kinetics in his project for coping with a world permeated by the tension between the intelligible and the irrational.

While ascertaining what knowing is not, they have, according to Socrates, discovered what sort of thing it is in a general way: what the soul itself by itself does when it concerns itself with things that exist. Theaetetus calls this opining. Responding to Socrates' suggestion that they start over, using the gains of their recent progress, Theaetetus modifies the proposal that knowledge is opinion to say instead that knowledge is true opinion, the false kind being obviously ineligible.

Now (187D) Socrates professes himself puzzled, and often before to have been puzzled, by "false opinion." What is this *pathos* that affects human beings, and in what way does it come to be? We in turn are unprepared for his perplexity. His argument against the kinetics included the observation that for them, every perception is its own incontrovertible truth, with the possibility of false opinion becoming instantly problematic. But Socrates is the conqueror of kineticism. Why should "false" be a problem for him, and at so late a date in his life when he has exploded innumerable opinions (including kineticism) as false? What appears is that he does not doubt the being of false, he simply claims not to understand it, its "how" and "what." Apparently, it is possible to know the being of something and at the same time not to know the thing as it is and what it is.

Unable to define false opinion as a failure to know what one knows, or not to know what one knows, or any other paradoxical combination of knowledge and ignorance, Socrates is enabled to move the inquiry away from knowing and not knowing to being and not being, which is to say that he can view part of the territory claimed by the venerated Parmenides. It would seem that holding a false opinion is to hold an opinion of "what is not," i.e., of non-entity; but an opinion must be about or of something, some one thing, not about a non-thing. If then it is impossible to opine about a non-being, opining about non-being cannot be the ground of false opinion. The application of Parmenides' warning against thinking about what is not has not led to the explanation of what false opinion is but rather to what it is not—a point worth noting, if at all, in view of what may be called the significant rehabilitation of the negative that the Eleatic Stranger, a revisionist Parmenidean, will launch in *Sophist.* In simply declaring that opining is always about some one thing, Socrates has preempted the argument of a hypothetical Parmenidean who might suppose that all error in thinking arises from attempting to perform the impossible act of thinking about a nonbeing. For us, the conclusion is that a problem or confusion generated by the principal axiom of the kinetics—only becoming is—is incapable of solution by the application of the principal axiom of the statics—only rest is.

Socrates leads the discussion on through the suggestion that error arises when the mind supposes a thing to be some other thing which it is not. In order to carry on the inquiry, Socrates offers at last a definition of opinion: it is the conclusion reached by the mind at the end of that silent internal discourse which is thought. Since no one ever reasons to the conclusion that one thing known is another thing known, or that something known is a thing unknown, or vice versa, this attempt to define error as mistaken identity must be rejected in turn.

Socrates is apprehensive that they will have to accept certain follies if they fail to account for false opinion. We are interested in this minor passage (190E–191A) because it gives Socrates occasion to say that he and his companions should solve the problem of false opinion themselves before taxing "others" with the follies that are implicit in theories which render false opinion inexplicable. To this point, the indications present in the dialogue point to the Protagorean kinetics and the Parmenidean statics as the most likely "others" of Socrates' reference, which strengthens our speculation that at least one aim of the dialogue is to set Socratic philosophy alongside its weightiest alternatives so that it and they may all be tried alike.

Socrates embarks next on a tortuously detailed effort to elucidate false opinion by introducing the factor of memory. Of the things that we perceive we retain images, which he compares to the impressions that would be made, more or less distinctly depending on the quality of the impressionable material, in some substance like wax. Thereafter when we perceive an object, we refer it to its own impression, if we had perceived it before, or to the impression of a different object. In the latter case, we suppose something that we perceive and—so far as perceiving something is knowing it—know, to be something else, which we remember and—so far as remembering something is knowing it—know. This chiasma of immediate and retained perceptions is the newly proposed source or meaning of false opinion. People with faulty memory apparatus are the ones who will be prone to false opinion.

If we have not noticed that this account of false opinion proceeds on the premise that perception is the element of knowledge, Socrates will now make this known to us in a speech of intense self-mortification (195). On he must go in order to deal with the obvious fact, apparent to us we know not how, that false opinion exists in the realm of thoughts themselves, which are not perceptions and do not arise from them. This could have occurred to us if we had reflected on our recent experience as readers, which has been a tour through one demonstrated and then rejected conclusion after another, culminating in the genesis before our eyes of Socrates' false opinion about false opinion, all on the plane of thought and imperfect recollection. Error has been avoided. Socrates somehow knew that his conclusion, what he "knew" provisionally, was not true and thus was not knowledge. In this sense, he knew what he did not know.

Socrates and Theaetetus have been searching for false opinion unsuccessfully, all the time knowing *that* it is but not *what* it is. Now (196D) Socrates reminds them that their purpose from the beginning has been to discover what knowledge is; they have not answered the question yet they have repeatedly spoken of knowing as if they knew what it meant. They have carried on as if they did not know that they did not know what knowledge is. The self-awareness, honesty, and modesty that prompt Socrates' self-correction are the moral accompaniment of philosophy that must contribute to the definition of that elusive thing and to its difference from sophistic.

What is knowing? Socrates reports a current answer: knowing is "having knowledge." Socrates proposes to modify this formula, which seems to have everything wrong with it for which he had just reproved their former speech; but the point of his suggested refinement is otherwise. He introduces a distinction that accords with the difference in English between owning and possessing. One may own something without being in present possession of it. One has it "somehow," but it is not now in one's grasp or control. To elucidate this, Socrates conjures the famous image of the cage in which one keeps all manner of birds, all of which one owns indeed but any one of which might on a certain occasion be elusive, so that one reaches into the cage intending to seize a pigeon but comes up in possession of a crow instead. We start life with an empty birdcage, which we stock by inquiring and learning, acquiring knowledge and ending by knowing. The usefulness of this image lies in the future if anywhere, for in itself it is as tautological as any of the rejected explanations that have gone before. In any case, it enables Socrates to pronounce that one cannot not-know what one knows, for the knowledge in question is present in the cage of the mind, or, as one might say, in a state of latent memory. It is possible, though, to bring out of latency a knowledge of some certain thing when one has wished to grasp a knowledge of some other thing. The example we are given shows a man grasping for knowledge of eleven and seizing instead knowledge of twelve. Presumably this means that a man subtracting ten from twenty-one would be "grasping for knowledge of eleven" but would for some reason arrive at "knowledge (perhaps one might say 'active consciousness') of twelve" instead. This would be to entertain a false opinion of the difference between ten and twenty-one. If this is what Socrates means, then an opinion, false or true, would be an affirmation or judgment that something is something in the sense, for example, that "the leaf is green." With a view to the fact that Socrates will leave the present scene in order to proceed to the offices of the king archon, one might, if only fleetingly, consider whether such an opinion as "thunder is a god" may also come within Socrates' reference to a grasping for one thing known and coming up with something else.

In any case, Socrates' reasonings on knowledge and the state of the knowing mind, however inconclusive they are proving to be, rely conspicuously on the difference between a mental content that is in a state of latency and the same that has been made patent. This conception of knowledge is consistent with Socrates' familiar insistence that, as a midwife or mere interrogator, what he does is not to implant anything but only to evoke it. It is consistent even with the myth of anamnesis, by which the soul learns what it knows while it is detached from the body, and then "remembers" more or less imperfectly in its incarnated condition, as the latent is brought to the surface by experience of one kind or another.

Out of all the effort, Socrates claims (199C) that at least they are clear on the subject of our not knowing what we know: we may be wrong, but we have what we have. He seems to lose the opportunity to take up the crucial alternative, that "a man either can or cannot know what he does not know," to which only one answer can comport with the philosophizing of Socrates.

Still dissatisfied (199D) with their work, Socrates muses on the strangeness of their provisional conclusion: they have found falseness in minds in which there is nothing but knowledge. Theaetetus would like to help by suggesting that perhaps there are birds of positive nonknowledge as well as birds of knowledge in the psychic aviary, but Socrates must turn the suggestion aside, and in so doing attend to the philosophic formula that he seemed to neglect. He argues as follows. A man who reached into his birdcage and caught a bird of nonknowledge would think that he had grasped a knowledge; he would not know that he was not-knowing. But the explanation of this common occurrence by that hypothesis of a positive existence of the negation of knowledge fails. If there were a noetic entity called notknowing, it would by definition be a "known-thing," and the man in whose mind it was lodged would have to think that one thing he knew (an item of knowledge) was another thing he knew (an item of nonknowledge), which is no more possible than his thinking that an elephant, which he knows, is a flea, which he also knows. The explicit point is that we do not yet understand false opinion, and are paying the price of seeking to do so before satisfactorily responding to the question, What is knowledge? The implicit point is that this welter of speculation is Plato's representation of Socrates, at the end of his life, trying to make perfectly clear in his own mind what he means when he says that his wisdom is in his knowing that he does not know—an apparent paradox that could encapsulate what is problematic in philosophy as such.

We start over (200D). What is knowledge? Knowledge is true opinion. No, it is not, according to the rhetors and pleaders, the slaves to the clock, to whom we now return after a long parting. They enter the discussion in a peculiar way. They have the art of persuading—which Socrates distinguishes from teaching—the judges in litigation of the force of a particular decision. They do this in a time too short, and in the inevitable absence of ocular evidence (perception) on the part of the judges, for knowledge proper to become present in the mind of the judges. In brief, the judges may be persuaded to the truth of the matter without having knowledge of it. We are to understand that opinion as such is not knowledge, the truth of opinion does not convert opinion into knowledge, and true opinion therefore is not knowledge. The judge who has been persuaded cannot give a perfect reason for his opinion, as he could if he had seen the thief take the gold from the temple.

Theaetetus tries again. He had forgotten but now remembers having heard it said that true opinion with reason is knowledge, without reason it is not knowledge. The rational is the knowable, the irrational is the unknowable. Socrates, who might have asked what are the rational and irrational, asks what are the knowable and unknowable, and is obliged to address the question himself. In so doing, he does arrive at the rational and irrational. His discourse, which he presents as a "dream in return for a dream," turns on the following issue. Are there absolutely primary, irreducible elements of being or being known which, precisely because they are irreducible to anything more primary in terms of which they themselves might have to be explained, cannot be explained at all, since the explanation, or "reason," of something means the account that can be given of it by reference to something else, of which, for example, it might be composed, or even to some attribute that belongs to it such as being itself? For the purposes of the argument, the primacy of the irreducible must be preserved by protecting it from any plurality in its constitution whatsoever, even such as is implied in saying of it that it is itself and *also* that it exists. The very characterization of it as "itself" is inadmissible, we are told (202A). Nothing can be said about the irreducible inexplicables, or uttered in relation to them; only their name can be said without impugning their absolutely elemental primacy. These elementaries are irrational or inexplicable (*aloga*) and unknowable (*agnosta*); they are only perceptible (*aisthēta*) (202B). Nothing is made of the fact that in one breath Socrates has denied that anything can be said of the elements and has affirmed that they are, among other things, perceptibles in some unexplained sense. This apparent oversight, however jarring in the immediate context, will prove to be consistent with the eventual refutation of the hypothesis, now being maintained, that the explanatory irreducible must itself be unintelligible. To explain his meaning, Socrates brings the example of the unitary letter and the syllable or composite of letters. The letters of the alphabet are reducible to or explainable by nothing simpler than themselves. The composite syllable can be "explained" by reference to the letters that compose it. But Socrates questions whether something knowable can be concocted of what is unknowable. At 203C, he asks whether the first syllable of his name, *So*, is the two letters of which it is composed or is "some one idea" (*mia tina idea*) that has come into being by their conjunction. On the assumption that the combination is "one idea" (*mia idea*) that has come into being, and that this might be so of words and of all other things, does it follow that this generated composite acquires the condition of a new unitary entity? If the composite becomes a true although generated One, can it and indeed must it be understood as a self-subsistent thing, or can it never escape being reduced to its component parts or elements, which, by the provisional hypothesis, are unintelligible, merely present, irreducibles?

Socrates considers (204A) that the new unit idea that has come into being out of its elements cannot, qua unit, have parts. His reason is that a thing composed of parts must remain simply "all the parts." This seems to open a distance between an "all" and a "whole," the latter sounding like a unitary entity. Socrates wonders next if there is a difference between "an all" as a collective noun and "all" in the plural sense of "all of them." It seems that there is not, if by "all of them" we mean the same totality that we have in mind when we say "all." In the same vein, a collectivity such as an army is, according to Socrates, the same as its "number," which is as much as to say that an army composed of a million men is a million just as much as it is a million men. But a number, a million, is inescapably a plurality, and there is thus no way to transcend its being a thing of parts. Yet part has meaning in relation to whole, and whole, like all, means the complete and comprehensively inclusive. The difference between whole and all is thus made to disappear. The inquiry favors the conclusion that the composite is a generated idea whose intelligibility is not tainted by the unintelligibility of its irreducible component parts.

If the syllable is not simply its letters but is a new Unit Idea, must the syllable not contain those letters in such a way that they should not be thought of as its "parts"? Or is it true that the syllable is of the same order of being as the letters and is therefore only as knowable as they are (205AB)? The latter being ruled out, and therefore the letters *not* being "parts" of the syllable, of what then is the syllable composed? The syllable must then be "some one idea without parts." But it had been agreed that the indivisible irreducible simple was not-rational (*alogon*) and unknowable (*agnoston*). Now syllable is impugned because it is not explicable by reference to something primary, whereas it had suffered previously because the primary to which it had been referred for explanation is itself necessarily unintelligible. Syllable and letter together collapse into the nonrational and unknowable. Theaetetus consents to this outcome with the telling proviso, "If we are persuaded by the argument."

Now Socrates demurs, finding their conclusion obnoxious to the experience of everyone who has learned to read. His point is that in the matters of which we have experience, like reading and music, it is the primary constituents, the letters and notes, that are much more clearly known to us than the composites, for learning the letters and the notes means knowing each one in its distinction from all the rest— not, by implication, tracing it to its components. If we were to make inferences from such indications to other matters, we would conclude that elements as a class (*genos*) are much more knowable than composites, and yield a more authoritative knowledge in the other sciences (*mathēmata*). If anyone were to say that the composite (syllable) is knowable but the element (letter) is by its nature (*pephukenai*) unknowable, we would suppose him to be playful, whether he meant to be or not (206B; cf. Aristotle *Metaphysics* 1086b, for example). If we were indeed to follow this suggestion, and apply the conclusion that favors the knowability of the element to the other *mathēmata*, for example to physics, we would find ourselves pointing to the intelligible atomism of finite divisibility as against the irrationality of the infinitesimal and incommensurable that lie at the heart of mathematics. Plato has taught that experience, which we cannot and should not try to escape, for it is a kind of knowledge, teaches us that the world is intelligible and livable, while speculation reveals that the world is an eternal and impenetrable mystery. It is noteworthy that where Protagoras spoke of perception, which is compromised by its metaphysic of flux and its degradation of judgment, Socrates speaks of experience (*empeiria*), which argues so persuasively if not always unequivocally. Philosophy, if Plato's Socrates exemplifies it, is what reveals and contemplates the accessible and the incommensurable in the whole, struggling to discern that boundary between the two that must itself necessarily belong among the mysteries.

Socrates reminds the company of the question that they are investigating: What is the meaning of the proposition that the most perfect knowledge comes into being by supplementing true opinion with reason? The ruling question is, What does this "reason" signify to us? There are three possibilities. It could mean, in the first place, explanation in speech, or "giving reasons" in support of the true opinion. Since everyone who has a right opinion can give a verbal account of it, there is no way for right opinion not already to be associated with "reason" in this sense. Therefore the so-called "addition" of reason to right opinion is a mere locution that conceals a tautology.

But, in the next place, perhaps "reason" is added to true opinion when to an inexpert definition of something like a cart is added a comprehensive, technically correct or "methodical" catalogue of all its parts, such as could be furnished by a carter. We seem to be thrown back upon the exhausted subject of the elementary ingredients, but Socrates' purpose here (207) is novel. He illustrates his thought with the example of someone who understands what is meant by spelling and writing and who spells "Theaetetus" correctly with a *thēta* but misspells "Theodorus" with a *tau*. In spelling "Theaetetus" correctly, he shows that he has right opinion, but in misspelling "Theodorus" he shows that he has not mastered *thēta* and *tau,* the elements. Thus he has right opinion and also, as understanding writing as the combination of letters to form words, i.e., understanding the "method," he also has reason. Still, he does not have knowledge, or so Socrates says and Theaetetus agrees. Therefore the definition of knowledge as true opinion with reason, on the present understanding of the meaning of reason, falls again.

There remains a third possibility, that knowledge will prove to be true opinion with reason if the reason of each thing is its singularity, that by which it is distinguished from every other thing in existence. To grasp that singularity and to express it is to give that account of the thing that is its explanation, or its "reason." But it is impossible to have an opinion about anything without having an opinion about that very thing that one has already picked out and identified as distinct from everything else. If one has true opinion about something, the "reason" that is supposed to be added to that opinion is already implicit in the having of the opinion. Therefore it is nonsense to speak of "adding" reason to true opinion if reason or explanation means what it has just been said to mean. The last hope that knowledge can be defined as true opinion together with reason has been exploded.

Theaetetus ends in aporia. That or how knowledge is problematic is demonstrated by the difficulty of knowing the meaning of knowledge itself. This demonstration is inseparably joined, through the medium of Socrates' pedagogical maieutics, with the crucial form of self-knowing, which is to know that or what one does not know. Especially because Socrates has told him a tale to the effect that his knowledge is latent within him, Theaetetus must learn a lesson of humility, if he learns nothing else, when a skillful and sympathetic midwife is unable to educe from him the knowledge desired above all else. Socrates says in his last remarks to Theaetetus: perhaps through all of this you will be enabled to think more fruitfully in the future, and if not, then you will be thoughtful enough not to think that you know what you do not know and you will be less harsh toward your companions. Socrates has prepared or sought to prepare Theaetetus for the life of inquiry into the irrational and incommensurable that Theaetetus in fact lived.

Socrates excuses himself at the end, saying that he must go to the office of the official, where he will respond to the indictment against him brought by Meletus, the only one of his accusers whom he mentions by name, the one who charged him on behalf of the poets, who are perhaps as vulnerable and sensitive as any men to criticism directed against those who manifest no doubts about their knowledge of the many and high things they pronounce on. The reference to the indictment moves the discourse from the abstract concerns that have dominated the conversation toward the realm of man's civil existence. Plato chose to make the transition by way of a discourse on the gods that occurs on the grounds of a judicial officer, where justice and divinity, the good on earth and the good aloft, would converge if the whole were disposed to their convergence, under the auspices of the state, the only human agency that combines deliberation with force.

III

EUTHYPHRO

PLATO'S SOCRATES EXCUSED HIMSELF FROM THE COMPANY OF THE
Theaetetus in order to proceed to the place of the king archon, the
Athenian officer to whom accusers and accused at law were required to present themselves. Now Socrates is at that place because
Meletus's indictment is pending against him. Thus we are made to
know that the trilogy *Theaetetus, Sophist,* and *Statesman,* which for its
content could have occurred at any time in Socrates' life, is immediately precedent to the trilogy that relates his trial, imprisonment,
and execution. The argument of *Euthyphro* should help to explain
Plato's conception of the two trilogies and their connecting member
as a consecutive whole. The imminence of Socrates' trial and the
theological-political issues that permeate it are ever present in the discourse of the *Euthyphro,* and may be taken as indicating Plato's conception of the seven dialogues as a whole: they portray the world of
man, the gods, the city, and philosophy.

According to its traditional subtitle, *Euthyphro* is about holiness
or the demands of piety, but it becomes evident quickly that the subject is not simply the holy but the holy in its relation to the just or the
right. As will appear, not all of the right is comprehended within the
holy, and the part that is so subsumed is in one aspect uncertain and
in another aspect available independently of any recourse to holiness
as a behest of gods. Thus *Euthyphro* maps the territory of the first trilogy, in which the mystery of knowledge itself, and inferentially of
knowledge of divinities, is thematic; and in which is shown the need
for the human beings to care for themselves in an atmosphere of justice prescribed by no god and no holiness. *Euthyphro* will at the same
time look forward to the second trilogy, the story of the predicament
of Socrates under indictment for offending, at the same time and in
the same act, against holiness or piety and justice or right, against the
gods and against the city.

As the conversation begins, Euthyphro is surprised to find
Socrates at the place of the king, and soon elicits from him the reason
for his being there. Socrates is under indictment by one Meletus, a
young man who is acting on behalf of the young, his contemporaries,
whose corruption by Socrates he would avenge with utmost severity.

Meletus would have it that Socrates ruins the young by making innovations in religion, rejecting the old gods and making new ones, then proceeding to demoralize the young with his heresy. The indictment demonstrates that a species of idolatry can be conceived even among pagan idolators, among whom the offense would be reprehended not as dishonoring a deity but as unsettling the city. We know from the opening of *Euthyphro* that Socrates' private theology, whatever it consisted of, was to be held against him for profane reasons, on behalf of public order, not from fear of the wrath of gods. Euthyphro is so far out of sympathy with the indictment as to declare that to harm Socrates would be to do a great evil to the city. It would seem at the outset that in Euthyphro's mind what truly deserves punishment are acts that are simply and in themselves offensive to the gods; but it will become increasingly evident that Euthyphro is in fear that the gods notice wrongdoing and will avenge it even to the extent of punishing those who do not take arms against it.

In this spirit, Euthyphro is on hand in order to indict his father of murder. To meet Socrates' amazement, Euthyphro explains. A drunken laborer on the family property murdered one of the household slaves. Euthyphro's father bound and confined the murderer, and sent for advice to the religious authority (*exēgētēs*) in Athens so that he might know how to proceed. The murderer died meanwhile under the rigors of his confinement, and Euthyphro considers his father to be culpable. That the source of death was his own parent and the dead man a besotted butcher is beside the point, and the one who does not denounce an evil makes himself complicitous in it, an abomination. Euthyphro recites persuasive arguments against what he is doing to his father, including that it is an offense against piety, but he is moved by none of them, for those who propound them do not know, as he declares himself to know exactly, about the holy and the unholy. Euthyphro is sustained by the confidence in his own righteousness and wisdom that always and everywhere stiffens the neck of zealotry. *Euthyphro* opens the way to the question whether "holiness" might be an apt rule of life in the city, for, as has already been seen, "holiness" is capable of promoting itself as the vain and self-righteous moralism of Euthyphro as well as the antipathy to philosophy of Meletus. Why the rule of godliness understood as recourse to the behest of heaven should be presented as problematic will become even clearer as the first trilogy unfolds and the story is told, in the

Statesman, of the god's abandonment of men to live by their own devices within an uncaring world of nature. Why piety should not rule over philosophy will be made clear in proportion to the clarity with which the meaning of philosophy itself will emerge through the dialogues.

Now Socrates would like to hear Euthyphro say what the holy and the unholy are, so that Socrates may be better prepared to confound Meletus at the trial. Euthyphro is ready with the answer: holiness is prosecuting evildoing whether on the part of one's parents or anyone else, and unholiness is not to prosecute. We have the example of Zeus, who acted against his infanticide father, the latter beforehand having emasculated *his* father in retribution for atrocious misbehavior. Euthyphro is so given to extracting holiness from the evenhanded rectitude of the gods in punishing their fathers that he overlooks the wickedness of the gods that drew on them the violence of their sons. Socrates now begins the interrogation that will show how problematic is the effort to infer the moral order from the doings of gods.

Euthyphro, in reply to the question, What are the holy and the unholy? has given examples. Socrates points out that what is wanted are definitions, not examples. First of all, in manifest incredulity, Socrates would like to know if Euthyphro truly believes that the gods acted as they are reported in poem and picture to have acted. When Euthyphro, again in the spirit of piety, pronounces himself a literal believer, the way is open to Socrates to point out that there is discord, to say nothing of active hostility, among the gods. Socrates will return to this fact presently, but for the moment he dwells on the need to find the form itself, the one idea (6D) of holy and unholy. Euthyphro replies with the famous definition of the holy as what is beloved of the gods and the unholy as what is not loved by them. Now it is time for Socrates to recall the discord among the gods regarding good and evil, virtue and vice. How is one to judge what the gods love when they can no more avoid disagreements about morality than we can? Thus far, godliness is no guide to our conduct. According to Socrates' formulation, holiness and unholiness have not yet been identified, since the same things can be simultaneously holy and unholy, at once loved and hated by gods.

Euthyphro tries to save his position by maintaining that all the gods would hold wrongful killing to be culpable. The question-begging does not escape Socrates, who reminds Euthyphro that not only gods but men too are unanimous in blaming wrongdoing and considering it punishable. For the purpose of going forward to provide a rule for human life, it is necessary to say what wrongdoing is, clearly enough so that each act may be judged right or wrong. In the case at hand, how does Euthyphro know that all the gods agree that his father's servant was the victim of a wrongful killing, in view of all the circumstances? In what follows (9BC), Socrates goes so far as to allow that all the gods might hate the killing of the drunken murderer and would all agree that Euthyphro's father was culpable. Yet Socrates declares that the definition of the holy and the unholy still eludes them. In the next portion of the argument he will explain why he is not satisfied with the current definition even in the improved form in which he will now render it, namely, that what all the gods hate is unholy and what they love is holy (9D). Socrates can allow this definition of the holy for the present because, as what follows will show, he means to raise a more radical question than any arising out of discord among gods, or out of polytheism as such. Socrates will be inquiring about the holy itself, not the holy under Olympus.

He proceeds by way of a question that proves to be inconclusive, although pregnant. How is the love of the gods for the holy to be understood? Is the holy loved by the gods because it is holy, or is it holy because it is loved by the gods (10A)? Socrates will have his way with this question by means of a strange logic. First, he will gain Euthyphro's agreement that the gods love the holy because it is holy, not that the holy is holy because it is what the gods love. By this reasoning, the holy is something that the gods approve and cherish but it is not consecrated by their mere loving of it: it must be good, or a thing to be loved, by reason of some merit. He goes on to argue that what is beloved of the gods is beloved by them by reason of their loving it—it is the object of their love because they are in the act of loving it—an undeniable tautology. Thus the holy is both loved by the gods because it is holy and because they love it. Whether this contretemps is meant to suggest the vulnerability of zealotry to sophistry is more than we shall ever know. Socrates simply does not trouble himself to explain that "because" is being used in mutually irrelevant senses. He is content to draw the conclusion that the holy cannot without equivocation be defined as what the gods love. Seeking to move beyond showing what the holy is not, Socrates puts the question in the perennial form of his own inquiry, namely, What is the holy itself, not how may it be defined through something that befalls it, like being loved, or that is accidental to it?

He opens this third phase of the inquiry by asking if everything holy is right (*dikaion*) and everything right is holy (11E–12A). Is there something that belongs to right that is not included in the pious, although everything that is pious might be right? Euthyphro confesses himself to be confused. Socrates explains painstakingly by means of an analogy. A poet whom Socrates does not name and whom he regards as mistaken declared that one must not speak the name of Zeus the Creator (the poet apparently excepted) because wherever there is fear, there also is reverence (*aidos*). Socrates explains that there is much fear without any reverence, as for example fear of illness or ill repute, although where there is reverence there also is fear. Euthyphro signifying that this is clear to him, Socrates goes on to point out that, similarly, there may be justice or right that is not included in holiness. In brief, holiness and right are not coextensive or identical, and justice or right is the larger entity of which holiness is a part, not the reverse. Euthyphro like many before him had complained earlier of being reduced to confusion by Socrates. He is now ready to give his assent to the subsuming of piety as a part of right. But what part of right is piety (14A)? Socrates would be greatly obliged if Euthyphro would tell him about holiness as a part of justice so that Socrates can fend off the injustices intended against him by Meletus. Euthyphro will gratify Socrates by enlightening him. Holiness and piety are that part of right that is about attendance (*therapeia*) to or on the gods, while the remaining part of right is about the same attending with regard to men.

Socrates believes that only one small detail needs to be cleared up, namely, What exactly is the meaning of the *therapeia* in Euthyphro's definition? Socrates explains his difficulty by bringing several examples of the use of the word, all eminently inapplicable to the gods. There is the "attending" of horse trainers, dog handlers, and cattlemen on their respective animals. It suits Socrates' immediate purpose to represent those arts as devoted to the advantage and improvement of the animals in question. Certainly there can be no thought of making the gods better, so *therapeia* must mean some other kind of attending. Euthyphro tries again, and proposes that attending to the gods means serving them in the way that a servant serves his master. Of course Socrates is eager to know what it is that human beings do for the gods in serving them. What end are the gods helped to achieve with the attending service of their human servants? Socrates could be understood to be asking, What do gods do? Euthyphro answers in generalities until pressed by Socrates, at which point he declares that in return for pleasing the gods with prayers and sacrifices, the gods are good to private households and civil communities. The opposite of what is gratifying (*kecharismenon*) to the gods is impiety, which overturns and destroys everything (14B). Impiety has ruinous results for men and cities. Euthyphro no less than Meletus has in mind the consequences for himself and mankind if they neglect the gods.

Socrates, with patient diligence, manages to comprehend that Euthyphro is proposing a mercenary relation between mortals and the divine. By means of sacrifice mortals give the gods what the latter need, and with their prayers mortals make their requests for the things that they would appreciate receiving in return. Piety is a system of commerce or exchange, is it not? Euthyphro gives a grudging assent. But Socrates has not finished. What can gods possibly need that we can supply, especially in view of the fact that every good that we enjoy emanates from then to begin with? Euthyphro, of course, cannot allow that we endow the gods with anything that is useful to them, but he can well maintain that we furnish them with honor, praise, and thanks (15A). But if these gifts of ours are not useful, what gives them their value? Is it that they are simply dear (*philon*) to the gods? Euthyphro thinks they are more dear than all things. Now Socrates closes the circle: we have returned to the definition of holiness as what is dear to the gods, the definition that collapsed long ago.

Socrates would begin again from the beginning. With elaborate courtesy he taunts the presumption of Euthyphro to know all things about the service of the gods, even to being confident that he was pleasing them by accusing his old father in the face of all human feeling, common sense, and common opinion. Socrates would prolong the skewering of the arrogant spokesman for a theology about which he understands not the first thing, which is the divine itself, but Euthyphro pleads other business, and flees. Socrates sends him on his way in a cloud of ceremonious contempt, ostentatiously regretting that he will not have the benefit of Euthyphro's wisdom to protect himself against Meletus.

The dialogue does not eventuate in a definition of piety, except perhaps by indirection. Piety is not arrogant presumption to know the mind of god, nor therefore can it be the self-righteous rigorism that parades itself as high-mindedness even as it is based on the blasphemy that reduces the gods to parties in a base exchange of bribes. Plato holds up a rectifying mirror to the distorted figure of Euthyphro, enabling the spectator to read piety in the negation of that man. In the great economy of the two trilogies that it links, *Euthyphro* serves the purpose of indicating the impoverishment and disorder of human life as it would be lived under the mindless, self-contradicting, and pitiless rule of Euthyphro's piety. If the poets and zealots who mantle themselves in godliness are not the authoritative guides to human well-being, who can be trusted to secure the human estate? There are the sages called sophists who make their own claim to a comprehensive and pragmatic human wisdom and to the skill of imparting it to any who would learn. There are also the statesmen, for whom it may be claimed that they, in their essence, possess the art of tending us as we could have hoped the gods themselves would do. And there are the philosophers, whose rule can be seen in the ether of the *Republic* but has never been observed in any other element. Socrates will return to godliness in his last hour, but the piety that he educes in the discourse reported by Phaedo has, as will be seen, little in common with that of Euthyphro. *Euthyphro* carries forward the lesson of modesty regarding knowledge that was taught in *Theaetetus*, while it prepares for the inquiry into the condition of man in a world so constituted as to leave humanity searching for its sovereign, its well-being, and its very nature.

IV

SOPHIST

THE TRANSITION TO THE *SOPHIST* IS MADE COMPLEX BY THE COM-
plexity of what precedes it, for this dialogue is preceded in one
way by *Theaetetus* and in another by *Euthyphro*. As preceded by
Theaetetus, the transition is from the atmosphere of Protagoras, conveyed through the medium of Theodorus and Theaetetus, to the
atmosphere of Parmenides, conveyed in the energy of the Eleatic
Stranger, with movement toward the definition of the philosopher.
As preceded by *Euthyphro*, the transition is from the corruptions of
vulgar piety toward the definition of the philosopher. At best, the
complex transition will contribute to the progress of the whole argument that constitutes the integrity of our group of dialogues, but of
this very much remains to be seen.

The *Sophist* opens with the reunion of "yesterday's" party, meaning the company that were gathered in *Theaetetus*. *Theaetetus*, it
should be recalled, was introduced by a scene that revealed that what
is before our eyes when we read *Theaetetus* is a report of a reading of a
report of a conversation that had taken place some thirty years earlier,
when Theaetetus was in his teens. The day on which the conversation
of the *Sophist* takes place is the one that follows the conversation, not
the reading, of *Theaetetus*. While we are told by what route, and with
what helping interventions on the part of Socrates, *Theaetetus* became
available to us, we are told nothing at all, certainly nothing comparable, about the *Sophist*. It presents itself to us unexplained, coming simply from the hand of Plato.

"Yesterday's" party is augmented by the Stranger from Elea,
nameless throughout yet "known" by his presence. It is the deviant
Protagorean, Theodorus, who introduces the lapsing Parmenidean
Stranger into the discussion, bringing together a persuadable fluxist,
an undogmatic static-monist, and Socrates. In a high-flown speech,
Socrates asks whether the Stranger is not some monitory god come
among them to correct their inquiry. His meaning is revealed when
Theodorus replies that the Stranger is no eristic wrangler but divine
only as a philosophic man is godlike. This response opens the way for
Socrates to announce, in effect, the central issue of the dialogue: how
hard it is to recognize these classes, of philosopher and god, for owing

to the ignorance of men, the philosopher is believed to appear in many guises (which Socrates refrains from saying of the god too)—sometimes in the image of statesman and sometimes of sophist, and sometimes even of lunatic. What is thought about these where the Stranger comes from, and by what names? When Theodorus wants to know his meaning, Socrates replies with "Sophist, statesman, philosopher." As will appear, the question of the nature of sophist and philosopher, and eventually of statesman, will become entwined with the question of the genera as such and the porosity or impermeability of their boundaries, of their mixing or blending or communicating with one another—as if the ignorance of men had a very deep foundation in a theoretical difficulty that leads easily to the confounding of sophist and philosopher. Perhaps it will prove to be true that the philosopher is marked by his power of coming to an adequate understanding of his genus—what it shares and what any class can share with another, and where such community must cease lest limit dissolve into chaos. That he must know his genus before he can know himself is more than likely.

Socrates makes it clear that he is interested in the divisions among things, and especially the relation between the names of things and their true differences, as if the names by which we know things must be examined to determine whether they are very truth or are, perhaps, mere conveniences, indistinct approximations, instruments of the unreflecting or scheming mind. Did the people of the Stranger's place regard sophist, statesman, and philosopher all as one, or two, or according to their names as being three, and did they divide (*diairoumenoi*) them into three genera, one genus for each name? This seemingly space-filling question gains in weight when one considers Socrates' conflating of the philosopher and the statesman / king in the *Republic* and the easy confounding of the sophist and the philosopher that will complicate the present effort to distinguish them, to say nothing for the moment of the ease with which the sophist might be mistaken for the statesman (cf. *Statesman* 291C). Are they one or many? In the end, sophist and statesman will prove to be alike in being defined by possession of a science. Will philosophy be capable of being defined by the possession of a certain knowledge or science, or will it not rather prove to have its nature in the possession of a peculiar ignorance and a moral virtue adapted to that state? The successive diremptions that are the instrument by which the Stranger will lead Theaetetus toward the definition or "discovery" of the sophist will be revealed to be an exercise toward proficiency in dialectic, the philosopher's method for defining what lies within his ken (cf. *Statesman* 286DE). The principles of diairesis will therefore be of special interest.

The Stranger speaks, allowing that where he comes from they consider the three named to be three, but determining what each one is is not small or easy work. Socrates now recruits the Stranger to be the leader of the inquiry into the ruling question, asking him whether he prefers to ask and be answered or to carry on by himself. Lest the Parmenidean connection be lost on us, Plato has Socrates recall being present once, when he was young and Parmenides was very old, on an occasion on which Parmenides led an excellent discussion by question and answer. The reference is of course an evocation of the *Parmenides*. The Stranger agrees, contrary to his preference, to proceed by question and answer, but lets it be understood that he would not like to be paired with a painful interlocutor. Presumably he means that he does not want to have to contend with a quibbler, but we cannot tell whether it is Socrates or some sophist that he wishes to be spared. Socrates advises him to choose one of the youths present, no doubt remembering his own recruitment to discussion with Parmenides many years earlier (*Parmenides* 137B). The Stranger consents to have Theaetetus as his partner in discourse, basing his willingness in part on conversation he has already had with the youngster. We do not know what that talk was about or when it took place or why it should be mentioned, but it seems to express the Parmenidean's judgment that the youth had not been sophisticated by his Protagorean upbringing and made thereby into a wrangling nuisance. In this small circumstance we receive the faintest repetition of the signal sounded by the Protagorean geometer's respectful introduction of the Parmenidean Stranger at the opening of the dialogue. Knowing, as we shall, that the first division of the dialogue proceeds by division and the second addresses the grounds of conjunction, we are readier to consider the possibility that Plato has in mind the ever-problematic status of philosophies within Philosophy.

The Stranger comes to the point. Putting what we take to be the Socratic question, he asks, "What is the sophist?" (218C). In a remark that is anything but routine, he says that what all agree on in this regard is the name "sophist," but as to what the thing named is, it is very hard to say. This seeming platitude means that there is much in a name, for we know enough, in knowing a name, to recognize the object of our ignorance. Everyone who refers to "sophist" has some notion of what he and his auditor mean by it. This reminder that anyone who talks about anything knows, in one sense at least, what he is talking about agrees with one argument that Socrates made against the definition of knowledge as right opinion with reason (*Theaetetus* 200). The Stranger will now proceed to lead Theaetetus through a series of diremptions, often fanciful, arbitrary, or tortured, toward a definition of sophist that has all the appearance of having been present to the Stranger's mind as a conclusion from the beginning. The Stranger, whose consent to participate by asking questions was unenthusiastic, makes no parade of being a midwife of knowledge who quickens the latencies of his interlocutor's mind. His proceedings demonstrate, if demonstration is necessary, that the "Socratic method" is not simply inquiry by interrogation but belongs to a profound conception of the human being as intelligent wonderer whose intelligence as well as its cosmic object will always withhold something of itself from his understanding.

The dialogue is set in motion by the simple question whether three names are attached to one, two, or three entities. Do the things named have everything, nothing, or some things in common?

Because the pursuit of the sophist will be so arduous, the Stranger proposes that they proceed along lines indicated by what everyone has known for a long time, namely, that one should prepare for doing big tasks by first doing smaller and easier ones. Before hunting the sophist, let us hunt something easier to catch. Let us hunt the angler, a very petty prey.

In this reversal of the method of Socrates in the *Republic* (find justice writ large in the city, that it might be understood writ small in the soul of a man), the Stranger is making a complicated suggestion. The angler proves to be more than the illustrative object of such an inquiry as would provide a model for their own larger inquiry. He proves also to be a kind of hunter, one who will provide a clue to the definition of the sophist as himself a kind of hunter (218E). Plato makes it clear that, in the mind of the principal interlocutor, little or nothing about this "inquiry" is random or arbitrary, and much or everything about it is anticipated and therefore in fact, though not in form, expository. How far this might be true of other philosophical interrogatories is a vexing question for Plato's readers. How far is Socrates the diligent hound, that philosophic dog who ranges backward and forward over scents false and promising until he strikes the one with the prize at its end, and how far is he rather the crafty pedagogue whose method is to pretend to confusion for the encouragement or humiliation, as needed, of his partner but who knows from the outset what is to be demonstrated? Whatever the answer to that question may be, it is presumably compatible with Socrates' claim to know what he does not know, and to enlighten his companions through interrogation that, as such, must quicken rather than endow the mind by means of suggestion having nothing to do with reminiscence on the part of an immortal soul (cf. *Phaedrus*).

But our present concern is with the doings of the Eleatic Stranger, who inaugurates a long series of diaireses by asking Theaetetus whether the angler is someone with an art or without an art (and if without, then having what other power). From his being a man with an art, the angler is further and minutely anatomized through a series of eccentric and tendentious disjunctions, such as between fish-striking from above (with a spear) and from below (with a hook). This exhibition of cunning and triviality has fulfilled the promise of the Stranger to seek a model in the small and uninteresting. It has also fulfilled his hope of finding a definition of the angler that would point toward the definition of the sophist. Recalling that they asked first whether the angler was simply a man (*idiotēs*) or rather a man with an art (suppressing now the alternative "and if without an art then with some other power"), they are prompted to ask not quite the same question regarding the sophist: is he just an undifferentiated someone (*idiotēs*) or is he indeed and truly a wise one (as *sophistēs* means)? Theaetetus now reveals what has been obvious enough from the beginning, namely, that the search for the definition of the sophist has as its premise a contempt for the sophist as a pretender to a wisdom he does not possess, for Theaetetus sees this absence of wisdom in the sophist as the Stranger's own view. Of course the Stranger has "known" all along that the sophist and the philosopher are not one and the same.

Theaetetus has answered agreeably that the sophist is not simply undifferentiated man and also is not the wise one. Then, by a suppressed logic, the Stranger concludes that the sophist, being neither without differentia nor differentiated by wisdom, must be differentiated by an art. The vigilant Theaetetus asks, What art? It is at this point that the Stranger amazes himself with the insight that the sophist resembles the angler: both are hunters, though it must be admitted that the resemblance is limited by the fact that the sophist's prey does not inhabit the waters. Here begins another chain of diaireses no more artless and spontaneous than the others, leading to a conclusion that we will soon encounter. But we have already seen enough of this method of diairesis, with its tendentious disjunctions purposefully contrived with a spacious unconcern for plausibility, to ask ourselves how the method can be reconciled with the artfulness of Plato. Is it a satire on sophistry itself? With *Euthydemus* in place, the point was already made. Is it jeu d'esprit? If so, it is surely one of the most leaden of its kind. Is it the misbegotten offspring of sophistic and philosophy, two whose possible mating we will be in a better position to contemplate after we have watched this grotesque "method" writhe to its sagacious conclusions? Perhaps. But likeliest of all is that it provides a demonstration in act of a dialectic that abandons the Socratic fable of teaching by midwifery and eliciting a knowledge by anamnesis. Anamnesis is the Socratic formula for the pre-presence in the mind of the truth that appears to be simply arrived at. The Stranger's method makes nakedly evident that "interrogation" is a ruse deployed when straightforward exposition is for one reason or another not to be used. In his practice, questioning is a rather time-consuming device whose bizarreries teach a lesson very different from anamnesis, namely, that the wisdom gained through observation of the world can be transmitted by innumerable chains of reasoning through a realm of speech in which nature marks out no one path to the truth.

In the course of refining the definition of the sophist as a hunter of the tame land-animal that is man, the Stranger procures the distinction between overcoming by force and by persuasion. Elaborating this, Plato broaches a notion (222DE) of singular scope and gravity. He causes the Stranger to say that putting together piracy, kidnapping, tyranny, and all warfare is defining them all as One, hunting by force; and joining together forensics, oratory, and conversation as One whole is to represent them as some One art of persuasion. Next we can say that there are two classes (*genē*) of persuasion, and each of these—private and public—becomes a class (*eidos*). We become aware that the Stranger has announced that the process of diairesis is in fact the formation of *eidē* or Forms by the act of human definition.

The progress of the process reveals the numerous, perhaps even innumerable, divisions of the realm of entities into two parts along rifts of infinite variety. We wonder who may be more safely trusted with the insight that the Whole can be bisected along an immeasurably huge number of planes—sophist, whatever he may prove to be, or philosopher, however he might be defined. And whose image of the Whole accords best with that explosive insight—that of the kinetic Protagoras, who yields to the manifold and concludes that man must be the measure of all, or that of the static Parmenides, who gazes past the quicksilver manifold and sees all of being and truth as concentrated in the One immovable; or is there a Socratic mean? It would be unsafe to propose an answer without a better understanding of "philosopher" than we can now claim.

Through many novel diremptions the discourse wends its way to the conclusion, albeit provisional (223B), that the sophist is the practitioner of "the part of the appropriative, coercive, hunting art which hunts animals, land animals, tame animals, man, privately, for pay, is paid in cash, claims to give education, and is a hunt after rich and promising youths."[1]

The end is not yet. The Stranger declares that there is another path to the sophist, one that begins at the division of acquisition between hunting and exchange. Last time they took the road of hunting. Now they must tread the other way. The reader becomes alarmed at the prospect of an infinite algorithm of algorithms, never knowing at how many stages of the diremption it will be found necessary to go the other way *also*, not alternatively; for the conclusions derived from these disjunctive excursions are cumulative. Thus the Stranger reaches a second conclusion descending from the art of acquisition as premise, following the hallowed opposition between taking all and giving in order to get, thus moving down the latter road of exchange. The definition of the sophist's art reached by this second way is "that part of acquisitive art, art of exchange, of trafficking, of merchandising, of soul-merchandising which deals in words and knowledge, and trades in virtue."[2] To this trenchant but by no means scandalizing characterization something must yet be added: some merchants deal in products of their own manufacture, some obtain from others the

1. Translated by Harold North Fowler in his Loeb Classical Library edition of *The Sophist* (Cambridge, MA: Harvard University Press, 1961), p. 289.

2. Ibid., p. 295.

things they sell. In both cases, the traffic is sophistic as long as the commerce is in knowledge.

More is to come. Beginning at 225A, the Stranger dissects the aggressive aspect of acquisitive art, distinguishing along the way between attacks on the body and disputation in speech, the latter in turn consisting of public speeches in a judicial setting and private conversation by question and answer. Unable to encounter "private conversation by question and answer" without the compound association "Socrates, dialectic, philosophy, and the present proceedings," we wonder how the Stranger will manage thence to arrive at sophistic rather than philosophy. He manages easily, by distinguishing ordinary confrontations of mutually opposed concrete interests on the one hand and, on the other, the formalized disputes carried on in technical terms about justice itself and injustice and other things. Now we wonder more keenly than before how the Stranger, following the latter branch, will escape defining the philosopher while thinking himself to be closing in on the sophist. It will prove premature to convict the Stranger of confusion. He calls the seemingly philosophic art "eristic" (225C). Why does he not stop there, and claim once more to have defined the sophist? If he does not, but takes one more step, he will leave the sophist joined with whoever else investigates justice and injustice, the two embalmed side by side in the amber *eidos* of eristic. But he does take one more step. Of the eristics, one kind becomes poorer and the other becomes richer. The former, who carry on for their own pleasure without regard to their prosperity, give pleasure to few of their auditors with their chatter. After this lightly embittered ironism, the Stranger can call the latter sophists, joining in the familiar disparagement of the sophists as dedicated fee-takers.

Since the premise of the entire discussion is the possibility or even the likelihood that philosopher and sophist may be confused with one another, we should not be surprised that the Stranger's hunt for the sophist is not an exercise in unrelieved vilipending. Possessing no definition of the philosopher but only a prejudice in his favor, we should have considered, once we had been introduced to diairesis, that the disjunction between sophist and philosopher might itself be comprehended within a higher *genos,* which is a taxological way of saying that they might participate or share in something that is common to them both. In this perception we merely return to what we "knew" at the outset, namely, that distinguishing them would be a task. We would have needed a prescient intuition to conceive that the one might prove to be the better nature rather than the simple antithesis of the other.

A new series of divisions opens (226B) with the reflexive category of division itself. In manual work there are many examples of processes like the separation of the wheat from the chaff. All are comprehended in *diakritikē*, say discrimination. Plato leaves it to us whether to make anything of the fact that he has practiced the art of bringing together as one the many instances of the sundering or separating art. The substantive point is to draw attention to the disjunction between separating worse from better and like from like. The reflexiveness of this line of diairesis is emphasized by the applicability of the immediate disjunction to the present *act* of disjunction: in separating sophist from philosopher, how far are they separating worse from better, and how far like from like? The involution of the discourse requires that the conversation be read by the light of its own subject, under the question whether what is emerging is a definition of the difference between sophist and philosopher, a demonstration of that difference, or, most likely, both.

Exactly in this vein, the Stranger pursues (226D) the differentiation of better and worse and the discarding of the worse by denominating the act a purification (*katharmos*). Of purifications, some pertain to base things like body and some to exalted things like soul, but "the method of argument" (*tē tōn logōn methodō*) is blind to such differences as between petty and grand. The Stranger illustrates his meaning by expressing, on behalf of "the method," a low opinion of a reasoner who went out of his way to use generalship rather than louse-hunting to exemplify venery. All that matters is collecting together all the purifications of what is without soul and separating them from the catharses of the soul. So saying, the Stranger seems to be evoking Parmenides of *Parmenides* 130E, where the old Eleatic rebukes what he sees as Socrates' juvenile subjection to common opinion in conjecturing that the Ideas pertain most certainly to the noble things, not to such as mud and hair. What can one infer from such a thought except that the very truth in Being is incommensurable with the very truth in Good? It is important to remain aware that Socrates is listening to all of this in utter silence, without remonstrance.

Returning to the argument, the Stranger begins an elaboration of the class of purifications that pertain to the soul. Purification is removal of evil; but evil is twofold: one sort is like disease in the body, and another is ugliness or deformity (*aischos*). Disease is assimilated to *stasis* or conflict, deformity to *ametria*, which is disproportion or incommensurability. The evil of the soul that is its disease lies in the *stasis* endemic among the opinions, passions, and other miscellany present in the wicked. The evil of the soul that is its deformity as distinguished from its disease is traced to the soul's folly, to the involuntary ignorance that underlies its failure to attain to truth. The deformity of the soul is simply declared by the Stranger to be a condition of disproportion, an absence of measure of the same kind that causes an archer to miss the target. It is left to us to gather from the context that an archer misses the target when he does not know the relation in space between himself and his object. The disproportion appears to exist between the true distance and his judgment of it. Shedding the metaphor, he aims at the truth but misses it because there is something he should know in order to attain it, but he does not have that knowledge. In brief, he does not know what he does not know. We have been taught by the Stranger that there is a defect of the soul that is moral, likened to disease, and a defect of the soul that is intellectual, likened to deformity and connected to disproportion. A perfect purification of the soul would purge it of defect in both kinds.

This portion of the inquiry moves toward its own portentous conclusion. To each kind of defect there is a specific remedy. The moral disease is corrected by punitive justice (*dikē*) and the intellectual deformity by didactic. But the ignorance addressed by Didactic is twofold, leading to the diairesis of Didactic itself. The Stranger now discloses, confirming what had been implicit in the foregoing, that the paramount and all-important ignorance is of our own ignorance: "not knowing what one supposes oneself to know, whereby it may be that all our failures of understanding arise" (229C). The part of didactic that treats this portion of deformity (namely *amathia*, stupidity) is called education (*paideia*) by Theaetetus, who appears to believe that the term is peculiar to "this place," apparently meaning Athens, and is so called by reason of "us." The Stranger does not allow this, declaring that it is so among practically all the Greeks, tacitly demonstrating on and to Theaetetus the point about presuming to know beyond one's knowledge.

Now education must be divided. There is a rough and ready

branch of it, much favored by fathers, by which the addressee is told more or less peremptorily what is wrong about him. The Stranger, perhaps regardful of Theaetetus's youth, refrains from calling attention to the uncertainty of this method's success. Socrates, for his part, made the point plainly in *Protagoras* (319E) that even such a figure as Pericles could not procure the improvement of his young ward by the ancestral positive method. The Stranger says that "some" have persuaded themselves that all stupidity (*amathia*) is involuntary, and therefore those stupid ones who are entrenched in the belief that they know what they do not know are impervious to correction. His implicit thought is that one does not learn without having first the will to learn: there is an inertia of ignorance that is to be overcome by a positive force that must operate within, although generated without. The defective human being must be induced himself to say the words that, when he hears them, expose to him the "deformity" of his mind. Hearing those words from the mouth of another does not, perhaps cannot, have the force that hearing them from one's own lips has. It is as if the human being must somehow be made to be his own teacher or, more exactly, to collaborate in his own instruction. One can hope to perform that function only when something has become or been made problematic for him that had not been so before, when what was fast in his mind has been jarred loose. It is by the method of interrogation that a mirror is held up to the soul's *amathia* and the indispensable self-dissatisfaction that leads to self-correction is induced. The Stranger has well represented Socrates, who listens in silence as he is personified in the "some" who have persuaded themselves in the manner described.

The Stranger seems to have been converted from his preference for uninterrupted exposition to an advocacy of the method of interrogation. It is true, though, that his advocacy of interrogation is expressed in an uninterrupted exposition (230B–D), also in the manner of Socrates. Thus it appears that the method of interrogation, the "Socratic" method, is based on a large but limited confidence in questioning as the device for instruction. After all has been asked and answered, there must be a summing up by which the questioner lets the respondent know in so many words what the latter has learned. The interrogation is the argument, the didactic peroration is the conclusion at which the enlightened one might not know he had arrived. It is conceivable that the pedagogic questioner might omit the disclosure to the learner of what he had in a manner of speaking learned, leaving the completion of the argument to the intelligence of the respondent. If every settled belief, every pronouncement of every real and supposed authority, may or must be made matter of inquiry or, to speak more plainly, of doubt, before the mind may be cured of its deformity and the shakiness of a man's convictions be revealed to him, there is room for a question whether in all cases the concluding peroration ought to be supplied. In what is to follow, the deformed who is complacent in his deformity is shown in contrast to the convalescent who is in the throes of a therapy that, incidentally, the fate of Socrates will show can be more perilous to the healer than helpful to the ailing: there is no guarantee that the method of interrogation will succeed any better than the method of admonition. The Stranger seems to be aware of the danger. As he continues to speak in the name of those who have persuaded themselves according to what is known to us as the view of Socrates, he observes that, unlike the fathers and other monitors whose admonitions fall fruitless on recalcitrant ground, the interrogators coax their deformed charges into the overt contradictions that may advertise to them the unwitting errors of their mind. Those so altered become harsh toward themselves and mild toward others, just as Socrates himself proclaimed to Theaetetus on taking leave of him "yesterday." As we reflect on what the Stranger is given to say, we realize that the education by interrogation has an extraordinary result. We are led to believe that the youth who seem to be made skeptical of everything settled and to doubt everything authoritative, in brief to be made uncivil, and in that sense corrupted, thereby experience in truth the civilizing growth of self-dissatisfaction in place of impatience or vehemence toward others. Can we fail to ask ourselves how Euthyphro would have been constituted, and how he would have behaved, if he had been interrogated sooner rather than later? He would presumably have hesitated before threatening his father. But any hesitation to proceed impiously against his father would have sprung from the same curtailment of self-confidence that puts in suspension dogmatic certainty about the city's gods and laws. Would one such as Euthyphro have been set on the road to a recovery by interrogation or would his mind have been sown with the seeds of antisocial insubordination, making of him an Alcibiades without genius? Is it conceivable that the two are inseparable? It seems clear that the humbling of the arrogant mind must be the condition precedent to some positive reconstruction if the self-dissatisfaction of the knowingly ignorant is not to emerge transmogrified as easygoing agnosticism in speculation, iron-shod conventionalism in politics, or uncontrollable hubris. This is to say nothing about the effects produced by Socrates' interrogations of his fellow citizens in the course of his pious efforts to vindicate the judgment of the god, who thought so highly of Socrates' wisdom. Soon enough, on trial for his life, he will be reporting that the widespread hatred of himself was in good part the consequence of the edifying humiliations he inflicted caringly on those around him who so much needed his gadfly ministrations. The "Socratic" method, which one is likely to associate directly with philosophy itself, is a thing of many questions.

The Stranger, having pronounced his panegyric on interrogation, now asks who the practitioners of that art are, declaring that he is afraid to say it is the sophists (231A). He fears esteeming them above their desert. Theaetetus alleges a similarity between the sophist and the educator just described by the Stranger, who replies with a warning regarding similarities: a wolf is also like a dog. The retort is not a mere sarcasm, but for the sake of the argument the Stranger sets aside the tacit disparagement of the sophists as predators and grants that the practitioners of the interrogatory art are the sophists. Now emerges the definition of sophist, or, more exactly, of his art, that has been yielded by the recent portion of the discourse: the sophist's skill or art is in the first place discrimination or distinction or separation (*diakritikē*) (231B), which, a reader might observe, includes diairesis. Of this art, one part is cathartic, purifying, eliminating the worse in favor of the better. The sophist practices the part of cathartic art that works on the soul rather than on body. He does this by teaching, but by the special mode of teaching that proceeds by questioning and that uplifts human beings, thereby by making them confront, acknowledge, and know their ignorances. This is the art of high-class, well-born (*gennaia*) sophistic (231B). Nothing is surprising about this definition except that it is given, even if tentatively, as the definition of sophistic rather than belonging to Socratism or philosophy. We shall have to consider the singular convergence of sophistic and philosophy presently, but in the meantime we must notice the recapitulation of the definitions that have emerged in such abundance that Theaetetus professes himself confused by them. There are six: paid hunter of the young and rich; merchant of knowledge for the soul; petty vendor of the same, also dealer in his own products; emphatically an athlete in verbal contests who appropriates the art of eristic; and finally, and granted reluctantly, the soul-purifier who expels stultifying opinions. We believe ourselves to have been shown a grasping, ambitious competitor with only one redeeming feature, and that most equivocally conceded: his salutary effect. Many centuries after Plato, political philosophy will discover, or rather rediscover, that unseemly selfishness can, in spite of itself, without "caring," do works of beneficence that are beyond the power of benevolence; and that an equivocal word can be said for the unprepossessing benefactor.

By 232A, the method of diairesis seems for the present to have done what was required of it, and the Stranger prepares to give the discussion a turn that, in a final act of diremption, divides the dialogue itself and sets it on a new course; but before we move off in the new direction we should pause to consider the protagonist who is no longer quite a stranger to us. Who or what, so far as we can tell, is the Eleatic Stranger? A few things strike us directly. First, he and Socrates have never set eyes on each other before—the Stranger is a stranger to Socrates. He is also a stranger to Athens, not only in the trivial sense that he is a citizen of another city but also in that he corrects a certain presumption on the part of Athens, the city soon to be the killer of Socrates, that it is the locus par excellence of philosophy (cf. p. 78 above). Further, he is a stranger in the emphatic sense that he is nameless. Yet he is not an absolute enigma, for of his mind we know at least two things. His "father" is Parmenides,[3] and his conception of dialogue and its relation to philosophic self-knowledge is Socratic. That he might signify the possibility of nonsectarian philosophy, of thought not limited by the genius of an eponymous founder, should not be dismissed. That he was a lapsed Parmenidean is as obvious as that whatever is "Socratic" or "Athenian" in his thought surely grew out of no acquaintance with Socrates and therefore no educational interrogation by the latter. This nameless one will in due time evince a solid knowledge of the schools and a well-developed judgment of them, but always with the detachment of an unenrolled inquirer, which is to say a Stranger. It would be rash to identify Plato with the

3. 241D, 242A. Cf. 237A, 242C, 244E, 258C.

Stranger without first making plausible a proto-Parmenideanism on Plato's part to match that of the nameless Eleatic—a task for a different occasion—and an unexpected Platonic objectivity in relation to Socrates; but if we could imagine a composite of the Eleatic and the Athenian Strangers, would we be envisioning Plato as he envisioned himself?

The plurality in the definition of the sophist that they have reached is a dissatisfaction to the Stranger, who declares that a man who appears to be a polymath is not well understood by anyone who calls him by the name of a single art; just as such an error would betoken a failure to understand the art itself, leading to the reciprocal error of calling the possessor of the art by many names rather than the one true one (232A). The Stranger has put himself in a position to revert to the early characterization of the sophist as a disputer (*antilogikos*) and a teacher of disputation. But about what? The answer is, about everything—about the gods, who are immanifest to the many, and about the manifest things on earth and in the heavens and such. And in private company, when the subject is universal becoming and being, we know him to be clever (*deinos*) in controversy and a teacher of the same skill, as also about the laws and politics. Of course we are put in mind of the passage early in his defense, where Socrates rehearses the long-standing resentment of himself as being that wise man (*sophos*) who reflects on the things aloft and investigates everything below the earth and makes the lesser argument the stronger (*Apology* 18B). We are encouraged to suppose that Socrates was condemned from a point of view that, without anxious discriminations, would consign "philosopher" and sophist equally to the odium so well expressed by the eunuch doorkeeper in the house of Callias. Yet sophists were not a scandal under every foot, well patronized as they were by the class that could pay; and it was a "philosopher," not a sophist, who was tried and executed. We must hope to understand at last how the innermost difference between philosopher and sophist, presumably so much to the advantage of the former, could comport with or even result in a vulgar understanding so deleterious to the nobler. Is it conceivable that sophistic is somehow vulgarized philosophy, akin in that respect to that self-satisfied piety which is the vulgarization of true veneration of what is first and highest? And if so, what in the nature of the human situation brings on or tolerates such flourishing defiance of truth and good?

The Stranger is offended by the sophists' presuming to know and pronounce on all things, and to commit their polymathy to writing in manuals, a practice of which Protagoras himself is declared guilty (232D). The Stranger concludes that the sophists' claim to speak and reason about everything convicts them ipso facto of having opinions rather than knowledge, for such knowledge is unattainable by man. The claim to omniscience is the claim to make and do all things, which we are given to understand is the power to represent the verity of all things in the cosmos. One form of this art specializes in exhibiting such imitations in speech to the young, who cannot judge of the images held up to them because the events of life that go so far to invert our early opinions have not yet come within their experience;[4] but the instant effect is to persuade them that the sophist is the wisest of men. We are led to conclude that in his pedagogy the sophist is a self-server not only as eristic lover of victory but as an impostor of wisdom. The Stranger will continue his efforts to guard Theaetetus in his youth against the corruption to which inexperience renders him vulnerable.

The Stranger reverts to diairesis. The sophist is an imitator, a prestidigitating maker of the images of things; but there are two kinds of images and image-makers: one makes literal reproductions, while the other, whose work is on the grand scale, deliberately deforms his representations of the noble or beautiful things. If he rendered those things in their true proportions, the verity of the image would become a distortion to the eye of the beholder whose view is from below, for he would see the uppermost portion of it as diminished by the greater distance, and the lowest things exaggerated in magnitude by their proximity to the lowly-placed beholder. To compensate for the greater distance of the higher, he represents it as larger than it is so that it may not appear to be smaller than it is, and conversely with what is at eye level. Plato is inviting us to believe that there is a literalness in rendering the highest and noblest that affects the mind like a lie, and a manipulation of the image of the noble or beautiful that, when seen from below, is more faithful to its subject than the literally true one. The artisan of the former is an uncompromising, perhaps narrow and perhaps indiscreet but surely incorruptible truth-lover who cannot be deflected from undecorated truth by any consider-

4. The reminder of the allegory of the Cave is somewhat strengthened by Plato's use of the image of descending (*katabantas*) (235B) into the divided image-making art.

ation of the appearance of the thing in the eye of the beholder, to whose impressions he makes no concession. The profound artisan of the latter is a truth-lover whose care for the noble and beautiful is so compelling that he must protect the object of his art against every appearance of being other than it is even and perhaps especially to the eyes of those who for one reason or another must view it from below, say from the plane of the citizen. Is the latter a fabricator of the noble lie, a lie on behalf of the noble, whose love of the truth encompasses a refusal to countenance the effectual distortion of its image before low-standing witnesses? Is his probity compromised or enhanced by his concern for the truth's mere appearance, as if that were itself another truth? Is his love of truth tarnished or made splendid by his noticing the state of the lowly-placed human beholders? And what high, noble, or beautiful things might be the subjects of the image-making that so puzzles us? Gods? Truth? Beauty? Good? Justice? Philosophy? If there are to be answers to these questions, they will have to emerge from the continuing search for the sophist in his relation of similarity and dissimilarity to the philosopher. We would do well to recall the earlier description of the sophist as practitioner of the wellborn art of purger of souls by the method of interrogation. But the sophist has also been exposed as the self-serving exhibitor of the imitations of things rather than of the being of the things themselves. What is the status of the verity of an imitation?

In pursuit of the sophist as claimant to imitate "everything" in speech, the Stranger has evolved the distinction between the imitation that produces literal likenesses but false appearances, and the art that imitates with perspective cunning, sacrificing literal truth in order to make truth appear. Let us call the former "iconic" (*eikastikē*) because of the accuracy of its representation, and the latter "apparitional" (*phantastikē*) because of the Stranger's emphasis on its concern with appearance (236), with making manifest. Now, like the Stranger, we are at a loss to decide which ambiguities, those of the iconic art or those of the apparitional art, should be assigned to the sophist (236D). The difficulty itself is, on reflection, rather creditable to the sophist, for the two artisans differ not in their respect for the truth but in their judgment of how it is best displayed to the world; and so it will prove in the end. In the meantime, we should be aware that the problem of defining the sophist by one or the other of the two parts of the imitative art will not be transcended but only suspended (until 264C) during the strenuous inquiry into being that the Stranger is about to inaugurate in furtherance of the speculation on truth.

If the inquiry into being is the inquiry into what truly is, then it is necessarily also the inquiry into what is not. "Is not" is the ground of "false," is it not, for what might "truly false" be if not the affirmation of what is not? But is not what is not Nothing? Is there speech about nonbeing that is not necessarily non-sense? But perhaps the difficulties surrounding being and nonbeing can be relieved by recognizing a neutral "in between"? These questions and others flowing from them will now arise, all of them pungent with Parmenideanism and all of them oriented on "the false." Both the iconic and the apparitional arts are infected with "the false," each because its peculiar mode of making truth manifest contains a deception. Then, if the disjunction iconic-apparitional corresponds with the disjunction sophistic-philosophic, both sophistic and philosophy are tainted with "the false." If sophistic is to be found in the apparitional branch, then sophistic is a politic art of noble lying, which is the art of Socrates. If sophistic is an iconic art, then its notorious preoccupation with politics is trivialized by the naïveté of a literal truthfulness that is ridiculously oblivious to life's truths. Perhaps there is a way to transcend an exhaustive disjunction by exploiting both its parts, occupying a figurative "in between," in the present case venerating the truth and representing it only as it is except when called on to represent it to those who must view it from below. Plato's own art would be to display the first and highest and philosophy as if they will be seen by some who must view them from below and by others to whom they can be shown in their verity without an exaggeration designed to compensate for the remoteness of the lofty.

At 236E, the Stranger formulates the problem that will guide much of the ensuing discussion: how to understand appearing (*phainesthai*) and merely supposing (*dokein*) as distinguished from proper being, and speaking as distinguished from speaking truth—all these things have always been very puzzling and are so to this day. How can one say that speaking and opining falsely really are, and not contradict himself? The Stranger immediately credits Parmenides (237A) with the insight that has exposed the difficulty, and we are now aware that the metaphysical ground of error which Socrates explored "yesterday" with Theaetetus in the context of Protagorean

kinetic pluralism is about to be explored by the Stranger with Theaetetus in the context of Parmenidean static monism.

Parmenides counseled against ever thinking that not-being is
(*einai mē onta*). When we consider that everything we say refers to
some particular something that exists, we incline to agree with
Parmenides: what is not is unthinkable and unsayable. After some
further argument to show the impossibility of speaking meaningfully
about not-being, about the unutterable, unsayable, irrational (*alogon*),
the Stranger notices a difficulty that is far from obscure: they themselves have been, as Parmenides assuredly had been, obliged to discuss what-is-not in order to prove that one cannot discuss what-is-
not. The Stranger admits that now, as always, he is hopelessly baffled
in his efforts to refute not-being. Theaetetus must do it instead.
Theaetetus must discuss not-being without ever speaking of what is
not or of things that are not, for such locutions attribute number, either singularity or plurality, to the not-being, which we know can
have nothing attributed to it (239B). The Stranger is in effect challeng-
ing Theaetetus or anyone else to speak of not-being without assigning
it to the One or the Many.

Now the Stranger judges that they are seeking the definition of
the sophist in an area of impenetrable confusion. This need not be
construed as a general depreciation of metaphysics as irrelevant to a
concrete question, but it does lead the Stranger to resume the inquiry
by recurring to the sophist's character as image-maker. What then is
an image (*eidolon*)? Theaetetus innocently defines an image as the sort
of thing seen on a reflecting surface and in works of art and so on
(239D). The Stranger informs him that a sophist would retort as if he
did not know what Theaetetus was talking about, as if he had no eyes
and had never actually seen any of the things that Theaetetus was referring to, and as if all that mattered were words (or reasonings, *logoi*)
and their implications. We might take the Stranger to be saying that a
sophist would reply in the manner of a metaphysician with an eristic
bent who replaces experience with logic-chopping. Instead, however,
of proceeding thence to the familiar disparagement of the sophist as a
verbal trickster, the Stranger gives the sophist's presumptive retort to
Theaetetus's attempted definition in such terms as to bear a disturbing resemblance to the characteristic Socratic response: you speak
about reflections here and there and representations in this and that

kind of art, and you call that unreduced plurality by the one name of image. Theaetetus has succumbed again to the common proneness to be content with an undigested manifold of examples—which is to say to appeal to unreflected experience, such as mere seeing—rather than to articulate the unity that is the reality and the truth, the speculative that feeds on the empirical. Socrates made this point (*Theaetetus* 146D) in the course of modifying the young man's Protagoreanism. Now the Stranger is making the same point in the name of the hypothetical sophist, in the course of criticizing the Parmenidean dictum that denies the being of the not-being. As the Stranger presses Theaetetus to try for a single characterization of "image," the two arrive at the conclusion that the copy or image of a real thing is not real and true as the original is, however much the copy presents itself as somehow being. If the original is the real or true that *is*, then of its mere image or copy one should be obliged to say that it "is not"; but one cannot say so since it is qua image and therefore it *is*. The Stranger blames the cunning sophist for having forced out of them this absurd admission that not-being, what-is-not, somehow is. Undiscussed is the bearing of this discourse on the doctrine that there are archetypal Ideas which truly are and are true, and there are the perceptible copies which are in flux apparently between being and its opposite. Socrates remains silent.

Can the sophist not be understood as the purveyor of false opinions, which are opinions that ascribe being to what is not and not-being to what is? The sophist will overturn this definition of himself by denying us access to the concept "false," for false implies not-being; and if we say "false," we are speaking and thinking about "what is-not," which implies that what-is-not in fact is. The sophist's best defense against the charge that he lives by the false is an appeal to a deduction of Parmenideanism: the false is not if false is the proclaiming of the not-being as being. Evidently, the possibility of "false" is compromised in one way by the fluxism of Protagoras and in another by the monism of Parmenides. If Socratism is to do better in understanding the false and thus the true, its doctrine of the Ideas should avoid the Protagorean and the Parmenidean denials of being and verity to the world itself. Should not the doctrine of Ideas, of the eternal and the true, be framed so temperately as not in its own way to sunder the intelligible and the empirical, parting them not so much by making it hard to think about the false (Parmenides) as by making it so hard to think about the true as that which is truly.

The Stranger indicates that defining the sophist through the ontic status of the false, on the premises they have been accepting, has not been successful. This covert disparagement of Parmenides prompts the Stranger to caution Theaetetus against supposing that he, the Stranger, is becoming a parricide (*patraloias*) of some kind in putting to the test (*basanizein*) the argument of his father Parmenides and maintaining forcefully (*biazesthai*) that what-is-not in some way is and what-is somehow is not (241D). We would accept casually this expression of conscientious inquisitiveness decently tempered with filial piety as no more than that if the present dialogue were not preceded by *Euthyphro* with its entailed literal parricide and its adumbration of the killing of Socrates. We may well wonder if *Euthyphro* is a story about the indecencies fostered by the false opinion that the Olympian gods, which we know to be examples of what-is-not, *are*. That Socrates will be the murdered victim of similar false opinion is our own widely shared opinion. False opinion, which qua false could be thought to not-be because it is about things that are-not, has a power over things like ourselves, to whose palpable welfare a dispute about being, on high metaphysical grounds that distinguish the eternal from the generated, may be irrelevant.

The Stranger sees that he must be severe with his father Parmenides' metaphysic lest the project for defining the sophist be abandoned (242A). The implication of this judgment is that sophistic can turn back upon itself any attack that defines the sophist as a falsifier if that attack is based on the Parmenidean axiom that not-being absolutely is not, is not thinkable, and is not utterable. The Stranger promises an attack on his father's reasoning; but what he launches is a critique of all the main schools of philosophy, classified according to their doctrines of entity. The Stranger's vastly broadened critique will imply that the whole panoply of Greek philosophy, and not only Parmenideanism, is poorly equipped to define and unmask the sophist. This may be taken as an intimation of a comprehensive parricide on the part of Plato himself.

As the Stranger tells it (242C et seq.), Parmenides and the others who have discussed the number and kinds of entities (*ta onta*) have gone on in a casual way and have treated their subject in fables or, as we would now say, in allegories. While Socrates saw reason to praise Parmenides as the sole exception to the fluxism rampant among the Greek wisemen (*Theaetetus* 152E), the Stranger makes no exception of Parmenides in the course of blaming the wisemen as loose-thinking mythologizers. What seems to be decisive for Socrates appears not to be so for the Stranger, which revives the question about the identity of the Stranger and his relation to his creator, Plato.

The Stranger recapitulates Greek metaphysics in about a page. There are those who make the irreducible entities three, those who make them two, and, of course, Parmenides, who makes it one. Of them, some posit strife and some love among the entities, which are hot and cold, or wet and dry. Then there are the synthesizers of the fables who declare that being is many and also one bound together in enmity and love. There are various tales of love and strife in the realm of entity. The Stranger does not take it on himself to judge the truth of any of this, but on one point he is confident: it is all unpersuasive. In other words, the fabulists of being did not take the trouble to teach. But "being" is what, above all else, we must be clear about. The Stranger sets forth with this clarity as his goal.

He will proceed by taking up first the theorists who allege that the All (*to pan*) is two or more, for example hot and cold. Their ontology and their cosmology break down together because recognizing or defining the one being that the plural irreducibles share would replace them with that truly primary, reducing them to one, or would increase their number by the new one that they cannot suppress. What then about the ontology of the theorists, of course Eleatic, who allege that the All is one and only one is? Is there something that they call by the name of being? Then is the one that is All the same as whatever one it is that they call being? Over and over, the difficulties whose resolution depends on solving the riddle of being will prove intractable because or so long as the impulse to speak as if being were itself an entity goes unsuppressed. Here is an early recognition of the thought that will resonate through the ages. Everything that is, is by virtue of "being." Then there must be "being," or "being" is. But "being" cannot be in the way that everything (else) that is, is. In our perplexity, we might be excused for relieving our confusion by declaring that we know Being through the things that are but cannot know it in itself; that its own being is for us only in or by virtue of a manner of speaking, yet we "know" that it is the intelligible because indispensable or necessary original ground of the All; and that it must forever be present everywhere, always as a mystery. It would have attributes that we have learned to expect of divinity, with the conspicuous exception of Mind. Within the context of the search for the sophist, the elucidation of being has become the prerequisite for the definition of that counterpart of the philosopher. We begin to wonder if the sophist, as the one who claims to be able to "make" everything, everything that "is," must not be characterized as the man who would have to know Being in order to be the master of all that is, but who does not know that his pretension must collapse because he is ignorant of his ignorance of being. Whether this comports with the Stranger's line of thinking remains to be seen.

It is not the sophist but the pluralists who have been under attack by the Stranger, who now turns his attention to the monists, of course preeminently Parmenides (244E). The pluralists broke down qua pluralist; the monist, we shall see, fails qua monist. The former foundered on Being; the latter will founder on Unity. Parmenides reflects on the Whole and calls it One, while seeing no reason to deny that it has parts. The Stranger objects that a unit can certainly have parts but then it should be thought of as being one, not as being Unity Itself. Reminding Theaetetus of Parmenides' conglomerating One, All, and Being, the Stranger points out that Unity has been made an attribute of Being and thus is not identical with Being, which leaves All standing as a two, Being and Unity, not a one. Moreover, if it is true that Being was not (successfully) made Whole through having been made One, and it is also true that the Whole itself is Being, then Being is not perfectly itself because it is not identical with Whole, which *is* Being (or also is Being). In this way, Being is also Not-being (245C). The Stranger sums up these and myriad similar puzzlements as all having their root in the thesis that Being Is, whether it be two or only one (245E). It appears to us that a covert hypostasis of Whole and All might also have contributed to the confusion of the discourse, which bears a disturbing resemblance to the logification of known sophists. These unpleasing resonances are accounted for by way of the Stranger's announcement that he is cutting short his analysis of those whom he describes as discussing being and not-being with accurate precision (*diakribologoumenous*). It must be supposed, if only from the peculiarity of his own language in interpreting them, that his characterization of them as accurate is tantamount to an indictment of them, including his father Parmenides, as pushing into the empyrean and pronouncing on it in detail, speaking myth as if it were wisdom.[5] Adopting their mode, the Stranger has "accurately" deduced and made deductions from what he had deduced until he consternated everything that the accurists had affirmed. For all their obvious indispensability, precision and accuracy in thought and speech are as capable of being confounded with pettifoggery as philosophy is with sophistry. Perhaps it is the precision of confident particularity unrestrained by contact with, or confirmation in, the realm of experience that eventuates in babble and offends philosophy. As to this we will know more presently, for the Stranger proposes now (245E) to go on beyond the accurists in order to show that it is no easier for the others to say what being is rather than not-being.

The Stranger's survey of Greek thought now takes up the contention between, on one hand, those who drag down to earth everything from heaven and the invisible, acknowledging the existence only of what is palpable[6] and defining body and being as one and the same; and, on the other hand, those who forcefully maintain the true being of the intelligible and incorporeal ideas (*eidē*), consigning the corporeal to the realm of becoming and change. The Protagoreans, with their doctrine of Man the measure, all is flux, and perception is truth, seem to be omitted, but we might be allowed to consider them subsumed under the materialists on the ground that both make perception the true evidence of being. To sum up, the Parmenideans affirm that to be is to be one, the materialists affirm that to be is to be body, and the idealists affirm that to be is to be intelligible. The Stranger proceeds to judgment.

What can the materialists and the idealists say for themselves? The former are an angry lot who can scarcely be imagined as willing to answer questions. What if anything this trait has to do with the substance of their theory is not discussed, so we are left to conjecture that their peculiar reliance on the senses is an aspect of a belief that the truth must grow up out of, and never lose direct contact with, the perceptible, which they consider obvious: they do indeed bring every-

5. It is worth remembering that when Plato causes Protagoras to speak in myth (*Protagoras* 320C et seq.) and Socrates to do the same (*Phaedrus* 246A et seq.), he makes the sophist in the former case and the philosopher in the latter declare that he is mythologizing.

6. See Socrates' reconstruction of Protagoreanism as materialism, *Theaetetus* 156.

thing down to earth. For the immediate purpose they will be imagined as less dogmatic and more open to being questioned. The absent Protagoras would be gratified by this tableau of melioration (cf. *Theaetetus* 166–168), and perhaps would not object to its being demonstrated on his own kind, though he could not derive much satisfaction from its being altogether imaginary. At any rate, responsiveness will not be an issue with the idealists, who are forceful in their own way but at home with interrogation.

The Stranger despatches the tamed materialists with a few rapid blows. There are mortal animals, they are bodies with souls, souls are endowed with virtues such as wisdom and justice and their opposite vices, and all such are imperceptible— or, as Theaetetus says in the voice of the stampeded materialists, almost all are imperceptible. What his hesitation refers to is the materialists' departure from dogmatism long enough to be in doubt whether the soul is not somehow somatic. Into this small aperture of uncertainty the Stranger will drive the argument that, once the materialists admit the existence of any incorporeal at all, they must go on to look for what is common to corporeal and incorporeal, which is Being. If the materialists happen to be at a loss to proceed, the Stranger is ready with a suggestion: being is power (*dunamis*), any power whatsoever to affect or be affected in any degree and no matter how seldom (247E). To be is to be potent for doing or for being done to, which means to be in the order of change either as agent or patient. This definition, which reverses the familiar identification (soon to emerge) of being with the changeless eternal, will be kept in reserve while the metaphysical doxography continues.

In what follows, the Eleatic Stranger will investigate those whom we have been calling idealists but whom he calls "lovers of the ideas" (*hoi tōn eidōn philoi* 248A). He will anatomize them in the presence of their chief, which should assure a faithful account. The Stranger continues to have Theaetetus answer for the school that is under scrutiny, an arrangement that produces such an oddity as the Stranger's saying to Theaetetus, "You maintain the distinction between becoming and being, do you not?" while Socrates himself sits close to Theaetetus's elbow as the teenager confirms this Socratic tenet. Thus Socrates' silence is preserved intact. The Stranger proceeds to a precis of idealist doctrine according to which we humans share (*koinonein*) in becoming through perception by means of body, and in ontic being through reason by means of soul. Being is forever identically the same, becoming changes. Now the Stranger raises the issue that Parmenides his father found difficult a half century or so earlier (*Parmenides* 131A): How is one to understand this sharing or participation (*koinonia*) of one thing in another? The Stranger recurs for the present purpose to his tentative definition of being as power: if power is to affect and to be affected,[7] then it is easy to see how the relation between what has the power to act and what has the power to be acted upon is a kind of *koinonia*, participation in each other of the agent and the patient. But the Stranger makes this suggestion knowing that it will not be acceptable to the lovers of the ideas, as we have expected and as will appear immediately. While in our impatience we might hasten to conjecture a common ground between the affirmation of Ideas and the eternal sameness of being, the Stranger takes a different direction and asks whether the idealists accept that the soul knows and being is known (248D). Of course they do. At the same time, though, they are committed to denying that knowing and being known are instances of acting and being acted upon, for these latter are implicated in change or motion, and the being-known of being cannot imply the passivity, hence mutability, of being. Now, invoking Olympian god, the Stranger figuratively throws up his hands at the thought that Being Itself could be conceived as without motion and life and soul and thought—awesome and sacred, dumb and inert. Without preparation that would involve theology in metaphysics, he calls on Zeus, who is held to be anything but dumb and inert, to witness this terrible suggestion to which venerable Socrates himself is the mute and inert witness. As between Socrates and Zeus, only the former has a demonstrated power to pronounce on metaphysics, which renders his silence more weighty, for his response would be a confirmation in act of the Stranger's hypothesis.

The Stranger seems to have proved that without motion there is neither soul nor life nor mind nor thought nor that which is moved. Ergo, being moved and moving are (249B), or belong, in being, a point that would seem in need of being made for the benefit of Parmenides rather than Socrates; but we have already been given an insight into the Stranger's reason for tacitly assimilating the idealists to the statics. Now (249CD) the Stranger summarizes the state of the issue:

7. As in the "Protagorean" account of sense perception given by Socrates (*Theaetetus* 156). Aristotle's impatience with the notion of "participation" (*metechein*) should be remembered (cf. *Metaphysics* 1079b25).

for the philosopher, who respects these things above all, it seems that they compel him to reject the demonstrations of those who maintain that, either as a one or as many Forms (*eidē*), the All is at rest, as he must also altogether refuse to listen to those who maintain that being is pervasive motion. Rather, all and being are the immovable and the moving things. The sequel will show that the words "it seems" (*hos eoiken*) are meant literally.

Theaetetus and we ourselves are inclined to welcome this irenic disposition of the matter, but the Stranger sees a possible difficulty, the one that afflicted those thinkers who found a duality such as heat and cold to be the ground of All. Motion cannot be reduced to rest, nor rest to motion, so each must exist not by virtue of the other but by virtue of being, which is not a composite of the two but a third that supports them rather than a one that is composed of them. The daunting conclusion is that Being, according to its own nature (*kata tēn hautou phusin*), neither rests nor moves (250C). But every single thing must be either at rest or in motion. The argument is at an impasse. We wish it had occurred to Theaetetus to ask whether the situation would improve if they were to leave off speaking of being as if it were in any way a thing, but it does not occur to him, and the dialogue takes what appears to be a different turn. The Stranger remarks that being now shares confusion equally with not-being, which prompts him to hope that any clarity they can gain about either will illuminate also the other; but if that fails, he hopes to be able to drive the argument through between them. This intimation that there is something discussable between being and not-being and thus outside a disjunction designed to include every conceivable thing lets us know that the question Theaetetus did not ask will somehow be considered.

The Stranger sets forth once again (251A), this time by asking what justifies us in calling a single thing by many names. He means to ask what in the nature of things supports predication, the possibility open to us to say of one man that he *is* short, good, plain, and many other things—to say of one that it is many. Some wranglers pay their respects to the diremption of one and many by insisting that the only valid statement is of the type "good is good" and "man is man." These the Stranger describes as fools who came by their wisdom before or after they were ripe, but he will not exclude even them from consideration. In fact, far from excluding them, he will make use of their absurdity to mark one extreme among the positions taken up in the discussion he intends to address to everyone who has said anything at all about being. The gravity of this declaration of his intention will be tested by the treatment that he, which is to say Plato, accords the ontology of the lovers of the ideas.

The Stranger poses his primary question in terms that signify a new approach to the riddle of being and not-being. He asks whether we can attribute (*prosaptomen*) being to motion and rest, or predicate anything else of any other thing, for as immiscibles (*amikta*) it is impossible for things to participate (*metalambanein*) in one another; or can everything join in combination (*epikoinonein*) with everything? Or is the world a combination of combining and not-combining (251D)? The argument from division or diairesis having proved inconclusive, the argument continues now in the terms of combination and participation that intruded when the effort was made to define the sophist as a dealer in what is not. The lapsed Parmenidean does not in so many words raise the explosive question of the "participation" of things in the Ideas, the question with which Parmenides so vexed the youthful Socrates (see again *Parmenides* 131).

The Stranger's first hypothesis is that nothing whatsoever combines in any way at all with anything else—the notion of the adolescent and the senile. Then motion and rest do not combine with being, thus they are not, and everything else also is not for want of power to combine with being. This would destroy the kinetics (Protagoras), the monist/statics (Parmenides), and the idealists, as well as those who see the world as a scene of ongoing combination and dissolution. The Stranger surprises by attending as long as he does to the implications of the absurd view that there is no combination of anything with anything, but he does so yet again to show that it contradicts itself each time it affirms anything about anything in explanation of its own view. The supposition that everything can combine with everything is disposed of instantly: rest and motion combining, rest would move and motion would not. The truth must be that some things will mingle (*summignusthai*) together and some will not. The example is the letters of the alphabet (253A).

The Stranger is in search of the science of the mingling and immiscibility of genera, with a view to discovering what pervasive principle governs the comminglings and what the disjoinings (*diairesis*) of the kinds of things. Now as the Stranger wonders how to name this science, he calls out to god as he recognizes the possibility that, in discovering this science, which he calls the possession of free men, they have stumbled on the philosopher while seeking the sophist. For is it not by the science of dialectic that division according to classes (*genē*) is known, and that the classes are known in their identity and in their difference? But what is this science if not what belongs to him who can see the one idea (*idea*) in the many units that lie separately from each other, and who is clear about the ascending enveloping unities among the ideas themselves toward a unity of All. This, which is dialectic, is the possession of the one who philosophizes purely and justly (253E).

Philosophizing is the pure and just striving to see every difference as and in its plurality, and every identity as and in its unity. As the dialogue testifies, it includes the effort to know itself, its relation to sophistic—how it differs from it and how it resembles it, and to seek that self-knowledge by practicing diairesis and investigating participation. There can be little doubt that philosophy is more enthusiastic about what distinguishes it from sophistic than how the two mingle, but this must be considered as consistent with purity and justice.

The Stranger explains why the philosopher and the sophist are hard to distinguish from one another. The sophist is hard to discern because he is shrouded in shadows as he makes his way about in the darkness of mere experience, which the Stranger does not hesitate to call not-being. The philosopher, always reasoning about the idea of being, lives in a region of light or, as we might say, of abstraction, where the soul of the multitude is blinded by the glory of the divine (254A). If the idea of being is the divine whose glory blinds the multitude, it should not be hard for us to see the mutual pertinence of *Euthyphro* and *Sophist,* or to grasp the thought that the popular piety must be one or another form of misunderstanding and its worship a pathetic blasphemy.

The Eleatic Stranger seems to have thrown in his lot with the lovers of the Ideas, thus to have agreed that the philosophic question, the ultimate question, has its beginning in the simplest, most naive, and most immediate question, namely, What are the things: What is this thing? What is that one? What is meant by being a certain something? Are they as different from each other as they seem to the senses to be? What traits do they have in common with which others? How do they stand forth by name? And what is and is the meaning of the one single ontic Constitutive of all the things and all the groupings of things—what is the truth, and what is truth? If this is philosophy, then philosophy is the inquisitive activity of the intelligent being who is passive in the presence of the given. As such, it is the paradigm of hermeneutics. Socratic idealism identifies itself as philosophy in the course of its distinguishing itself from sophistic; we recognize it as the alternative that mathematical physics, when it still had its way to make, was at such pains to distinguish from itself. We wonder how many alternatives to philosophy so defined exist, and thus how conclusive any definition of it can be if the definition confronts only one such alternative, such as sophistic. If the touchstone of philosophy is its ultimate orientation on Being, then modern physics and sophistic, without being identical, mingle in their indifference to what preoccupies philosophy. Whatever might divide them, Parmenidean monism and Socratic idealism share the preoccupation with Being as that which must be addressed above all—a fact that becomes visible in the Stranger's own synthetic or commingled allegiance. Is ontology, then, a superior class within which species of philosophy are included, or is philosophy a class in which ontology is included along with something else? What else might there be that could claim comparable standing with Being? Perhaps Good. In the political environment of the *Republic*, Socrates associates Being and Good in a sovereign place. Is there an Idea of philosophy that encompasses ontology and science of right—the Idea of Being and the Idea of Good? For the present we know only that the philosopher is always thinking about the Idea of Being.

The Stranger suggests (254B) that they might pursue the inquiry into the philosopher more precisely later on if they wish, but their concern now is with the sophist. He defines their immediate agenda: the subject will be the relevant forms or classes (*eidē, genē*), what each one is like and then their power of combining with one another. Thus they will be seeking clarity about being and not-being as well as they can by way of such an inquiry as their present one. The question the Stranger hopes to resolve is whether one can say that not-being is. It appears to us as if the Stranger would like to know how his subscribing to Socratic idealism would comport with his Parmenideanism as the latter is distilled in the denial that not-being is. If Socratic idealism and Parmenidean monism were themselves Ideas, as they would be if an Idea were a human cerebration, then any question on the part of the Stranger about the logic of his synthetic allegiance would be in fact a question about the miscibility of Ideas. But can this problem be kept separate from the question of truth and falseness? If the two "Ideas" are consistent, hence miscible, are they both true, alike qua true but not the same, each fructified by the truth of the other? Their truth would lie in their shared recognition of the questions to be asked rather than the answers provided, as the Protagoreans, Parmenideans, and Socratics occupy themselves with motion and rest, being and non-being, and rational and irrational. If they are immiscible, each falsified by the truth of the other, then philosophy is defined as binding commitment to a sect and rejection of the others rather than the critical interrogation of itself and all the others, as dialectic demands. The questions of mingling, truth, and being seem intertwined, in general and in the nature of philosophy.

We are now told that the greatest of the classes (*genē*) are being itself, rest, and motion (254D). Rest and motion cannot mix with each other, but being must mix with both, since they are. Together they make three, each being "other" (*heteron*) than the others but the "same" (*tauton*) as itself. Are "same" and "other" two more classes that mingle with the first three to make five? These concerns introduce a lengthy discussion in which two most pregnant questions will be moved: if classes mark the defining boundaries within which things fall and by their inclusion in which all things are known, can the classes themselves fall within one another's boundaries, or "mingle" with one another, to any extent or in some valid sense? And can there be a meaningful being of not-being? The first of these questions is the test of Socratic idealism, the second the test of Parmenidean monism.

The Stranger reasons as follows. Motion and rest cannot, each, be "other," for if they were, then motion, for example, by being "other" would be rest, and rest would have to abandon its own nature and be motion. That they cannot both be "same" is clear from the fact they are opposite to one another. Yet they do participate (*metecheton*) in the same and other (255B). Implicit is their participation in "same" on the ground that they remain what they are, they remain "the same." Also, being and "the same" cannot be one, for if they were, then any two such contraries as motion and rest would be "the same" by virtue of their both participating in being. Nor is being one and the same with "other," for some things depend for their existence, it is true, on their relation of distinctness from something else, but some things simply

99

are on their own without relative definition. Yet "other" is ubiquitous; for anything that is, is what it is by virtue of not being any of the innumerable things that it is not. The Stranger's locution for making the point is striking: each thing is other than the other things not by reason of its own nature but by reason of participating in the idea of the other (*ou dia tēn hautou phusin alla dia to metechein tēs ideas tēs thaterou*) (255E).

The Stranger recapitulates by example (255E–256B): motion is opposite to rest and is not rest, but it exists via participation in being. Again, motion is other than "the same" and is not "the same," yet it is the same via the participation of all things in the same. Thus, motion is same and not same—same as itself or selfsame, and not same because it must participate in other in order to be anything at all that is distinguishable. It must be other in order to be selfsame. Likewise, there must be some not irrational way of understanding motion as at rest. Ergo, there is a mixing of classes (*genē*) according to nature (*kata phusin*).

Moreover, motion is not "other," but it must also be "other." Motion is also other than being, hence it is not "being." This means in its way that motion is not. Yet it is, for it participates in being. The Stranger draws the conclusion that, as regards motion but also as regards all the classes, not-being is, because the nature of other (*hē thaterou phusis*) makes every one of them other than being *and therefore not-being* (256E). Evidently the Stranger has proved both that it is the nature of the classes to have communion in one another and that not-being exists (257A). The Stranger appears to have vindicated his synthetic subscription to Socratic idealism and Parmenidean monism by refuting each of them in its definitive proposition.

The Stranger will wish to go further into the manner of the being of not-being, but before following his discourse in that direction we should take note of a characteristic of the argument that precedes that development. Beginning at 255A, the Stranger relies repeatedly on an appeal to the "nature" of a class to account for its properties. Thus, motion and rest cannot become "other," for if they did, the nature of each must necessarily change. That is, each must cease to be what it irrevocably is. The ground not simply of its being but of its being what it is, and unchangeably, seems to be what the Stranger means by its nature. Then at 255E, it is the "nature" of other that is to be considered as having the status of a class (*eidos*). Again, the nature means the innermost or defining, the ultimate answer to the question, What is it? And when (256C) the Stranger reminds that some genera mix with others and some do not, he claims to have shown that this is "according to nature" (*kata phusin*), presumably by virtue of the inmost singularity of each class (*genos*). The same conception of nature operates at 256D ("the nature of other") and at 257A ("it is the nature of the genera that they have community [*koinōnia*] in one another"): it is by virtue of what they are.

Is it possible for us to decide whether "What is it?" is prior in principle to the awkward question "*Is* its being?"? Certainly it would seem that its being is prior in reason to its being a particular something. But do its defining qualities cling as attributes to its "being" or to it itself, as if its being were itself an attribute clinging to something more primary, something that might be called its "nature," which is so much its very own that it cannot be diluted by mixture with any other nature? We cannot tell; but it appears that the Socratic preoccupation is with the "nature," the What-is-it, and the Parmenidean preoccupation is with its "Being." Do they exclude one another if they are proposed as alternative answers to the question, What is the ground of all things? It would appear that they must if the question is one of primacy in reason. And it would appear further that a thing must be before it can be a something, that "being" is self-evidently primary. But what if its "being" were nothing more than a conceit that grows out of the what-it-is of each thing in its particularity? The stress between the Parmenidean and the Socratic preoccupations generated a question for philosophy that has not lost its energy through the millennia. Precisely because the question overrides the answer, philosophy overrides the sect unless the sect itself is in the profoundest way dedicated to questioning.

At 257B the Stranger begins what we may call the explication of the negative with a view to its rescue from Parmenides. His first point is quite simple: as not-large does not mean small but could mean anything between large and small, so not-being (*to mē on*) does not mean the opposite of being but rather what is different (*heteron*) from being. Of course, on this understanding, not-being is and is eminently discussable. Next, the nature (*phusis*) of other appears to the Stranger as cut up fine, like knowledge—a one that is many by virtue of its distribution among the numerous arts and sciences. So it is with the one entity "other" and the parts of the nature of "other." As has emerged already, the nature of the thing is its inmost identity, the answer to the question, What is it?—which is different from and, as we may say with the benefit of our most recent instruction, not necessarily the opposite to or the contradiction of the "Being" of the thing. We perceive a glimmer of the ground on which the Socratic and the Parmenidean preoccupations, Nature and Being, may be reconciled and the synthetic commitment of the Stranger be made intelligible.

The Stranger moves toward bringing these very questions into focus. Some part of "other" is "other than beautiful," which is nothing other than "the other of the nature of the beautiful" (257E). This not-beautiful, which is not an undiscussable non-being, must fall into some one class of being and also be in opposition to one such class. This is as much as to say that "not-beautiful" *is*, and is no less meaningfully or emphatically than "beautiful" is—and similarly with just and not-just and all the other pairs of affirmation and negation. The Stranger appears to believe that the ruling premise on which his conclusion rests is that the nature of other is an entity (258A). By this we may understand his conviction that the defining particularity of a thing or concept, the "what-it-is," itself *is* or is an entity. The Stranger appears to have argued that, contrary to Parmenides, it is not true that what is not is undiscussable, but rather that what can be defined (we might be inclined to say, that of which we can have a clear and distinct idea) is discussable and is *ipso facto* an entity, whether affected by negation or not. It is at least more plausible that the Stranger's argument means something like this rather than that there exist things that are not beautiful and acts that are not just. In the culmination of the present segment of the argument, the Stranger speaks (258B) of a possible opposition between the nature of a part of other and of being, thereby alluding to the "what-it-is" of being, the definition that still eludes us. It is possible for the Stranger to speak of the nature of being. We wonder whether it would be possible for him to speak of the being of being without absurdity, and whether, if he spoke of the being of a nature, he would not have to mean the *logos* or rational definition of the thing: the nature of its nature. Troubling is the question of primacy between nature and being, the respective preoccupations of Socrates and Parmenides. In the immediate context, the Stranger is intent on maintaining that the opposition between the nature of some part of other and the nature of being illustrates a relation between two genuine entities whose existence is guaranteed by the true being of all the parts of "other."

What purpose is served by all this intense ratiocination? According to the Stranger, it is the inquiry into the sophist that has led them to establish the existence of not-being, "which *is* securely and has its own nature" and is to be numbered as one class (*eidos*) among the many entities (258BC). Before the Stranger explains the bearing of the discussion on the definition of the sophist, he will make a large claim that bears heavily on the standing of Parmenides. Not only have they refuted Parmenides' denial of being to not-being but they have actually disclosed the class (*eidos*) of not-being; for they have demonstrated the existence of the nature of other (*tēn thaterou phusin*), cut up fine and present in every entity as against every other. It is the Stranger's claim that not-being, in the form of "other" or being other than, not only is but is the basis of the being of every entity. From this we can easily deduce that the being of an entity is exactly its distinctness from everything that it is not: its definition, its circumference, the answer to the question What is it?—in brief, its nature. It would appear that Being is reducible to Nature. In the past, presumably when he was a strict Parmenidean, the Stranger forbore to speak of not-being, but now he not only discusses it but can insist that what he has shown about the being of not-being is inextricably bound up with the miscibility of the classes (*hoti summignutai te allēlois ta genē*) (259A): being and other mingle, with other having a secure ontic basis through its "participation" (*metaschon, methexin, meteschen*) in being, while being by its nature not-being. Evidently, the classes are not the impenetrable, mutually immiscible Ideas that metaphorically inhabit an empyrean and in which the transitory things must in some obscure way "participate" in order to have their identity or nature. The classes or *eidē* have the character of attributes rather than substances. The youthful Socrates of the *Parmenides* could see easily enough that a particular entity would participate in many Ideas, but he did not admit the participation of any Idea in another. The Stranger argues otherwise.

He returns to the polemic against the logic-choppers who speak the language of same and other with mock earnestness to no purpose but the confounding of discourse. His speech tends to assure us that we have not ourselves been the dupes of a calculated obscurantism.

The particular offense of the logic-choppers is to try to separate every-thing from everything else, that is, to render "participation" or predi-cation unintelligible. To do so is the negation of the philosophic (*aphilosophos*), or, as we might now be inclined to say, it is the being of not-philosophy. The Stranger declares emphatically that the disjunc-tion of everything from everything is the complete destruction of all discourse: "for our discourse arises through the interweaving (*sum-ploken*) of the forms (*eidon*) with one another" (259E). This striking passage does more than reiterate the miscibility of the classes. It refers to that commingling as an "interweaving," a term that will have a profound specifically political significance in the subsequent dia-logue (e.g., *Statesman* 305E), wherein the Stranger will look for the na-ture of the statesman as an interweaver of disparate and even opposing classes that must be distinguished according to their dis-similarity and united to form a whole. We are invited to keep in mind a question whether there is something in the nature of things in gen-eral that is repeated on the plane of political life—a version of the question whether or in what sense there is a cosmic order that can be brought to earth as the best regime.

The Stranger now (260A) reveals that his purpose in insisting that the classes commingle has been to show that discourse or reason (*logos*) is one of the classes of entities, of things that are, for without *logos* the greatest disaster would befall, namely, the loss of philoso-phy itself. But what is discourse? We must be certain that it is not dis-solved in nonbeing, and that there is commingling of things, for the absence of these conditions would render discourse or reasoning im-possible. The Stranger proceeds by arguing that not-being must mingle with opinion and *logos*, for if it did not, everything would nec-essarily be true and there would be no such thing as the false, which is the thought or utterance of what is not. The false leads to deceit, and the existence of deceit leads astonishingly to the Stranger's conclu-sion that therefore all things are necessarily full of images, likenesses, and fantasies (*eidōlōn, eikonōn, phantasias*) (260C). That there is folly and deception in the world is not a conclusion of deep insight, but that there is at least as much not-being in the world as there is being is more noteworthy. It is a thought that accords well with the grand myth of the Age of Kronos and the Age of Zeus that the Stranger will generate in the ensuing dialogue of the *Statesman* (269B et seq.).

We are thrown back to the point very early in the dialogue (236) at

which the Stranger was contemplating the sophist's falsifications under the burden of Parmenides' injunction against thinking not-being.
As it seems, the great effort put forth in the central bulk of the dialogue was expended in the interest of proving, via the refutation of
Parmenides, that false truly is. We cannot avoid the suspicion that
some thought less obvious than that there are lies and errors in the
world constitutes a tacit agenda. If the Stranger were to be taken literally to mean that the totality, *panta*, is by some necessity impregnated
with the seed of deceit and the false, it would be his task to make clear
how that fact about the nature of things or of the world enters the human condition. This he now proceeds to do by drawing *logos* and error together. Every intimation of the irrational and incommensurable
that invades the constitution of the world looks back toward the geometry of Theaetetus and forward to the Age of Zeus (*Statesman* 269B
et seq.).

At 260D (referring to 254A), the Stranger recalls their agreement
that the sophist defends himself against the charge of being a falsifier
by denying being to the false, on the ground that not-being can be
neither thought nor spoken for it does not participate in being. Thus
the Stranger makes Parmenides complicitous in sophistry because of
the implications for truth of his staticism / monism, while Socrates
had made Parmenides the sole distinguished exception to the prevalence of kineticism, the doctrine of Protagoras the sophist that threatened truth by making man the measure of it (*Theaetetus* 152E). As
Plato presents the matter, Socrates sees the danger to philosophy as
coming from Motion while the Stranger sees it as coming from impervious Rest. At any rate, the Stranger presents the sophist as continuing to deny the being of the false by maintaining that, whatever might
mingle with what, and however firmly established the being of not-
being may be, still speech and opinion do not mingle with not-being.
The immediate task then is to say what is speech, what is opinion, and
what is the apparitional art, the materials of sophistic that the sophist
says are not subject to falseness.

The Stranger will proceed by an inquiry into words (*onomata*)
(261D), more exactly into which combinations of them signify and
which do not. Again, the issue is conjunction: what communes with
what. The Stranger refers to their discussion of ideas and letters (presumably at 253A) as indicating where the present investigation will
lead. Hindered by his absence from the preceding day's discourse, he

is unaware that Socrates, on the track of the definition of knowledge, was attempting to find its distinguishing characteristic, the "what-it-is" of knowledge, by differentiating it from everything that it resembles closely; and in the course of so doing, it will be remembered, he compared the intelligibility of an element and the composite of elements, which latter he called "one single idea" (*Theaetetus* 203C). His illustration ran in the familiar terms of the letters and the syllables. Thus, there are two discussions of the ideas and letters, that of Socrates and that of the Eleatic Stranger. That of Socrates was part of an inconclusive inquiry that had as its premise the absolutization of the one immutable, immiscible, differentiating idea, by way of arguments that kept Protagoras in view as the target. That of the Stranger is part of a strenuous attempt to correct that premise, as has been maintained, by way of arguments that kept Parmenides in view as the target. Plato's art calls on the reader to bring together the closing of *Theaetetus* and the closing of *Sophist* in the repeated recourse to the figure of the letters and the ideas.

The Stranger continues his new argument with the disjunction of what we call nouns (*onomata*) and verbs (*rhēmata*). He proves that a sentence says something about something that is, and does so by interweaving (*sumplekon*) certain verbs and nouns that lend themselves to combination. Then, by comparison of "Theaetetus is sitting" with "Theaetetus, with whom I am now conversing, is flying" the Stranger elicits the observation that the true statement reported as *being* certain things that are, while the false one reported as *being* certain things that are not. Thus a true statement is one that affirms what *is* about some subject, with the understanding that such a thing as its running or sitting is comprehended as entity. Now we know what a false statement is, and how its definition depends on the being of not-being. But what about the falseness of thought, discourse and imagination (*phantasia*)? The Stranger must say first what they are (*ti pot' esti* 263DE). We as observers know that if he says truly what they are, he will have disclosed their being in discovering their *eidos*.

Thought and discourse are the same, thought being the soundless dialogue of the soul with itself. What issues forth therefrom in a vocal flow through the mouth is called speech. It will be remembered that Socrates, in *Theaetetus* (189E–190D, 206D), proposed these very definitions of thought and discourse, although at *Theaetetus* 189B he had argued that "one cannot opine what is not, neither about things nor about it itself," and thus had to move on to other premises in his inconclusive search for the truth about knowledge. Socrates, like the Stranger, was on the attack against those whose doctrines made error and the false unintelligible, though he aimed in the opposite direction. As for the Stranger, he proceeds to define discourse as affirmation and negation (*phasis, apophasis*), or assertion and denial. When present silently in the soul as thought, this is opinion. When present not simply by itself but through sense perception, it is imagination (*phantasia*). But all of these, as derivative from *logos,* are, like *logos,* susceptible to being false, which is what was to be demonstrated. Thus the Stranger has in his own way contradicted the Protagorean proposition that there can be no falsifying a perception, a notion that rests on the thought that each thing indubitably is to the perceiver of it exactly as he has perceived it and cannot be otherwise.

The Stranger prepares to conclude the discourse by recurring to diairesis according to classes (*eidē*) (264C). A man of art, the sophist had been characterized first through successive dissections of the art of acquisition, then of the art of production. The sophist was portrayed as claiming the art of producing verbal images of all things, an art (*eidōlopoiikē*) that consists of two others, one that generates a literal likeness that diminishes the appearance of the uppermost when seen from below, and another that departs from the true dimensions of the thing so that the higher will appear in its greatness when viewed from below (233E et seq.). Thereafter, the question of the truly false, in the form of the question of the being of not-being, came to preoccupy the discussion. But now the nature and being of the false has been laid bare, and the nature of the sophist's imitative art can be determined through the final anatomization of the art of production (*poietikē*).

The Stranger introduces a new diremption as he divides the productive into divine and human art (265B). For Theaetetus's benefit, he explains that the plants and animals and other terrestrial material could be thought to have come into being through god's workmanship (*theou dēmiourgountos*) or, as according to the popular belief, caused by mechanical mindless nature.[8] He prompts the youth toward the explanation that depends on reason and divine knowledge, and praises him for his ready acceptance of that pious opinion. The

8. Once again, the reader must look ahead to the myth of Kronos and Zeus, and its teaching of the god's inattention in the present state of the whole.

praise itself becomes problematic for the reader because the Stranger includes in it the remark that Theaetetus's nature (*phusis*) inclines him toward the pious opinion. If the mindful and the natural causes are indeed alternative, then the Stranger's praise renders his own piety and Theaetetus's judgment problematic at the same time. The Stranger goes on to say that he will posit (*thēso*) that what is said to be natural is produced by divine art, and what is made from such products by men is by human art. This is the diremption that he will proceed to treat in an unprecedented way. Conjuring a figure that has been divided vertically into parts corresponding to divine and human, he calls for a further lateral division into parts corresponding respectively to authentic things and to images. He has made four classes—a human authentic and iconic and a divine authentic and iconic. The divine authentic art produces whatever we call natural— the animals, the elements, and so on. The divine imaging art produces dreams, shadows and reflections of things, images not only of divinely made things but of artificial ones as well, as we know and the Stranger does not say. Then there is human art, which makes authentic things like houses, and iconic things like pictures of houses, "like artificial dreams for the waking" (266C). It goes without saying, which perhaps explains the Stranger's silence, that the human iconic art can imitate divine productions as well as human ones by reproduction on canvas or in stone. It has become clear that the Stranger's version of piety, which reverently attributes everything "natural" to divine intelligence, must implicate divinity in the deceptions practiced on visionary mankind. Of course, the Cartesian reflections on the possibility of a deceptive omnipotence did not depend on an ambience enlightened by revelation in order to arise.

It serves the Stranger's purpose to revert to the division of the image-making art (presumably the human not the divine branch thereof) and to focus on the apparitional part of it (*phantastikē*), which he is entitled to do because he has demonstrated the true being of the false. He concentrates on that subpart of *phantastikē* that is practiced by one who mimics the shape or voice of another, an impersonator. From this description we would expect to be told about one who wishes to look or sound like someone whom he pretends to be, in the most egregious case a fraud who conceals himself behind a curtain and intones like a god, or in the more innocent case a person who appears on the stage and declaims the speeches of men and gods. Instead, with shocking disregard for the expectation he has aroused, the Stranger reveals that it is justice, and virtue in general, that he had in mind when speaking of a shape (*schēma*) and voice that a mimic impersonates by himself, that is, in act and by his speech. Now some know, and some do not know but have only an opinion of the thing they affect to imitate, though the latter may nonetheless succeed in their mimicry. Because the men of old were casual in distinguishing things according to their *eidē*, the Stranger must commit neologism in order to name the mimesis by opinion and the mimesis by knowledge. The sophist is known to operate on opinion, not knowledge, so it is the opinion-based imitation (*doxomimetikē*) that must be analyzed. The "doxomimetikos" may be of the kind that does not know that he has only opinion to rely on, but on the other hand he might be a man who much suspects and fears that he is ignorant of what he discourses about. It is to this latter class of the sophist who knows or suspects that he does not know that the Stranger turns. Some members of it orate at length before crowds while the others do it privately, and with short speeches compel their interlocutor to contradict himself. Is one of the former a statesman (*politikos*) or a popular orator (*dēmologikos*)? Popular orator, of course. The latter—is he the wise (*sophos*) or is he sophist? He cannot be called wise because he is ignorant. Therefore he is sophist, revealed at last as the mimic of the wise.

The sophist cannot be called wise because he is ignorant. But Socrates too is ignorant, and is known for saying so. Therefore Socrates is no more *sophos* than the sophist. But the question at the outset was not whether the sophist and the *sophos* are the same but whether the sophist and the *philosophos* are the same. That question has not been answered explicitly in the conclusion. What we know is that Socrates, who may be the very pattern of the philosopher, does not deceive about his ignorance but makes something of a show of being the merest midwife, although he is willing enough to countenance and recommend deception in the practical world in the form of the so-called noble lie. But Socrates is as famous for his irony as for his modesty: the world well suspects that not all of his self-depreciation is seriously meant. Has the difference between sophist and philosopher, the difference between the mimic and the original, been reduced to the concealment on the one part and the confession on the other of important ignorances? The core of that difference, as we reflect on it, was indicated long since by the remark of the Stranger at 231A, when he tells Theaetetus that, for all the similarity between sophist and philosopher, the one is like the other as the wolf is like the dog. The difference between them is a moral difference.

Much, and, as we reflect on it, perhaps everything has been made of the sophist's motives. He seeks out rich young men, he charges for his instruction, he is crafty, he is incorrigibly eristic, and more along the same line. But he is not unintelligent, he need not be ignorant of his ignorance, and he is not identified simply as one who is wrong about important things: Parmenides might have been profoundly wrong about the most important thing, but he was at worst a resource for the sophists and not one of them. The sophists are known by and blamed for the state of their soul, not merely the condition of their mind. The sophist's traits reveal, in their negation, the nature of the philosopher. The latter is insatiable in his passion for *logos* and at the same time imperturbably serene in his skepsis of the whole. He is profoundly selfless and unassuming, passionate not for prevailing but for clarity, yet caring very much for the condition of his own soul. He cares for his city and for its youth, but he cares nothing for the wealth, power, and renown that are the city's gifts. He is, in brief, the paradigm of selfless egoism, impassioned serenity—the bringer of light in a hooded lantern. If a commingling of incommensurables were not possible, there would be no philosopher, and, if no philosopher, then no incarnation of measured caring.

The Stranger concludes the conversation by recapitulating the long series of disparagements that descended from the analytic diairesis of productive art. He calls the unflattering total the character of the veritable sophist. The gist of the whole awkward catena is that for the sophist, interestedness extinguishes caring and appearance takes precedence of being. The sophist is terrestrialized man whose view of the human being's earthly existence does not take in the exposedness of the whole human kind and humanity's need for a care that is born on earth. In the conversation that follows, on the *politikos*, the theme of human caring for humanity will be extended from the persona of the sophist, who fails as carer, to that of the statesman, whose aptitude in that capacity is the issue of the dialogue. How the theme will be carried into the defense of Socrates before the Athenians is known to all.

V

STATESMAN

PLATO MAKES THE *STATESMAN* TAKE PLACE LATER ON THE SAME day as the *Sophist,* with the same named characters present, Theodorus still somehow in the chair, the Eleatic Stranger again to act as senior interlocutor, but Theaetetus about to be replaced as respondent by his contemporary and friend, a youth named Socrates. The replacement of Theaetetus by Young Socrates occurs after an opening scene in which the elder Socrates thanks Theodorus for having introduced him to Theaetetus and the Stranger. Theodorus incautiously says that Socrates will be thrice indebted after the Stranger has elucidated the statesman and the philosopher. Socrates, seemingly playfully, reproves the geometer for his faulty mathematics: no proportion relates sophist, statesman, philosopher; they are incommensurable, though doubtless subject to ranking and comparison. When Theodorus acknowledges the acuity of Socrates' hit, he swears by Ammon, the deity invoked in *Meno* when Socrates elicits the doubling of the square from the slave boy and, therewith, the positing of a line whose length is the square root of two, that recurrent reminder of the irrational / incommensurable that lies near the heart of mathematics itself. This dark omen, the square root of two, will materialize again when the Stranger deploys it in accomplishing the somatic, derationalized definition of man as featherless biped, a description that, whatever its oddity, cannot be dismissed as unnatural, for it declares plain facts of nature. That an act of judgment dictates the selection of the natural facts that constitute a definition will soon be demonstrated in the series of algorithmic diremptions by which the Stranger affects to discover the definition of the statesman. It will become obvious that both the choice of classes that the Stranger selects for diremption, and the choice in each case of the branch to be divided further, determined by the Stranger without the pretense of eliciting them by questioning, are guided by a certain discernment of the end that is to be arrived at, a definition already had in mind in some form at the outset, the *quod erat demonstrandum* of a geometer's proof. That there is nothing sinister or deceptive in this process is guaranteed by the truism, already stated in *Theaetetus,* that there would be no way to raise the question, What is a statesman? if one

111

could not recognize a statesman well enough to raise the question. The Stranger is no more in the dark, at the beginning, about the statesman than he was, at the same stage, about the sophist. The long and tedious process of diremption seems to have as its aim the refinement of an indistinct opinion to the state of precise knowledge. In fact, the meaning of diairesis will be revealed to us later in so many words: it is to improve its practitioners as dialecticians, which means disclosing to the inquirer the most important things about the ground of all inquiry. If diairesis is *the* method of inquiry, then something about the way of forming distinctions must be crucial. What follows will exhibit the dialectician in the rightful exercise of his authority over the argument and thereby over his interlocutor. A portrait of the caring ruler in the realm of discourse will emerge in due course, as Socrates' original invitation to contrast statesman and philosopher continues to shape the dialogue.

The replacement of Theaetetus by Young Socrates prompts Socrates to remark that the two youths are in some ways his kinsmen, one by virtue of his name and the other because of the "similarity in the nature of his visage" (257D). One should get to know one's relations through argument or observation, as Socrates has already done with Theaetetus, but, as he says, he, Socrates, does not know the other Socrates in either way. He will at some later time question him. As it is obvious that a casual "natural" resemblance of features and a fortuitous "conventional" identity of name are slender or no evidence of kinship, we are induced to consider Socrates' remark either as a witticism or as a weak intimation that apparent similarities, both natural and nominal, can mislead. In any case, the time never comes for Socrates to question his namesake, the future proving as impenetrable as the square root of two; and Socrates says nothing further in the course of the *Statesman*.

The Stranger begins his colloquy with Young Socrates by proposing to seek out the statesman and to do so by identifying the statesman's peculiar "science" or knowledge (*epistēmē*). If one knows what the statesman singularly knows, one knows what the statesman singularly is. Since the task is now to isolate a science, the Stranger must proceed to the division of all science, following the method he has just used in the investigation of the sophist. This time, however, the dissection will not be according to the same divisions as before. Young Socrates asks, "How, then?" The answer, surprising in one way and not in another, is "Differently." Unless we are to pass over this response as a gratuitous rudeness or a fatuous joke, we can consider it an indication that the continent of all the sciences is available to be mapped in any one of innumerable ways depending on the purpose of the cartographer. Is there one and only one naturally authentic taxonomy of the sciences? Much to the contrary, it would appear that there are as many paths of diremption as there are beings to be defined if they are to be defined according to their science. The Stranger formulates the task as follows: to find the statesman's way, to isolate it from the others, to stamp it as one idea (*idea*), and to designate all the others collectively as one kind or species (*eidos*), making our soul conceive of all the sciences as being of two kinds (*eidē*)—one "kind" consisting of one member and the other "kind" containing some large number of members. If the Stranger's project could be understood as a paradigm for all inquiry that aims at definition, we would have to conclude that the Ideas and the classes are conceits that the human beings construct and then impose on their soul. Violent as this notion may seem, in itself and as a supposed thought of Plato's, it will nevertheless receive support as the argument unfolds to reveal the state of man in the condition of mere nature.

The Stranger begins the dissection of all science by pointing to certain arts (*technai*) like arithmetic that are bare of any practical use but provide only knowledge (258D). The Stranger will refer interchangeably to arts and sciences throughout the dialogue, as if an art and the knowledge that defines it can be considered to be a one. Thus, "all science" is of two "kinds" or species (*eidē*), one practical, the other solely knowing, or gnostic. To make the point unmistakable, Young Socrates confirms it by consenting that the premise of their discussion be that the two "kinds" or species (*eidē*) of the one "whole" of science are the ones mentioned. Having posited that statesmanship and regality (the difference in names is dismissed as not significant) are a science, the Stranger can now deduce that anyone who possesses the art or science deserves the title, whether he rules a state or not, which enables "us" to combine or synthesize the statesmanly and the statesman, and the kingly and the king, all together as one (259D)—a fine example of constructive unification. In maintaining that king, statesman, and grand householder all possess one single art or science, the Stranger seems to have invented the science of administration, transcending the distinction of public and private. He appears to know that the science of the statesman, *politikos,* informs the one general art of superordination, of mastery or authority.

In order to proceed, the Stranger proposes that they look for some natural disjunction (*diaphuē*) along which to divide the gnostic science (259D). Making this suggestion, the Stranger has presented the whole field of their inquiry as an ensemble composed of parts that are distinguished by nature but are ready to the hand of man for arrangement as *genē* under concepts that are Ideas imposed by man not only on the material but on his soul. Within a few lines, the Stranger will procure Young Socrates' assent to the proposition that the gnostic sciences are divided between those that simply take notice and form judgments of things, and those that give orders about them. The former is described as including the contemplative (*theatē*), the latter the commanding and masterly, thus the royal. Two facts are striking: first, the Stranger makes this the occasion to remark that what matters for their discourse is that they agree, without regard to any opinion of others. Young Socrates' assent is the sign that the inquirers have succeeded in imposing on their soul the same schema that they have together imposed on the field of their inquiry. Also, if they were in pursuit of the philosopher rather than the statesman, and had generated the same algorithm that they have used to this point, they would have to move down the path that they must now avoid, thus separating philosopher and king beyond reconjunction and threatening the famous schema of the *Republic.*

When the Stranger arrives at the point of asking Young Socrates whether the statesman gives orders—his own orders, not those of any other possible higher source of commandment—for the sake of bringing things about among living or inanimate beings, we cannot doubt that the answer prompts the question and not the question the answer. Of course, the statesman is identified as a commander among living beings, and, more particularly, gregarious living beings. The Stranger proves to have an interest in presenting the statesman as one who can be described as caring for a herd. The next step in the inquiry is striking precisely because there could not be a doubt that the statesman governs human beings; yet the Stranger will rebuke Young Socrates for saying so when the youth is encouraged to bisect the herdsman's art and does so by distinguishing the herding of men and the herding of beasts. The Stranger has a quite different taxonomy in mind. Ostensibly, he objects to the self-preference that is exemplified in the Greeks' creation of a tiny class consisting of themselves and an enormous class consisting of everyone else, whom they denominate barbarians. It would be better to divide humanity according to the distinction male-female—what we would today call a purely biological, natural, or morally neutral disjunction. But as Greeks speak of Greek and barbarian, so do men speak of man and beasts. Young Socrates wonders how to tell the difference between a proper class (*genos*) of things and a mere part (*meros*) of a true class or order of things. The Stranger cannot stop to work this out for the youth but offers the information that *eidos* or species (with which he replaces *genos* of the original question) might also be a part, indeed it must be a part of whatever it is that it is the *eidos* of, although the *eidos* as such need not be a part of anything. If *eidos* could be understood as Idea (or "Form"), then we would be seeing a resurgence of the Stranger's Parmenideanism in the shape of an intimation that the Idea is immanent in the object just as a part is in and of the thing of which it is a part, the *eidos* being unintelligible as being outside its object. This notion harmonizes well with the thought already noticed that Ideas are imposed or stamped upon a passive material and on the soul, by men for their own purposes.

At this point (263C), the Stranger resumes the hunt for the peculiar animal that is herded according to the science that defines the king. Proceeding through a succession of such unexpected disjunctions as wet-herding and dry-herding, horned and hornless, cloven-hooved and otherwise, cross-breeding and endogenetic, the Stranger comes in sight of his intended goal, the human being. There are, however, more oddities to be explored before the end is reached. The Stranger can apparently think of no better way to drive the diairesis into man's two-footedness than by implicating our *nature* in the square root of two (266B). Someone less bent on introducing the irrational into the search might have suggested that the very process of rational inquiry is shown, as by their immediate doings, to rest on division into two; but the decisive digit is deployed in its irrational association rather than through any rational reference. To drive the point home, the Stranger compares the human being with some animal that he leaves unnamed but that man resembles in nobility and in a kind of affable slowness, the inference having been drawn for many years that the animal in question is the pig. "Nobility" may be supposed to be part of the joke. The Stranger notices that this flattery of the subject casts a distinguishing light also on the king who rides herd on the excellent swine. He notes further that, as in the investigation of the sophist, their present mode of inquiry is impartial between the more and less dignified, caring only for the truth whether it is to be found through the noble or the base. Persuasively illustrating this observation, the Stranger brings this section of the dialogue to its conclusion by pronouncing the famous definition of the king's human subject as the featherless biped (267E), a description that purges man of his pride as it locates the human being within a nature eminently neutral or indifferent to man and perfectly suited to investigation by a mode of inquiry that abstracts from the distinction of noble and base in the interest of truth.

The Stranger has portrayed the human being in two very different ways: as the active intelligence that stamps intelligibility on dumb nature, and also as so little distinguished from that dumb nature as to be susceptible to the derationalized definition of "featherless biped." The former description characterizes man as inquirer or dialectician and, even more radically, as his own artifact. The latter description characterizes him as the object of government in civil society.

The Stranger has succeeded in procuring the definition of the king as a herdsman; he must now distinguish the royal herdsman from all the others. The point of distinction appears to lie in the fact that, alone among herdsmen, only the herdsman of the featherless biped is susceptible to the rivalry of members of the herd itself who might claim to be the providers of certain cares and functions required by the herdsfolk. No sheep challenges the shepherd's eugenic program, or offers to play inspiriting or calming music to the flock. This would seem to establish the peculiarity, and thus the definition, of the royal drover, but of course it does not. It distinguishes him well enough from the literal herdsmen, those who rule animals unlike himself, but precisely in doing that, it shows him exposed to rivalry on the part of his subjects, who are just like himself and among whom, for example, there may indeed be a featherless who takes it on himself to sing significant tunes to the generality. Thus it will be necessary to define the statesman's art in such a way that it excludes those arts that belong in principle to the human being as such rather than to the ruler or the subject as such, the member of civil society—in brief, to the natural featherless biped. It is because Plato is in search of man in the condition of mere nature that he now makes the Eleatic Stranger introduce the grand myth of the *Statesman*.

The Stranger calls on them to start from a new beginning (268D) and to proceed by a different way. By way of new beginning, he will not now start with science as the mark of definition, and he will not proceed to anatomize science by diairesis (although he promises that he will return to those devices after the ensuing "interlude"). What he does provide is nothing less than two portraits of the universe, one that is recognizable as our own experience, the other resembling our natural life as much as Adam's in Eden resembled his existence after his expulsion. It is helpful to note that before the Stranger begins his tale, he says that much of this great story will be purposeful. We will have to judge eventually what is extraneous, why a storyteller would plan to include what he announces will be superfluous, and what therefore is the positive meaning of the allegedly superfluous.

The Stranger begins in the mood of "once upon a time," evoking the old story of Atreus and Thyestes, two who claimed the same throne. Hermes and Zeus intervened in the affair, the latter giving a sign of his preference for the cause of Atreus by reversing the course of the sun and stars. Inured to the extravagances that are the theology of gods whose existence consisted only in their names, we might overlook the impiety in the apotheosis of such figments and the blasphemy of avowing their scandalous interventions in human life. Immersed in their atmosphere as we are not, and constrained by convention to observe the cultic proprieties, the Stranger is more sensitive than we might be to what is problematic in such theology. At any rate, he promises to integrate three stories and connect them all for the very first time with a single incident. He will draw together the stories of the counterrotation of the heavens, of the reign of Kronos, and of the autochthony of the earliest men. The focal incident to which he will connect all three will prove to be the abandonment of the universe by the god.

In a few lines (269CD), the Stranger tells the story of the whole. At some earlier time, Kronos governed the revolution of the universe, but when the measure of its turnings had somehow been accomplished, he abdicated his control and released the cosmos, a living thing with a mind of its own, which then took its way according to its necessary nature. No longer constrained, the whole adopted the reverse or perverse revolution; for whatever the mind of the world might have dictated, it is the corporeality and hence corruption of the world-animal that prevailed. Thus the Stranger has disclosed the truth of the natural world: composed not only of body, its way or decisive turning is yet dominated by the necessity of body, and it is not such a way as would be dictated by a god.

In the beginning of the former age of the world, when the god assumed the rule of the cosmos and led it to labor according to its then nature, the heavens reversed their motion, the universe was convulsed and time ran backward. The old were rejuvenated, the young returned to infancy and vanished, and the only pregnancy was the earth's, which cast forth the resurrected dead to live their retrograde lives. The untilled earth brought forth an abundance, each kind (*genos*) of animal was herded by a divinity to the end that there was no violence, there was no eating of flesh, the lamb was untroubled by the lion, and god was man's shepherd. Families were unknown because man sprang from the dust, and there were no cities, for they were not needed, for there was no bloodshed. If we have to explain to ourselves the deepest ground or ruling fact of the condition of life in the age of Kronos, we would find it in the absence of need from all animal life. The existence of man is portrayed as an effortless trajectory, from painless extrusion out of earth to an unconscious evanescence, and in the interval a tranquil sufficiency shared by all that breathed. As there was no need that impelled, so there was no fear, not even, so it appears, of the shepherd himself.

It occurs to the Stranger (272B) to wonder which life is the happier, that of the men in the age of Kronos or that of our own experience in the age of Zeus. He can only speculate. If the men of the other age used their advantages to increase their knowledge, then it is obvious that they were vastly happier; but we cannot tell if they did. What is clear to us is that the happiness, such as it was, of the other folk came to an end because the age itself expired, and their painlessness did not cease through the sin of seeking to better themselves by seeking knowledge.

The god let go the helm of the world and remanded the cosmos and all its denizens to their own care, under the tutelage now not of divinity but of the nature that we know, so that they might grow and procreate and thrive in autarky as best they might (274A). The mind of Zeus is elsewhere.

It is time for the Stranger to explain the bearing of the grand myth on the inquiry into statesmanship. Men in the realm of nature alone are above all else in peril, artless prey to the beasts and to need. Old stories relate that the helpless primitives were rescued by divinities who imparted fire and the productive arts to mankind, but such tales do not accord well with the Stranger's portrait of men's abandonment to utter autarky by indifferent god, nor with the divine punishment of Prometheus for his philanthropy. As the Stranger remarks, it is from fire and arts and seed that everything arises that furnishes human life, the gods having deserted us.

In this, the human condition in the age of negligent Zeus, which is the only condition that matters to us, there is nothing in the world that takes care of us as Kronos did as our shepherd and the shepherd of all the living things in the time of his sovereignty. Assuredly, there is no human being and thus no king who does or could provide so for us. The myth therefore serves to teach us that the king is our shepherd in some merely limited way (275A). But this cannot be the whole reason for the telling of the fable because the point had already been well made (268BC) when the king was shown to have any number of human rivals for the title of provider for the human beings. Indeed the Stranger gives another reason: the story presented the image of the veritable carer for human beings, that carer whom no king can equal in caring. We are encouraged to conclude that, as the sophist was a defective imitation of the philosopher, so the king is a defective imitation of the paradigm of a fictive divine carer. The best regime available to us will be a defective imitation of its own excellent pattern, and we will eventually learn that law is a defective imitation of reason. The inhabited world contemplated by the Stranger is rife with actual defect. In no case is the defective entity represented to be the flawed imitation of an "idea"—perhaps because the Stranger is a lapsed Parmenidean, not a converted apostate.

The grand myth furnishes an account of the life of man in the condition of mere nature, and it discloses the terms of that nature which, being the disposition of the cosmos itself, is the inevitable matrix of our present life. These massive truths are the premise on which the Stranger grounds the question, brought to light by the myth, that propels the discourse into its next phase: if the king does not rule as Kronos could, then what is the manner of his rule, and who in principle is that royal ruler? We might restate the question in this way:

given the precariousness of the human existence under the influence of nature rather than in the care of god, and allowing that we are somehow endowed with the elementary arts, what is the human agent of rule that we must supply out of our human resources in order to thrive on earth? Before following the Stranger into the territory opened by his latest question, we should consider that his depiction of our unprovided condition under the blank eye of Zeus bears heavily on what has developed on the theme of piety in the preceding dialogues, as well as on what will emerge in subsequent earnest discourses on the same subject.

The Stranger will apply his new knowledge to the project for isolating the herdsman of men by pointing out that the statesman is not a herdsman as the others are because they do and he does not feed his charges, though he may care for them in sundry other ways. Of course, each human being bears the burden of assuaging his most primary neediness: only a god could do it for him, the god has excused himself from the task, and the king is no more a god than is his needy subject. This understood, the Stranger appears to move on another tack—the distinction between rule by force and rule with consent (276D). The caretaking of kings should therefore be distinguished from that of tyrants. The Stranger wonders whether they have not at last sufficiently defined the statesman. Young Socrates thinks they have; the Stranger thinks they have not. Knowing as we do that in the latter part of the dialogue the Stranger will openly depreciate the distinction between the royal rule over subjects who consent to their regimen and the rule that simply compels them to obey, on the ground that a superior criterion is the merit of what is prescribed, we can surmise why the Stranger is not satisfied that the distinction between accommodating rule and coercive rule is decisive.

Yet the Stranger declares to Young Socrates (277A) that, for the point to be settled, not only one of them must accept it but both must be of the same opinion. At best the Stranger is hinting that his authority over Young Socrates should be of the consensual rather than the tyrannical kind, as if the ruler of the discourse can prevail by either convincing his subject with truths or subduing him with whatever means are available for compelling surrender. When it is recalled that, according to the Stranger himself in the preceding conversation with Theaetetus, there is a higher truth for representing the higher things, it becomes apparent that the philosopher commands a device for gaining agreement that is not in the unequivocal sense truthful and thus is not simply free. That there is a ground that is common to the philosophic and the political ruler adds depth to the question whether sophist, statesman, and philosopher are the same or different. Philosophers and statesmen are caretaking rulers who may rule with consent over free subjects or may rule otherwise on occasion. To speak in a language already familiar to us, if the monarch rules in his own interest he is an uncaring tyrant, and if the reasoner rules the discourse in order to prevail he is an interested, uncaring sophist. That Socrates' imminent apology will turn so insistently on his caring should help us to see how far the human loneliness in the cosmos, which pervades our being and throws humanity back on its own caring resources, guides us in distinguishing good and evil, just and wicked.

The Stranger aims to begin anew, but his introduction to the new beginning reveals a close continuity with what has gone immediately before. The preceding passage projected a judgment in favor of rule exercised on willing, or free, subjects, a judgment that will be modified later on because of perceived limitations on the human subject's capacity for knowing. The forthcoming passage reflects on our manner and power of knowing, setting in train a lengthy ratiocination that will culminate in a definition of the statesman as a man whose task it is to deal with human beings not in their rational but in their passionate constitution. It is as if Aristotle's variant definitions of man as rational animal and political animal were anticipated in their failure to coincide exactly.

The Stranger professes dissatisfaction with their—which means his—use of the myth (277B). They used a very large paradigm (*paradeigma*) to explicate a smaller object, and they used a sort of picture, although it is better to employ articulate logic (*lexei kai logō*) for those who are able to follow, while addressing the others by means of contrivances (*cheirourgiōn*). Now the Stranger admits that it is hard to explain the larger thoughts except by the use of paradigms or illustrative parallels, which are undoubted contrivances. This is the case because each of us is in a dreamlike state regarding everything that we know and do not know, which is Plato's way of saying that our clear and distinct ideas are very few. To make this similitude clear, he must, he says, use a paradigm to elucidate this paradigm. The illustration that he uses is one that we have met in *Theaetetus:* the letters and the syllables. Here the Stranger sets as the exemplary task teaching a child to recognize letters already familiar to him in simple syllables when they occur in new and difficult syllables. The Stranger makes explicit what the illustration does not emphasize, namely, that the child's "knowledge" of the letters to begin with is no more than right opinion. How, indeed, could one's "knowledge" of *thēta* be anything but right opinion? Then, starting with the right opinion of *thēta*, the learner will perceive the likeness of the same letters and the unlikeness of the different ones as he meets with more syllables. Recognizing the similarity or identity of two unconnected entities, of which the human being has right opinion, leads to a conclusion in "one true opinion" (278C). By this paradigm, the advancement of knowledge consists of a progress from a simple right opinion to a complex true opinion. In this "paradigm" of our epistemology, the Stranger has done two things. He has adumbrated the method he will use to reach the definition of the statesman, starting with a little thing with which we are familiar in order to reach the greater thing that it resembles, so that we will have presumably a true opinion of the two in conjunction; and he has told us something crucial about the being who is subject to the statesman's rule, a being who dwells together with his equally human ruler in the dreamy realm of opinion and is to be governed accordingly. The Stranger thinks that, in saying these things about the status of our knowledge, he has described to us "the nature of our soul in its relation to the elements [*stoicheia*, meaning also "letters"] of all things" (278C).

The Stranger has thus prepared for his choice of weaving as the minor paradigm that will disclose the nature of its major correlate, statesmanship. It is immediately obvious that a necessary condition for his choice of weaving is his having at the outset at least a right opinion of what decisive attribute of statesmanship must be brought to light, and how the weaving art embodies that in little. That the Stranger understands this is clear from his remark that in what they are about to do, they will be illuminating the nature of paradigm as well as the nature of statesmanship (278E).

The Stranger affects to pick weaving at random. Weaving suits his purpose because it aims at procuring something useful as a means to avoid a suffering or being done to, not to make possible a doing. Knowing what we know about man's exposedness and the harms to which that leads, we can discern something of the Stranger's purpose in guiding the definition of statesmanship in the direction of an art that fends off, or defends, for the preservation of the human beings, as the woven web does against the natural elements of wind and water. But weaving is not the only art that produces protective covering for men; it is the art of that kind that uses wool as its material. And before it does its characteristic act of joining components of wool together, it must first resort to ancillary arts and processes of separating—namely, carding—and then of spinning, which means the spinning of warp and woof, of stiff and soft yarn. We are expected to form an image of an art that practices a separation on its primary material and then an intertwining that joins the hard and soft components drawn from that material to form a strong integument, which is man's shelter in the face of nature. Stated so generally, the structure of weaving will prove to adumbrate the structure of statesmanship.

After extruding the definition of weaving from a detailed scrutiny of that art, the Stranger wonders why they did not get more expeditiously to the point. Perhaps suspecting a trap, the youth declines the invitation to criticize the minuteness of the inquiry. This earns him a homily on too much and too little which becomes a long and important discourse on excess, deficiency, and the mean (283C et seq.). The Stranger begins by enfolding the subjects of long and short, excess and deficiency, within the art of measurement (*metrikē*), which art is to be divided along the line of a most pregnant distinction: there is longer in relation to something shorter, and vice versa, as with all more and less; but also there are long and short in relation to the "nature of the mean" that is indispensable to the coming into being of things. By the latter the Stranger seems to mean that a man fifteen feet tall would exceed the measure of a human being by so much as to lack the human nature, for the mean or measure lies at the heart or nature or definition of the thing in question. The Stranger has it that the relative standard of longer and shorter, too much and too little, measured only against one another, is by nature (*kata phusin*) (283D). But he goes on to ask whether we must not say also that exceeding the nature of measure, excess itself, in words or deeds, really exists, the measure or mean being that by which we differentiate between bad men and good. This same measure is of the essence of what is necessary for the coming to be of things: it is, as the Stranger says, indispensable for the being of all the arts of bringing about or bringing into being, including the art of statesmanship. There must be a measure more positive than the merely comparative or relative one described as being by nature, or all the expedients of humanity on its own behalf would be brought to nought in the destruction of praxis (284A). In representing the natural measure of mere relation as destructive of the practical arts, the Stranger would have it that nature's indifference regarding the human good falls somewhat below strict impartiality, for it appears that the emphatically natural basis for judging the superfluous and the insufficient does not supply what is needful for man's makings and judgings, namely, the regulative measure.

In order to save the existence of the art of statesmanship it is necessary that there be the mean or measure that is the condition for the being of all art. As in the matter of the sophist, the Stranger says, we imposed the necessity that not-being be, so in the present matter we must impose the necessity that not only the relative measure but also the mean measure exist (284BC).[1] The Stranger's extraordinary task is proving to be to define the ground on which man may live—judging and doing, and saving himself—if man is not the measure, if the natural measure is inadequate, and if the god is as inattentive as nature is indifferent. It remains for philosophy, as its practical task, to make the case for the mean measure that supports man's praxis and accounts for the good and the beautiful in human doing. Someday the mean measure will have to be demonstrated with precision, but for the present it is splendidly proved by its indispensability for the existence of the arts, including the art of the statesman (284D). What the Stranger refers to continually as the measure seems to replace what Socrates might speak of as an Idea. The Stranger's measure receives a corroboration, solid if only provisional, in the undeniable existence of the arts. The Ideas of Socrates are burdened with the mystery of "participation" that troubled Aristotle as well as Parmenides.

It might be inferred that the mean measure exists as the instrumental means to the end served by the arts, including the art of statesmanship, which is the human good. But can the human good be known except in terms of a mean measure that is not merely comparative? Is the mean measure good because it serves the human end, or is the human end good because it is defined by the mean measure? We hear an echo of the question that ruled over the *Euthyphro*. The

---

1. The awkwardness of "impose the necessity" results from the Greek *prosenagkasamen* and *prosanagkasteon*.

Stranger has implied this question in the course of leaving it for disposition "someday" when the superior measure will be investigated thoroughly. In the meantime, the arts, and especially the art of statesmanship, are guided by the superior mean which, in supporting praxis, supports humanity in the realm of nature, wherein the overriding consideration is necessitousness, not good or beauty.

The Stranger proceeds to the diremption of the science of measurement (*metrikē*) along the lines so elaborately prepared: the arts that measure number, length, depth, breadth, and thickness in relation to their opposite, and the arts that measure them in relation to the measured (*metrion*), the fitting, the opportune, that which should be (*deon*), and all such as lie at the mean between extremes (284E). Declaring that all things should be regarded in their similarities and distinctions, the Stranger makes a particular point of advising that the two kinds of measure be kept well in mind. This is as good a place as any to note that the arts of the natural, relative mean operate in the realm of the comparison of quantities, where the incommensurable irrationals have their demonstrated being, while the measured mean between the extremes informs the arts by which humanity draws itself above the level of mere nature; yet the humanizing measure is the object of a precise demonstration reserved for an indeterminate "someday." The division of responsibility between statesman and philosopher for the care of man is at this point still to be made clear, but if in the end it is philosophy that must nurture the ennobling measure which fosters human doing, then the philosopher might eventually make a claim to be an authentic carer that is not without merit.

The Stranger now (285C) seems to change the subject abruptly, but it will appear that he has not so much changed the subject as devised a stimulating way of advancing it. He maintains that their inquiry about the statesman is not for the sake of this subject but rather in order to become more dialectical, say, more rationally investigative, about all things. He remarks that no one in his right mind would be interested for its own sake in such an inquiry into weaving as the one they recently completed. Why then must such things be endured? Because "most people" (*tous pleistous*) can be taught to understand the meaning of something by being shown its resemblance to something else that they do already know, so to speak. This kind of explanation no more calls upon a power of ratiocination than did the indication of the letter *thēta* in an unfamiliar syllable. It is pedagogy through pointing at what is to be perceived and re-cognized—taken notice of again. But there are things to be defined for which there is no perceptible schema, nothing to point to, incorporeal things of which there are no images (*eidōlon*). These are the greatest things, the most to be revered, the most beautiful and, again, the greatest, to be explained only through reasoning. Authorities as various as the Bible and Spinoza have likewise reproved the error of supposing the highest or the intelligible to be imaginable. The Stranger lets it be known that everything that has been said is for the better understanding of the most beautiful and the greatest things. But what has been gone into at such length has been weaving and the turning of the whole, as well as the being of not-being (286B). Of weaving and the cosmic turning it can be said that they are image-paradigms inseparable from body, one smaller and the other larger than the statesmanship intended to be illuminated. Of course, statesmanship is not one of the most beautiful or greatest of things: consider the means by which it has been "explained." The being of not-being stands higher, for it was demonstrated by reasoning, not by the paradigm of corporeal things. At any rate, the Stranger alleges that what he has said has been aimed at warding off impatience, that is, judging the discourse to be too long for the purpose, especially when it seems to meander. It might be noted that Young Socrates, far from showing signs of impatience, had been passively submissive as the mysteries of weaving were unfolded. However that may be, the Stranger has succeeded in maintaining unbroken the thread of the argument from the distinction of the relative and absolute measures of such things as long and short, thus too long and too short, to the present point. He concludes his discourse on excess and deficiency by making it very clear that judgment on the length and brevity of speeches is dominated by a mean or measure that regards one thing above all, namely, the demands of the method of diairesis according to classes (*eidē*) (286DE). It is left to us to infer that the measure for judging the length of reasonings is a measure of the absolute kind, one we might define for ourselves as prescribing what is necessary and sufficient for the intended purpose of bringing a truth to light. Such a mean or measure is a formula whose concrete meaning is supplied on every occasion by the experience of the occasion. Because it is so obvious that an inquiry should be as long as it must be and not longer, we are forced to wonder why the demonstration of this self-evident truth is itself so protracted when the mere statement of it would have gained plausible assent. Drawn out as it is, this performance could serve as a rebuke to old Socrates, who made so much of the length of Protagoras's speeches (*Protagoras*) on the mildly amusing ground that he could hardly remember the beginning of a long speech by the time the end of it was reached. It was for Protagoras to say that his speeches must be as long as their purpose required. Plato assigns no intervention here to Socrates, the regular advocate of short speeches who occasionally delivers himself of monologues.

The Stranger announces (287A) that the king has been sufficiently distinguished with regard to herding. That is to say, we know beyond a doubt that the king is a somehow caretaker of the human beings, a weak image of any numenous provider but one who, as it happens, for all his being a mere image, confers a benefit on mankind that his authentic prototype in heaven neglects to dispense. Distinguished from what may be described as above him, it remains to be shown how he is distinguished from those who may be described as below him, those practitioners of the civilian arts which are the necessary conditions for the existence of statesmanship and of the state itself without themselves being part of statesmanship. The Stranger now particularizes the arts and commodities that provide and form the material infrastructure of the political society. The distinction of all of this from statesmanship itself once again draws attention to the chasm between statesmanship and provision of the means of human survival. Then there are the servile or ministerial arts and their practitioners, ranging from slaves through those freemen who sell their services, some as laborers, some as ancillaries to commerce. It should be pointed out with serious emphasis that these humble beings, so remote from rule as never to be seen as rivals to the statesman, are those on whose shoulders lies the entire burden, abdicated by god and beyond the art of kings, of providing for the survival of their kind. It is only in democracy that they receive their tacit recognition.

The Stranger moves on through the civil servants to a class of servitors that, as the Stranger allows (290C), deserves special consideration. These are the mantics and the priests, servants because they carry on the commerce between men and gods. The Stranger uses the context to remind the Athenians of the intrusion of hierophancy into their public life, referring particularly to the magistrate king (the king archon) on whose premises, as it happens, Socrates and Euthyphro had encountered one another on the preceding day. These and the sophists are now about to come under scrutiny as claimants to possess the royal art; but first the sophists.

The Stranger's exposition on the sophists is extraordinary for its length and its matter. It extends from 291A to 303C, and until the last word of the last line of this passage on the sophists is reached, the reader is compelled to supply his own reasons for believing that the subject has not been lost in digression. Our recent learning prepares us to believe that the passage is of the precise length necessary for its purpose, and we come to understand that there is no way to separate the length of an argument from its content; nevertheless, nothing explicit prepares us for the denouement.

The Stranger begins by affecting to descry an elusive motley of men, beasts, and grotesques, many leonine but very many who are weak and crafty. By dint of peering, he becomes conscious that these are the meddlers in political affairs, those among the sophists most able to counterfeit the statesman and king and therefore most urgently to be distinguished from these latter. In the *Sophist* we learned that the sophist is a close mimic of the philosopher. We are about to learn that he is an apt mimic of the statesman. In what follows, the Stranger will treat of such sovereign matters as the schema of the regimes and the status of law itself, as well as other political matters; but he is steadily in the course of elucidating the sophist, so that the statesman may be distinguished from that counterfeit. We recall the homily on definition by similarity and difference.

The Stranger proceeds forthwith. There is rule by one, few, and many; and there is rule affected by the opposition between coercion and consent, poverty and wealth, lawfulness and lawlessness. Thus arise royalty and tyranny, aristocracy and oligarchy, and democracy, the last undifferentiated with regard to the three named antitheses. Is any of the five the "right" polity, and, if so, which? But the question cannot be answered in the terms proposed because the decisive criterion for defining statesmanship itself is "science," not freedom, wealth, legality, or numbers at the head. The right regime will be the one in which the ruling science par excellence is in authority. Since that science can never be possessed by many, it is clear that the right regime is to be sought in royalty or aristocracy, although from this it certainly does not follow that everyone who possesses the science will surely rule (292E). The Stranger enlarges on his general theme by adducing the physician, who rules his patient with a sole view to the patient's well-being and without regard to the patient's concurrence in the treatment or to his wealth, and indeed without regard to any written rules. The health of the city is not the highest law, it is beyond law. Right rule is truly beneficent rule, we might dare to say caring rule, constrained only by science and justice. The Stranger goes so far as to declare the regimes that are not this right one do not properly exist, for they have only so much of being as can lodge in a mere imitation of something that is right or true, i.e., that truly is (293E). The Stranger is in fact judging the regimes by the standard of the absolute measure revealed earlier, according to which the technic end to be achieved governs the propriety of the means to be deployed. For the present practical purpose, the purpose served by the absolute measure, he neglects the proposition so laboriously demonstrated that affirms the being of the not-being. The criterion of being is subordinated to the criterion of the good for needy mankind.

Young Socrates recoils from what he perceives to be a teaching that, in the best case, rule would be without law. His scruple initiates a major discussion on the place of law in human society. The Stranger avers that the circumstances of life are too complex and mutable to be subject to the simplicity and rigidity of law, which he likens to a headstrong and stupid man who tolerates nothing but his own dictate, regardless of any reasons for relenting. How then explain the need for law? On our own behalf, we might restate the question by asking, Whence the necessity of the mean or measure that applies the rigid and thus killing standard, rather than the supple and discreet one, to the art of ruling? The plain answer is that the wisdom to rule by discretion without written law is either lacking or would, if available, be suspected and rejected. It may be noted that the Stranger now refers to the governed once again, after a long interval, as herds (294E). Evidently, the Stranger includes in his reflection on the necessity of written law a reflection on the nature of those who must become subject to it as well as of those who would be eager to rule without it.

The law prescribes to all alike, regardless of persons and circumstances (which in truth Euthyphro, but not only he, could urge as its merit), and resists revision though circumstances change. Would not the lawgiver himself, after an absence, be moved to make changes in the constitution?—a question for consideration by theorists of original intent. But there must be a rigid uniformity in the law, "for how,

Socrates, could someone stay at the side of each person throughout his life and lay down precisely what he should do?" (295AB). (The question anticipates the fantasy of *Emile*.) It is of course not the laws that resist amendment but the people who demand to be persuaded of the need to make the changes. In what follows, still thinking of the criterion of voluntary as against coercive rule, the Stranger declares that meliorations of the body politic, as of the body natural, are no less meliorations for being irregular and crammed down the throat of an unwilling patient. With this the Stranger completes the part of his argument that subordinates written law and the antitheses of coercion and persuasion, of wealth and poverty, of legality and its alternative to the criterion of the good of the city and the people as a wise and good man would provide for it. The Stranger's version of the argument for rule by the philosopher king has as its premise *salus populi suprema lex*. He joins the preservation of the citizens and their being made better, their earthly salvation, when he concludes his promotion of knowledge and art to superiority over the written law (297B). If Eden existed, it would be ruled by caring philosophy. The conjunction of God and Law as paradigm of the highest and best for man and world belongs to another dispensation.

The Stranger remarks on the scarcity among men of the science that would make intelligent government possible. It follows that regimes that look for rule elsewhere than in one man, or a few must fall short. They are called better or worse imitations of the one right polity, imitations in that they adopt as written laws the intelligent formulations of the one right polity. Thus they embody whatever defects adhere to the heedlessness of what is committed to writing; but in exchange they gain the indispensable benefits of a rigid, unmistakable code with penalties of utmost severity for violations. It is this legal expedient that the Stranger calls "second," meaning second best (297E). The legal definition of crime and punishment regulates the life of man so far as poverty of wisdom in his soul must be made up by the infliction of pains on his body, in the manner of a beast of burden. Whoever knowingly takes it on himself to care for mankind does so with knowledge of the defect as well as the claims of the object of his benevolence.

Why the prevalence of the second best among mankind? The immediate cause is that the generality of men mistrust those in power over them and insist on having matters in their own hands, installing their own opinions as law or custom. It is as if the crew on board ship or the patients of the physician rose up in resentment and suspicion against the discipline imposed on them by the knowledgeable expert and insisted on taking matters into their own hands. The insubordinate crowd would commit their ignorant notions of war and peace, health and illness to writing, or install them as tradition. Then they would reassert their hegemony annually by subjecting the captains and physicians to scrutiny in public for accusation by anyone in the crowd. Driving home the point that law is the instrument of the ignorant against the qualified, the law will have to punish those who inquire about it and about the nature that surrounds it, so that anyone guilty of these things will be called a ruminator on things aloft (299B) and a maundering sophist, subject to accusation by any citizen of corrupting the young, and remanded to the dicasts for judgment, even capital judgment, because nothing or no one is to be wiser than the laws. The Stranger has brought the critique of written law to a sharp point in the criticism of the Athenian democracy in general but also specifically as the enemy of Socrates. Plato cannot plausibly accuse democratic Athens of inveterate hostility to philosophy, which raises the question whether the singularly rigorous caring of Socrates for the city and its citizens was decisive for his fate. The caring must be careful in the manner of their caring. The dire inference is that mankind, left ungoverned by god and nature, resists the salvation that might be sought for it through the care and government of man by man.

The Stranger has it that no art could be conducted under the constraint of written rules rather than by means of knowledge and technical skill. Announcing this (299E), he has made known a second requisite for the existence of art. First was the being of a mean or measure that is fixed or certain, not merely of the kind that defines long as having no meaning other than "longer than something that is shorter." Now we learn that fixed or rigid prescriptions of practice are the death of art. It is not hard for us to find the ground that removes the apparent contradiction between the two formulas for the existence of art and, therewith, of the statesmanly art. The first formulation, as we saw, means the discovery by discretion of the measure made necessary by the nature of the end to be achieved. The second formulation demands the presence of that knowledge or discretion by which the concrete may be emancipated from the general. The two formulations are in fact a conjoint pair.

The Stranger has disparaged the laws at length, but he does justice to them in acknowledging that they provide mankind with an indispensable second best in the form of a careful distillation of much experience to which those who are subject to the laws have given their assent. Whatever damage may come from the writing of laws, the damage from violating them is certainly greater (300B). Moreover, those who amend the laws are doing only what the wisest legislator would do were he to revise his constitution in an empirical light. The writers of laws compose imitations of truth, and the amenders of laws, as amendment is required, are imitators of the true statesman, the one who truly is. The Stranger harks again to the doctrine that being and truth belong to or inhere in the veritable possessor of the science and practitioner of the art in question, in the present case the science and art of the statesman. The true and real statesman commutes a standing knowledge of what is to be desired into a mutable code that responds to the incessant mutation of the world. If there were an immortal legislator, the statesman would be his defective mimic. As it is, the actual statesmen that we know are the defective mimics of the truly being statesman. The Stranger does not call the pattern of the statesman "the idea of the statesman" but rather "the essential statesman" (*ton ontōs politikon*) (300C) and the "true one" (300D). By the criterion of second best, those regimes would be the best within possibility which adhered strictly to the laws and to what the Stranger calls their ancestral ways (*patria ethē*) (301A). We have no means of knowing whether Plato intended the Stranger's remark to remind the elder Socrates that his inquiry into everything, while good in itself, was problematic if it shook the ancestral ways, which for all we know to the contrary include the received religion. We are on safer ground if we suppose that Plato intended us to reflect on the profundity of the wisdom that would reconcile the demand for amendment with the inviolability of the ways of the fathers.

The Stranger disqualifies the many and the rich per se as possible repositories of the definitive science, but allows that a royal monarch or a few aristocratic rich might possess it. He had long since proposed the fivefold schema of the regimes (291DE) according to the distinction of rule by one, few, or many and with regard to freedom, wealth, and lawfulness. At that point the Stranger's theme was the wizardry of the sophist in insinuating himself as mimic or pseudostatesman. Now the argument has progressed through the resistance of the governed to the government of the authentic and wise, and the scarcity among mankind of the wisdom requisite for government. The Stranger revives the schema of the five regimes (lawful monarchy of knowledge or opinion; lawless monarchy of appetite and ignorance, which is tyranny; aristocracy of the rich by law; lawless oligarchy of the rich; and democracy) in order now to characterize these defective polities as imitations of the one true and real one. The Stranger's dialectical strategy becomes clear: expose the imitation statesmen and the imitation regimes in order to discover the true statesman and regime, the ones that truly are. The meaning of a heuristic that proceeds upstream from imitation to original can be conceived if one thinks of a project for defining a diamond on the part of someone who has had experience only of glass. He would discover diamond by the method of hypothesis: if there were a material perfect in clarity, brilliance, and hardness, qualities present only meagerly in glass, that material would be diamond. As it happens, we have experience of diamond and therefore have no need to discover it by ascending to it by hypothesis from its inferior "imitation." The case of the true statesman and true regime is different. The Republic and its monarch have never been seen on earth, and everything that the Stranger relates is a testimony that they never will be—to answer again the plaintive question of the *Republic* whether the perfect polity is possible in experience. There may be no illogic in proceeding from an imperfect empirical to a constructed higher conception; but to name the former an imitation and the latter an archetype adds the implication that the latter not only exists but exceeds the former in reality. The essence of the locutions "imitation" and "original" is that what is flawlessly conceived, both conceived perfectly and conceived as perfect, *is* by virtue of the necessity of reason. It is because it must be: its truth and its eternal being guarantee each other by the mediation of necessity. Not only the logic of the argument must be flawless but the judgment of what constitutes a flaw must be perfect. A truth cannot ever not-be, therefore it must be, as the Pythagorean theorem was, is, and will be forever. The modern "I think, therefore I am" should be coupled with the ancient "It is veritable thought, therefore it is." The Stranger demonstrates the progression from defective to necessary and perfect by replacing, in speech, the defects of the empirical with their respective negations. It is evident that he must have some norm or measure by which to recognize a true and real defect, for if his dissatisfactions with existing rulers and polities grew out of anything but veritable reality, his construction of the right by correction of the negative wrong would fail. At this point the foresight of the Stranger, i.e., of Plato, becomes evident: the extensive demonstration of the being of the not-being now bears fruit in supporting the veritable reality of the defects in the empirical regimes, and thus their standing as objects of veritable thought. It would appear that in the age of Zeus we experience only the flawed imitations of the flawless constructions, because our besetting passions as needy beings frustrate the science that exists in the minds of the helpless few who know. The nadir of the Stranger's formulary of regimes is reached when he adds the monarchy of the man whose governing is ruled by desire and ignorance— the tyrant (301C). Tyranny has been named after all the others were subsumed under a unity, and the tyrant has thereby been set apart from the other governors. Plato's distinguishing the tyrant is followed immediately by a passage in which all the defective regimes, including tyranny, are assembled and their presence among men to the exclusion of the veritable royalty is explained by the human beings' disbelief in the possibility of the veritable king. In brief, they see only another such as themselves when asked to behold the wise and good man, and they scorn the suggestion even if they do not tax it with duplicity: the tyrant is the cause and the vindication of their mistrust. It is as we have already been told: the human shepherd is congener with his flock, and if truly he rises above them, they are not equipped by wisdom or encouraged by experience to be aware of it. As the portrait of the human condition has taken shape, it shows us abandoned by the god, implanted in an inhospitable nature, left to our own resources, and now discovering that we ourselves, as rulers and as ruled, are an obstacle to our happy preservation. The light in this crepuscular scene is provided by the theory of noetic originals, the thinkable entities whose unchanging being is guaranteed by their distillation from the empirical dross which they measure. There is great temptation to conjure a life where the archetypes are the perceived, where the distinction between the empirical as perceived and the known is obliterated because nothing exists there but the intelligible. For this purpose it is necessary to posit the immortality of the soul, of whose life among the perfect entities the life of the mortal philosopher is an imperfect image, a rehearsal for death. Socrates will say as much, as his end draws near. Unsupported by revelation, the belief in the immortality of the soul, according to the paradigm of original and imitation, is an inference from the dictum that the existence of imperfection is proof of the being of the perfect. But the being so proved is in the mind, and in the placeless realm of necessity, precisely and because not in the realm of experience. The image of the immortality of the soul expresses the conversion of a reflection on experience into a fact of experience by the mediation of imagination. The human predicament on earth is in itself the reason that our experience of imperfection cannot be the ground for the expectation of the experience of perfection. If the best regime exists as Idea, then its perfection is itself the guarantee that there will never materialize an empirical city that "participates" in that true, good and eternal conception, for the Idea is simply the denial of our undeniable woes. Yet whatever may be the practical dangers of Utopianism, they cannot exceed those of passive submission to evils as if they were imposed by nature or gods. Perhaps political philosophy is the wisdom that distinguishes the inevitable and the corrigible defects of life in common, and the philosopher king the imaginary man who would govern by the light of that wisdom.

If we wonder at the evils that are inseparable from government under written law and unknowing custom, we should wonder all the more at the natural (*phusei*) (302A) strength of the state that enables those polities that survive with such defects to do so. In this spirit, rather than seek to describe the best regime, the Stranger will try to identify the least burdensome one of the six actual polities as those are defined according to the number of those in power—one, few, many—and by the lawfulness or lawlessness of rule in each. In a remark that reflects the somber perspective of the discourse as a whole, the Stranger admits that their search for the least burdensome form of government is marginal (*parergon*) (302B) to the project for defining the best polity, but that after all, and to our enlightenment and astonishment, it is probably the search for the least bad form that really drives their entire enterprise. The *Statesman* and the *Republic* are reciprocal complements.

Monarchy, then, is the best regime when lawful, the worst when lawless. Democracy, in which power is so dispersed in a multitude as to render the polity ineffectual, is exactly for that reason the best, i.e., least bad, of the lawless regimes but the worst of the lawful. The two governments by the few fall somewhere between. Unprotesting, the indicted Socrates may be supposed to allow the Stranger's faint praise of direct democracy as the regime with the most limited capacity to accomplish its mischief. In a curious way, the small majority by which Socrates will be convicted and condemned confirms the depiction of the populace as indecisive for ill. If the Stranger were free to extend the *parergon*, he would explain the indecisiveness of the *demos* as caused or strengthened by the people's subjection to persuading speech. Hence the harm that comes from heedless, uncaring, and corrupting rhetoric, and the danger to the city that arises from the difficulty of distinguishing between wise and unwise counsel. At any rate, the Stranger makes the viability by nature of some of the defective regimes a matter of the burdensomeness or tolerableness of life within them; and that criterion he converts in turn into the measure of their relative merit, the latter measured by the two standards of effectiveness and legality. His implication is that the natural reward of survival is conferred on those regimes that sit most bearably on their subjects because the polity respects the law and keeps undivided counsel. The former virtue should check hostility from within and the latter confront hostility from without. The Stranger concludes that of the six empirical regimes, the lawful monarchy is by far the best to live under and thus presumably offers the examples of the most viable of the polities. Whatever might have been the burdens of living in democratic Athens, they were not so heavy as either to induce Socrates to emigrate or to drive out the gifted and intelligent men who made the city more illustrious than any monarchy the Eleatic could have mentioned. Yet the best of the Athenians lived under the shadow of ostracism and the dicastery, that is, of popular judgment armed with power. Plato had seen enough of the workings of the two institutions to surmise, apparently, that they damage the city's prospect. In general, the proper definition of the statesman and his art recognizes that survival is the natural reward that signals the presence of true and authentic statesmanship. This proposition by itself tells a very long story: the centuries-long survival of a Sparta or an Athens could not possibly result from the rule of an unbroken succession of true and real statesmen when even one such is an extraordinary exception in the course of human events. The longevity of the actual regimes must be attributed to those legal systems that crystallize the approximations to wisdom that the occasional Solons and Lycurguses contribute to the government of their city. The inevitable decline and fall of regimes is a perpetual reminder that mortality is the shadow of vitality according to the rule that governs in the realm of nature.

Having discussed the regimes and their rulers in their respective imperfections, the Stranger returns (303BC) to the task of distinguishing the veritable statesman from any others who seem to possess his art and to perform the functions of true kingship. First to be eliminated are those who associate in the rule of the six defective polities. The Stranger has not for a moment departed from his strategy of defining the statesman by reference to the nonstatesman. He merely interrupted his culling of the mimics with the discourse on the imitation regimes so that he might resume it with reference to the false regimes and their rulers, who are now described as factionists, party men (*stasiastikous*) (303C1), not real statesmen. In describing them as factionists he is blaming them for being bound to what became known two millennia later as the particular rather than the general interest. It is striking that the Stranger does not exempt law-abiding rulers from the stigma of partiality. If his silence on the subject is witting and just, it means that law, for all its generality, necessarily speaks for the lawmaker and aims to protect him and his law. It is a paradox that law must fall short of universality because it must defend the law-abiding lawgiver, who, in the case of the monarch, is closest to that true monarch who rises above all partiality and rules by the light of caring wisdom that is above all law.

The Stranger has denounced the actual rulers as the greatest of partisans and shams and therefore the greatest illusionists, sophists of the sophists, as he says (303C). He is free now to distinguish statesmanship from the few remaining sciences, those the highest and closest to it, with which it might be confounded and to which he must now turn: that of the military leader, that of the judge, and that rhetoric which, in common with kingship, persuades to justice. As has been the case from the beginning, the Stranger does not ask whether these arts are to be distinguished from statesmanship but shapes an argument to show wherein they differ from it: he must in some way know what statesmanship is in order to know that he does not yet know it precisely enough, and also to know that he is advancing to-

ward and not receding from that precise knowledge. It is easy for the
Stranger to convince Young Socrates that rhetoric is under the government of statesmanship and is therefore not itself statesmanship,
but in the course of the argument the Stranger characterizes rhetoric
as the science of persuading the mob by mythologizing, not by teaching. Perhaps it could be deduced that a science for persuading the
multitude by teaching would not be subordinate to the command of
kingship, but it seems more probable that the Stranger's formulation
implies that there is no such science to be discussed. That there is a
science or an art of didactic persuasion that is not subject to statesmanship and has much in common with philosophy is demonstrated
by the conversation itself; but the sense in which that art or science is
not subordinate to statesmanship is tempered by the power of the
state to put such a persuading teacher as Socrates to death. After
showing that the ordinary art of persuasion is subject to statesmanship, the Stranger shows that the art of coercion, of military command, the art of war and peace, is similarly subject. The remaining art
is that of the upright judges, the arbitrators of civil disputes who are
impervious to every blandishment and every sentiment in their impartial fidelity to the law and its regal legislator—to whose science
theirs is, of course, subordinate and hence not party. The Stranger
draws a conclusion: the royal and statesmanly art does not itself do
things but rather causes things to be done by the ministerial arts that
have the capability to do them. The royal statesman is the human ec-
type of the divine archetype that sets all things in motion without itself moving or being moved. His effects are an emanation from his
mind conveyed in speech, the hegemony of *logos* over the practical
arts. If this is a fair characterization of the veritable ruler, then the conduct of rule in Athens stands rebuked in almost every way, for in that
city the authoritative *dēmos* is swayed by its rhetors and mythologizers rather than controlling them, and it serves as its own
dicasts, far from immune to the passions that deflect their attention
from the demands of the law itself. These rebukes, implicit in the portrait of the true ruler, will be confirmed in the trial of Socrates.

The Stranger puts a period to his depiction of the statesmanly
king when (305E) he describes that personage as caring for the laws
and for all things in the city and most rightly weaving together the
many kinds or classes (*genē*) in the polity that have been brought to
light. In the course of showing the being of the things that are not

statesmanship, not only has he shown what everything but states-manship is, he has also depicted a many that it remains for statesman-ship to weave together into a one. There is a royal weaving that appears to operate on the great multiplicity that is the whole appa-ratus of human skills and powers. But that image of the royal person's doing is modified immediately when the Stranger implies that the de-fining task of the royal art is dominated by the fact that not merely is one part of virtue somehow different from another but the two are in a state of great mutual hostility in many things, unpopular as this no-tion might be (306BC). The warring virtues constitute the primordial duo that takes precedence of the manifold of nonroyal arts in provid-ing the matter of the statesmanly weaving, which is an art for the combination of two.

The Stranger reveals immediately (306A) the elements of the duo and the difficulty that they will pose for the royal weaver. There is a part (*meros*) of virtue that is somehow in tension with a species (*eidos*) of virtue, by which the Stranger means concretely that courage or manliness or aggressiveness (*andreia*) is in conflict with restraint or accommodation or passivity (*sōphrosunē*), each being a virtue or a part or kind of virtue. Earlier (263AB), the Stranger had reason to pro-nounce on the difference between *meros* and *eidos* when rejecting Young Socrates' forthright disjunction of man and beasts, a rapid di-airesis that, it will be remembered, would have circumvented the most unflattering depictions of man as a simply natural animal. In that context, the Stranger illuminated this difficult subject with a highly allusive formula to the effect that whenever there is an *eidos* of something, that *eidos* must necessarily be a *meros* (part) of whatever the *eidos* is said to be the *eidos* of; but a *meros* is not itself necessarily an *eidos* or formal species. On no account must he be understood to mean that *meros* and *eidos* are simply alternative to one another (*heteron al-lēlōn*) (262B), a thought that follows easily enough from his having said that a "species" is a part of whatever thing of which it is the spe-cies, or specific identity, or *eidos*. It would appear that this is a tactful way of declaring that the *eidos*, qua part, is immanent in and not exter-nal to the thing of which it is the *eidos*. (We understand that the Stranger is always free to revert to his original Parmenideanism, how-ever he may have lapsed from it in some particulars.) At that point in the dialogue the Stranger was busy with the construction of *eidē*, dis-secting the subject material and forming classes according to the needs of the conclusion to be reached, and especially forming *eidē* in order to construct unities by selective aggregation. Whatever an *eidos* might mean in general, it seems to mean in the Stranger's vocabulary a category formed plausibly and usefully for the dialectic occasion. In the present context, the disjunction of *meros* and *eidos* appears to be overridden within the Stranger's assertion that a part (*meros*) of virtue is in tension with a species (*eidos*) of virtue, aggressiveness and accommodation respectively, with neither virtue being inclusive of the other and neither metaphysical entity supervening over the other. Were the Stranger to mean rather that a part of virtue is in conflict with the whole of it, he would have to identify *eidos* with *holon* and either *andreia* or *sōphrosunē* with the whole of virtue, both options being unsupported in reason and in the context. Before returning to the argument proper, it should be noticed that Plato has represented Socrates as sitting silently through discourse that has addressed the being of statesmanship by confirming the being of the body of non-statesmanship, and has demoted the immanent *eidos* to the point of equality with *meros.* Plato has taken for granted the existence of virtue as a thing having parts, the latter point being the position taken by Protagoras against Socrates. Plato has made the Stranger his instrument for obtruding these Parmenidean and Protagorean (respectively) elements into the presence of Socrates. The eventual definition of statesmanship will thus rest on the tacit overriding of the Socratic propositions for whose contradiction Socrates is given no voice.

The Stranger proceeds with his argument (306C). The courageous, vigorous, sharp, and forthcoming, all encompassed in *andreia* (and all reminiscent for us of the gymnastic education), are praised as virtue when present in word or deed; and the gentle, considerate, retiring, restrained, all encompassed in *sōphrosunē* (and all reminiscent for us of the music education), too are praised as virtue when present in word or deed. They are praised, that is, when they are appropriate, for each is positively blameworthy if practiced when the other is called for. Each is a "nature" (307C), they are in conflict with one another, and each is a virtue or a vice depending on the circumstances or, as Machiavelli will have it, on the times. The measure by which each speech or deed is consigned to virtue or vice is not a mean that is fixed between extremes but rather the suitability of the speech or deed to some occasion; and the hostility between the two natures exists not only between them as human dispositions but between the human beings in whom the dispositions acquire their urgent political relevance. In tacit recurrence to the question mooted in the *Sophist* concerning the miscibility of one thing with another, the Stranger declares that the human beings of such contrary dispositions no more can mix with one another than can their hostile characters. It is part of the human predicament that indispensable virtues clash and their carriers conflict.

This paradox of moral nature has evident political effects. The retiring folk live at peace with their neighbors, mind their own business, and would move the city always to do likewise in relation to other states. If converted into public policy, this access of love, as the Stranger denotes it (307E) would be ruinous, for it would unfit the young for war and thus threaten the city with slavery from foreign aggression. We note in passing that minding one's own business, the eventual definition of justice in the *Republic,* is portrayed here as political vice when practiced in its untempered extreme, which is to say when unmindful of the demands of the occasion and of the nature of things. This view of the state of human society is consistent with that presupposed by Socrates when, in the *Timaeus* (19BC), he asks to see the excellent city depicted in its activity, which is conflictual.

If the efflux of lovingkindness, privacy, and forbearance would pose a threat to political prosperity from one side, so the excess of aggressiveness, bluster, and hardheartedness would pose the same threat from the opposite side, for in the Stranger's judgment inveterate militarism would either impose slavery from within or invite it in eventual defeat from without. It is obvious now that a critical task, if not the defining task of statesmanship, is to contrive a union of the perpetually hostile classes that are constituted by their infusion with parts of virtue that conflict by nature (*phusei*) (308B). True statesmanship according to nature (*kata phusin*) will see to the moral education of the citizenry and will procure the removal of any who, insusceptible to courage and restraint, are borne by the force of evil nature (*kakēs phuseōs*) (309A) into godlessness, insolence, and injustice. Those who prove incapable of rising above utter abasement of spirit go to slavery. To this point, the Stranger has implicated nature in the irreconcilable conflict of parts of virtue and in the wickedness of the incorrigible bullies, as well as in the true statesmanship that might save the polity from the perils of excess. Nature is simply the ocean of ills and remedies in which man is immersed and in which he can sink or from which he can draw his salvation, without help from the god or from a beneficent tide. The compassion and the brutality, the nobility and the baseness of men are alike theirs by nature, and if their higher inclination is also by nature, so too is the helplessness of the noble when, as the fate of Socrates demonstrates, the lower is set against the higher.

It remains for the Stranger to describe the statesmanly art of weaving by which the hard-natured and soft-natured are united as warp and woof to form the protective web of state, procuring the mingling that uncorrected nature would preclude. The essence of the human art for saving man proves to be a practice on the prepared souls of the people who have shown themselves to be of an adaptable nature. The Stranger has it that the statesman must work on his subjects' souls and bodies, but it will become apparent that it is their souls or natures that he is affecting throughout, a startling intimation that in the realm of human sociality, law, or convention has and must exercise an unexpected power over nature. The statesman joins the discordant souls with a "divine bond," by which the Stranger means inculcating in them true and firm opinion about the noble, just, and good things and their opposites. The Stranger is at pains to connect these true opinions with the divine in man, and at the same time to drive home the point that the statesman is the one and only source of such edification in doxic divinity (309D). With exemplary candor, the Stranger does not so much as hint that what the statesman deploys for his subjects' improvement will exist in their minds as "knowledge." In the way described, the two discordant natures will be moderated and made fit for civil life, the discordant parts of virtue bound together by the ties that are the more divine by comparison with those which will be described next—the singularly human ones that operate through the union of bodies.

The Stranger has discovered a way of linking the mutually repellent characters by manipulating the natural process of procreation and repressing the natural attractions of affection by controlling the bond of matrimony and family relations in general. He disapproves the arrangement of marriages and adoptions for mercenary or other selfish reasons, and deplores the prevalent tendency of men to seek wives and sons-in-law of their own character. Both mistakes ignore the nature of the offspring of such marriages. Under the Stranger's legislation, the courageous and the restrained would be induced to intermarry, and their discordant virtues would be mingled by the

natural eugenic of managed procreation. This device, which yokes together individuals belonging in effect to hostile tribes, is at first glance
unpromising with regard to domestic tranquillity. It would seem calculated to produce couples of which one member must by definition
be of the overbearing and the other of the submissive disposition; but
the Stranger, apparently foreseeing this obstacle in the way of human
happiness, puts such hopes as he has for the success of this scheme in
the doxic edification to which the parties will have been exposed
(310E). Evidently the indoctrination in true opinion, while necessary,
is not seen as sufficient but requires the support of the natural somatic
or genetic mechanism by which the moral traits are communicated
and modified. One may wonder therefore if the Stranger has it mind
that the traits of character lodge in some primitive way in the body's
constitution.

The Stranger makes it clear that everything depends on the
statesman's ability to bring the two natures into association with each
other under the arch of common opinion. This is the royal weaving,
and on it depends the successful administration of the public as well
as the private affairs. As he says, the considerate people are strong in
concern for justice but lack the executive impulse, while the aggressive are effectual in action but not obsessive about right. Each needs
the other for a reason that causes them each to repel and to be repelled
by the other, which is a disastrous condition that could be thought to
be the work of malign nature, remediable only by a precarious human
enterprise. It is appropriate to notice that Plato has enabled the modified Parmenidean to arrive at a parallel alternative to the "consequentialist hedonism" erected by Socrates on the foundation of
Protagoras's myth in *Protagoras*. There, the unteachability of virtue
eventuated in the need to find a natural mechanism of motive to replace the virtue so hard to inculcate and so necessary to decent preservation. Here the devices deployed are indoctrination in true opinion
and the natural mechanism of morally inspired eugenics.

Thus the account of the royal statesman's art and science has been
accomplished. The practitioner of that art exercises it in a world in
which the god is absent and nature is morally indifferent. The statesman's task is the inculcation of true opinion, which is the knowledge
and piety of the subjects of the state and the sine qua non of civil con-
cord. Plato begins with a view of a state of nature rife with danger and
hostility, and argues to an unrivaled monarch with authority over the

orthodoxy of the subjects. He never advances to a project for the rationalization of citizen life beyond opinion, withal true opinion; and what freedom he sees in the natural condition is inseparable if not indistinguishable from the openness of the human being to error as well as to correction. The Platonic Enlightenment is not properly understood as visionary, utopian, or dogmatically rationalist. Whatever the ancient Enlightenment might share with the modern, it is the modern Enlightenment, contrary to its self-understanding, that has been capable of an informing optimism that reached climactic extremes in visions of the end of history.

VI

APOLOGY OF
SOCRATES

THE *STATESMAN* RECORDS PLATO'S VIEW OF THE CONDITION OF HU-
manity and its political estate in terms so unclouded by illusion
of optimism as to form the immediate and proper proemium to
the story of the fate of Socrates, a man driven by a singular piety to
imperil himself in a defective polity of a kind described in the preceding dialogue. The *Apology* is the speech of a worthy man under attack
by the agency that is supposed to be our human shield, about to demonstrate that the only honorable defense he can make is to cast his
indictment in the teeth of his accusers and judges. The *Apology* is not
the key to the confrontation between philosophy and the city or between the citizen and the human being, because Athens is not simply
"the city," it is a democracy, and the citizen of Athens cannot therefore be simply "the citizen." The *Apology* can, however, be understood as illustrating that incommensurability between the philosopher and the many human beings that has already been pointed out
in the *Statesman* when the Stranger explains the layman's natural mistrust of the physician. What emerges in the *Apology* is the contumely
reciprocated between the almost helpless though still caring philosopher and the generality of mankind. To the merely limited human understanding it would seem that things would be different in this
respect if the cosmos were in the hand of authoritative reason; but we
have been informed by the Eleatic Stranger that, at present, it is not.
To this must be added that throughout its length the *Apology* is increasingly a homily on death, indeed the proemium to the extended
discourse on death that continues in *Crito* and *Phaedo.* How much of
man's living, or of the human condition, is revealed in man's dying
remains to be seen.

Socrates opens his defense with a profession of ineptitude in
speech, a claim that he will enlarge by repelling the insinuation that
he is wise in any positive way. One wisdom of which he cannot dis-
embarrass himself is the certainty that his hope lies in removing as far
as possible his judges' sense that he knows himself to be their human
superior. All the more telling is the boldness with which he confronts

them, as his speech unfolds, with his trial of them and his finding them wanting—the act of a man who has little hope. It is well to know at the outset that the Apology of Socrates might well have been titled the Indictment of the People. For the moment, Socrates would like to be thought a forensic naïf, though he will reveal that he has been a spectator of many a trial. The present self-depreciation of Socrates, a purposeful instrument of testimony to his superiority, should be taken as the consummate instance of the famous Socratic irony.

Socrates' disclaimer of rhetorical cunning has as its obverse his claim that he will speak only truth. This inexpensive promise might be allowed to pass unregarded if it were not folded together with a certain admonition to the judges: concentrate on whether what I say is just or not and nothing else, for that is the virtue of a judge, as to speak truth is that of the speaker (18A). This edification should be brought back to mind when Socrates argues, as he will, that a man would be ill advised to corrupt his fellow denizens because his safety depends on their goodness. Many are the ways in which Socrates' defense consists not of simple refutations but of counterindictments. His conviction on the capital charge will convict his judges of indeed having been corrupted, as he will now begin to argue in so many words.

Socrates considers himself to be doubly indicted, once in the immediate court, formally, but also, over a long period, by a horde of anonymous traducers who have made him hateful to the generality of Athens. Those men, of whom he can name only Aristophanes, have long represented him as a stargazer and earth prober whose peregrinations aloft and ruminations below passed from ridiculous to subversive when he found nothing underfoot or in heaven that is serviceable to the popular beliefs and hence to the social order. If the Eleatic Stranger is not a figment of Plato's creation, and even more so if he is, then someone in the ambit of Socrates saw heaven devoid of providence; but it is Socrates who was brought to judgment, and it behooves him first to reveal to his judges that and why they hold him in odium, so that they may judge fairly as judges should do. He is an indefatigable corrector, perhaps because his well-being depends on the virtue of those around him, perhaps because for some reason he cannot help caring about them. In any case, his tenacious accusers have long blamed him also for perverting reason, making the lesser argument the stronger (18B). It may be understood that the calumniators charged him in total with what we would call sophistry in the propagation of unbelief. It is to this ancient accusation, augmented in Socrates' repetition of it with the offense of teaching his mischief to others, that he addresses himself first.

Socrates' response to the shadow indictment is that it is a lie from beginning to end. He has not investigated the things meteorological and subterranean, he has not discussed such things with anyone, and he has never taught anyone and taken money for doing so. In a substantial passage (19D–20C) he argues, declares, and insists in so many words that he is no sophist, lest the indictment that floats on the air in Athens carry with it, and cast upon him, that additional obloquy. Unlike the foreigners who come to hawk their educational wares and depart with their silver, Socrates stays home and edifies gratis. In distinguishing himself widely from the sophists, he insinuates the selflessness of his purposes and his rootedness in Athens, in the hope perhaps that a showing of civic loyalty might weigh in the balance against endemic suspicion of wisdom. The belief grows on us that the opening of Socrates' defense of himself is in fact a demonstration that he is not a sophist, that in so doing he is presenting an argument that grows out of the strenuous labor of the *Sophist* and *Statesman*, strengthening the bond that joins the two trilogies together. Socrates is in the course of arguing, in effect, that the philosopher, unlike the sophist, is singularly in a position to care for the civil society unselfishly, for the philosopher understands more clearly than anyone else the human need for human caring, a caring that must find expression through the agency of political life.

Whatever else it may do, the rhetoric of Socrates, if that can be distinguished from his reasoning, serves to reveal his judgment of his audience, more exactly of his judges. In order to improve the court's self-understanding, he undertakes to explain how he came by his damaging reputation for wisdom, and how the general animosity toward him arose—in brief, how the judges came by their prejudice. It all began when his old friend, Chaerephon, asked the Delphic oracle if anyone was wiser than Socrates and was given no for an answer. Incredulously, Socrates took to moving among the Athenians in the hope and expectation of finding men wiser than himself. In this exercise of modesty that included the pious endeavor to prove the god a liar, he found himself frustrated by the invincible folly of the Athenians from high to low. He went first to the politicians, who were full of their own wisdom but who did poorly under questioning. With patience and consideration, Socrates apparently did what he could to inform those distinguished citizens that they were self-satisfied fools. They learned to hate him, as did "many others." In exchange for their hatred, however, Socrates was acquiring respect for the god's insight: if there is wisdom, albeit a merely human wisdom, in the consciousness of one's limited wisdom, then Socrates might concede something to the oracle's response, for the one thing that Socrates claimed confidently to know is that he knew very little.

Socrates means to carry his quest through the strata of Athenian culture and society. On his way to the poets, possibly including the writers of comedies, he claims to be acting in accordance with the god (*kata ton theon*) (22B), having apparently converted his project for refuting the god into one prompted by the god. He finds to his surprise that the writers of poetry are unable to give an intelligible account of their own meaning. They literally do not know what they are talking about because "they produce what they produce not by wisdom but by nature and inspiration, like soothsayers and oraculists" (22C). We are being told that the spokesmen for the god do not know their own meaning; and they are moved by nature and inspiration, which seem to come to the same thing. Apparently then it is for some human being to say what the god would have meant by his words if the god had had a clear meaning in mind to begin with. Indeed, Socrates' interrogation of his fellow citizens is proving to have just this purpose, and it is in this sense that he is acting for the god: he is translating the dictum that no one is wiser than he to the formula that all the rest, in their foolish presumption, are less wise than he. We have learned also that what comes forth as the saying of the god is in fact an emanation from nature having only so much authority, wisdom, or prescience as resides in the source. Whatever the judges might have been able to make of this, we receive the impression that Socrates is in the course of demonstrating that the intelligence in prophetic utterance is imparted to it by a philosophic mind, which acts piously as it rescues the divine speech from the appearance of natural babble.

Socrates completes his interrogation of the Athenians by interviewing the artisans who possess a genuine knowledge but, like all the others, perhaps even like the oracle, do not know what they do not know. Socrates admits to asking himself "on behalf of the oracle" (*huper tou chresmou*) (22E) whether it would be better for him to be as they are or as he is, and he answers himself and the oracle that it were

better that he remain as he is. We have no way of knowing whether
the court noticed that Socrates put the question to himself and not to
the god, and that instead of soliciting the god's wisdom Socrates be-
stows his own on the deity. What follows is Socrates' report to the
judges that his deflating activities made him exceedingly unpopular,
to the degree that he is slandered as a wise man. He protests that it
might be that the god is indeed right, in a sense, but only if understood to mean that anyone, say for example Socrates, is wisest if he
knows the insignificance of his merely human wisdom. We suppose
this to mean that there is a wisdom that so far transcends the merely
human kind as to reduce the latter to near worthlessness, but nothing
that has come to light so far has suggested where that wisdom re-
poses. To put a point on his present argument, Socrates declares that
he will continue to interrogate whoever seems wise, and on the god's
errand he will expose such as fail his test. This diligence keeps him so
busy that he neglects the city's affairs and his own, with the result that
he is terribly poor because of his service to the god (*dia tēn tou theou
latreian*) (23C). His judges might possibly have been expected to believe that his lifelong practice was a testimony to his piety. If they did
so, and construed piety in a sense favorable to his acquittal, then it
would go well with his cause. For us who read without hating him, it
is easy to be persuaded of his piety if we are willing to derive the definition of piety from his lifelong conduct.

Now Socrates looks at the charge that he is a bad influence on the
young (23C). He admits that the golden youth of Athens attend on his
interrogations and enjoy his skewering of the pretenders to wisdom,
among whom some of their elders were probably to be found. The
young men go forth and do likewise, causing their victims to be in a
rage against Socrates rather than against themselves. While this cannot have surprised Socrates, his remarks to Theaetetus at the end of
that dialogue notwithstanding, he says nothing about any effort on
his part to restrain or discourage his youthful mimics. When the exasperated seniors blame him for corrupting the young, he says they can
point to nothing that he has taught the youths, but they fall back instead on those formulas routinely applied to the philosophers, suggesting the erosion of religion through rational science and of honest
reasoning through logic-chopping trickery. It is quite evident that
Socrates can truthfully claim not to have taught anybody anything,
while being unable truthfully to deny that many have learned a great

deal from him. An artful indicter might conceivably have exploited that distinction, which was so telling in Socrates' disagreement with Protagoras over whether virtue is teachable or only learnable, and accused him of making the lesser argument the stronger by confusing the relation between teaching by precept and teaching by example, at which latter Socrates was an adept. (In due time, after his sentencing, Socrates will indeed admit and claim the influence he has had upon the young men in restraining them in such ways that the city will regret his destruction.)

Can a man be thought guilty if he discloses his worthy self in places where it is subject to emulation? As the *Apology* will record and as the *Statesman* anticipated, he can indeed be guilty before the law and be praiseworthy in some other forum. It is especially to be noted that this thought, so familiar in the contexts of a higher law or a natural law, is present in the body of our dialogues without the hypothesis of either a divine or a natural legislation. We are compelled to face the fact that Socrates has just disparaged "the merely human wisdom" while at the same time appearing to rely on precisely such a wisdom as our last best hope, the god and nature being disqualified either by preoccupation or ambiguity. So confident is he in his merely human wisdom, which includes man's ignorance of any life *post mortem*, that he will insist that nothing whatsoever will stay him from his settled course, which is that of philosophy, as long as life is in him. This prepares us to learn from the *Apology* that the philosophic life has as its end a wisdom desired above all other good things, pursued in full acceptance that the quest must remain unconsummated and that therefore the necessary condition of the best life is a certain high-heartedness, the spiritedness of patience, the *thumos* that encompasses courage and comports with the submissiveness or acceptance fostered on the political plane by the complete statesman. Socrates' sustained speech to the people helps us, however it might not have helped them, to see, as the single truth that defines human life on the disparate planes of philosophy and politics, that without courage and its restraining opposite all is lost—the lesson for common life taught in the *Statesman* and demonstrated again in the moral regimen of Socrates.

Socrates prepares to address the legal indictment, which he describes as derivative from the defamation that has pursued him during much of his life. He names his accusers and their several con-

stituencies: Meletus for the poets, Anytus for the craftsmen and politicians, and Lykon for the rhetors. He singles out Meletus for rebuttal,
as he had singled out Aristophanes by name as one who had ma-
ligned him to the public. It would seem that Socrates saw the poets as
his most dangerous enemies, as indeed they would be if they were the
creators of the Olympian lore and thus, at the source of the popular
orthodoxy, defining the popular piety. That the polity is in danger
when the human commerce with the gods is not regulated by the political authority has been argued in Socrates' presence by the Eleatic
Stranger; but this is an insight that Socrates could not well have urged
in his defense upon the demos, the political authority that can hardly
do otherwise than to ratify the prophecy of the poets. We see in the
trial of Socrates why the Stranger might have reasoned to the conclusion that the state is at risk if the souls of the people are educated at
hazard, that is, by private usurpers of a public duty. We can see also
that Socrates would have exposed himself to embarrassment if he
had made such an argument while vaunting his own industry as the
censor of his fellow citizens' morals. In light of the theme next to be
broached, it is worth considering whether Socrates' persistent efforts
at remaking the Athenians in his own image, as subphilosophical
knowers of their ignorance, was an act of suicidal innocence, inordinate caring, or profound prudence.

Meletus charges Socrates with corrupting the young and with
heterodoxy or, as a later age would have it, with heresy (24B).
Socrates makes use of his legal right to question his accuser, with the
apparent intention of showing Meletus to have been guilty of bringing a frivolous action, itself a punishable offense. The burden of
Socrates' argument is that Meletus's understanding of the long-
standing issues is so shallow and his involvement in them so recent
that his intervention cannot be conscientious. Over and over, Socrates
will say that Meletus does not *care*, which is to pun on the meaning of
Meletus's name. In order to demonstrate Meletus's confusion, hence
the groundlessness and thus the frivolity of the indictment, Socrates
will first draw him out on the subject of corrupting the young. If
Socrates makes them worse, who makes them better? Meletus would
like to say "the laws," but Socrates insists on his answering in terms of
human beings, and thus receives from Meletus the reply that the
dicasts, the audience, the councilmen, the assemblymen all make the
youth better and Socrates alone makes them worse. Socrates enlarges

on the absurdity of this response without conceding anything to the plausibility of its supposition that the legislative and deliberative apparatus might have an improving effect on the young and possibly even on the old. As for the audience, the ordinary folk of the city, they probably do what they can to teach their children at least the common proprieties of decent behavior. If Socrates were not in court and therefore enslaved to the hourglass, he might have drawn Meletus into a discussion of the teachability of virtue, which is the very same subject as the melioration of the young. Were he to have done so, would he have had reason to elicit the conclusion that neither the laws nor the officials nor the common folk can teach what can only be learned? Teaching implies that the decisive activity is on the part of the teacher, learning implies that the decisive activity is on the part of the learner. What better figure to symbolize the primacy of the learner than the myth of the immortal soul that returns from the heaven above heaven illuminated or gravid with the knowledge gained there, needing only to be "reminded" or, in the other figure, delivered of its burden by a patient obstetrician. Maybe for want of time but maybe because no good would come to him or to them by his doing so, he makes no representation to the people that their effort to improve their young is the cultivation of a soil they can plow but have no means to fertilize.

Socrates moves on to extract from Meletus the admission that any sensible person would rather live among good people than among those who could be harmful to him. Then how could anyone in his senses willingly and knowingly make those around him worse? Yet Meletus accuses Socrates of just that misdeed, which is folly before it is crime. Socrates can reply in triumph that he either did not corrupt the young or, if he did, it must surely have been involuntarily and thus subject to private instruction rather than punishment by the city. Socrates would like the court to interpret the folly of Meletus's charge as a sign that Meletus never cared about these matters. Why does Socrates go beyond the implausibility of the charge to the unseriousness of the accuser, adding an *ad hominem* stroke to a pertinent one? Looking for the answer within the immediate context of the discourse, it is easy enough to see that the peril in which Socrates has been placed by Meletus is a demonstration of Socrates' argument that a man is threatened by wickedness in his environment and therefore would not knowingly contribute to it; but the point is strengthened when applied to the concrete case. It might not be going too far to suggest that Socrates' defense to this point has rested heavily on the proposition that one such as himself is imperiled by the indifferent quality of his human environment. Except in desperation, he could hardly be expected to tell his judges in so many words that his fellows in the city, namely themselves, were already so far from perfect, that is to say so dangerous to himself, that he would have to have been suicidal or insensible to go about corrupting them, i.e., corrupting them further. As an argument for acquittal, though, it contains its own refutation: the judges are there before him in their presently incorrigible condition of decay. It is important to note how closely the course of the *Apology* follows upon the argument of the *Statesman:* Socrates is defending himself as much against the court and its defects, which is to say against the *demos* and the city, as against the indicters who share the same defects.

Socrates turns to the accusation that he corrupts the young by teaching them not to believe in the gods the city believes in but in other new divinities (26B). This is the charge of impiety, or civil impiety, that Socrates draws Meletus into enlarging to include simple atheism. Although it is easy for Socrates to show that he cannot be an atheist if he believes in divinities of any kind, he draws out his demonstration at such painful length that no dicast could miss the point. Along the way, he takes up Meletus's charge that he did not believe the sun and moon to be gods and refutes it by *asking* whether that was in fact Meletus's accusation. As for teaching that sun and moon are stone and earth, Socrates deflects the charge by pointing out that the doctrine is not his but was published by Anaxagoras and is outlandish anyhow. What remains is that Socrates believes in divinity of some kind. Meletus swears twice by Zeus (26DE), while Socrates, who has promised to say nothing but the truth, says nothing at all about the Olympian gods. He closes this part of his defense by returning to the long-standing popular hatred of himself and declares that that hatred on the part of "the many" (28A) will convict him if anything does. When he adds that the same cause has killed many other good men and will do so in the future, he is telling his judges something about themselves—helping them to know themselves, so to speak—that could conceivably improve his lot and theirs. Not in doubt is his intimation that the popular or civic religion, the intended instrument of edification, provokes the multitude of mankind against some of the best of men. Presumably, if all teaching about gods were governed by the authentic statesman according to the prescription of the Eleatic Stranger, the city's cult would generate no hatred of the good and the good would have no reason to deny the city's belief.

Socrates wonders if someone might ask him whether he is not disgraced by having followed such a course as has put him in the way of capital punishment. He retorts the suggestion on the questioner: he, like the heroes at Troy (he calls them demigods), would be disgraced if he turned coward in a just cause. As it happens, the just cause of Achilles, whose example Socrates calls to witness (28D), is to avenge the death of his friend Patroclus at the hands of Hector—to return evil for evil and to do good to friends and harm to enemies. However obvious the justice of Achilles would seem to the court, it could only merit reproof from the Socrates of the early pages of the *Republic*. But Socrates makes Achilles say more: he prefers death to the disrepute, indeed the scorn, that he would have to endure if he chose a dishonorable life. Is it possible that Socrates sets a value on his reputation for courage among those many whom he has been assiduously disparaging to their face? Or perhaps he fears the odium of the few good men whose opinion he respects. There is a clue to the state of his mind in what follows. He pronounces it a duty to remain where one has been placed by due authority or by oneself. In so pronouncing, he gains credit for his steadfastness in battle under the democracy's generals by the same principle that justifies his intransigent refusal to quit his philosophizing way of life. He would have it that he was under orders from "the god," according to his own mind and conception (28E), leaving it to the court to consider, if it occurred to them, whether there was a material difference between his being commanded to a philosophizing life by the god or by himself.

These reflections form part of Socrates' extended discourse on death and reputation or honor. He passes from the vulgar disgrace of cowardice in the face of death to what must be for him the greater disgrace of pretending to know when one does not know, which is the offense of those who fear death as an evil though its goodness or badness cannot be known. About the netherworld he is accused of investigating he does not know enough, and he knows that; but of the present world he does know that it is wicked and disgraceful to do wrong and to defy one's betters, whether god or man. Therefore, in view of his doubt whether death be a good or evil, and his certainty that betraying his conviction that philosophizing is a great good

154

would indeed be a great evil, he would not abandon his way of life if the court were to promise him life in exchange for ceasing to live as he has lived. Although he assures his judges that he is not acting contumaciously toward them, he could hardly have made it clearer that in rejecting their supposititious command he in no way conceived himself to be defying his betters. Not only will he continue to inquire and philosophize as he has done but he will continue to accost the pedestrians of Athens in order to improve their moral outlook. "The god" desires him to draw the attention of the generality, especially his fellow citizens, to their petty preference for wealth, reputation, and honor over wisdom, truth, and the improvement of the soul, so that they may be ashamed and mend their ways. Nothing, he says, and certainly not the fear of death, will deflect him from his improving course. If this defines corrupting the young, then so be it. His speech can be reduced to its essence in brief compass: he has a mission which is the cure of souls, he hearkens in this to "the god," he denounces the worldly things because the love of them corrupts, he wanders among his fellow men to afflict them out of his care for them, and he will die willingly rather than forsake his mission. Presently he will describe himself as the gift of the god; and he will go so far as to say of himself that his caring for the souls of his fellow men is more than human: witness his poverty (31BC). Whatever else may occur to us, we cannot fail to consider that his plight was a comment on the success of the ministry to which he had appointed himself. He had not discovered an instrument for operating the natural machinery that regulated the minds of his auditors. He promised them, besides their moral melioration, wealth and other good things that follow upon virtue, as if he were not a demonstration before their eyes that what he understood to be virtue would produce for them such good things as they would not dream of wishing to possess.

Well aware that his forensic effort is exasperating rather than edulcorating his judges, Socrates goes on to assure them that, by some higher prescription of right (*themis*), the worse cannot harm the better, and that therefore they do not have it in their power to harm him, though they might well kill him. On the contrary, it is themselves that they would harm (30C). They would have deprived themselves of that bizarre irritant, the spiritual gadfly, sent to stir them out of their moral lethargy—a mission for their benefit that he performed to the total neglect of his own affairs. He charged never a fee—let them infer that he was no sophist. How could they not trust him if he can produce the evidence of poverty to argue for him and for his disinterestedness. Surely he can expect them to believe his asseverated claim to have been sent to them by "the god." If his hearers believe him literally, they will think themselves and not him to be guilty of impiety. The verdict will reveal how far he is and has been preaching to the wind, now and throughout his life.

The jurors and we have been given to understand both that Socrates considers most men to be his inferiors in some decisive respect and that he has ever toiled for their good at the risk of his life and in the face of their suspicion, rejection, and even hatred. Such doings are, as he himself said, not in the human way. It could be thought that they are not rational. That he did not regret and would not alter his living leaves beyond doubt that he considered his life good. Could he imaginably consider it good if it benefited only others, and those his inferiors who will bring him to his doom? He must be believed if he repeats so insistently that he has cared for them, but it must have been a loveless caring that may, for all we can know, have been had in mind by Aristotle as he considered whether the better can love the worse. What drove Socrates, and to what end? If he is to be believed, it was philosophy and "the god" that drove him. "The god" was a god known to no one but him, a private deity whose only miracle was to inspire Socrates to appoint himself the meliorator of the people's souls, to assume the mantle of the true caretaking statesman. It will be remembered that the perfectly royal statesman would be an object of suspicion on the part of popular mankind who, abandoned to the rigors of an uncaring nature, learned the wariness of the imperiled. Socrates is thus far the semblable of the philosophic statesman of the preceding dialogue. We are entitled to suppose that the life to which he had called himself benefited himself, whatever good it might have conferred on others, in endowing him with the riches, power, and happiness inherent in the self-knowledge of what he did not know. We are aware that through his commerce with others, he saw by the light of their vain conceit of knowledge the verity in his own diffidence in the same regard. This would be a genuine but qualified reward to intelligence and effort, hardly requiring a lifetime's experience and much in need of augmentation with something more positive. Are we thrown back on a speculation that philosophy is its own reward, as the young in the *Republic* are admonished to believe that moral virtue is simply good? Perhaps the conjunction of philosophy and "the god" is intended to convey to us that the good of the philosopher and the good of the others are so bound together as to have driven Socrates to counterfeit the statesman. It is, I think, impossible to account for the extraordinary doings of so wise and healthy a man except on the premise that he was governed by an innate inclination toward right and good, toward a cosmetic world, an inclination or disposition that had in him the force of necessity in the appearance of altruism. It is of utmost importance to recognize in this disposition what deserves to be called his natur¬, so that we may be reminded that nature sends the better angels of caring and nobility as well as the afflictions of cruelty and baseness. If there was any seriousness in his implication of "the god" in his doings, it lay in the microcosmic resemblance of his own caring to that which the absent Olympian was withholding from mankind. His life and doom were to illustrate the probable and perverse fate of goodness on the plane of popular polity and, more largely, the limited power of mankind to give heaven an earthly venue.

Socrates makes this plausible in the next passage of his speech (31C et seq.). Why is he officious in private and mute in the assembly? Because he is attentive to the voice of his godlike familiar, the singular nay-saying daimon that has addressed him since childhood only to restrain him from what he might be considering, not to make suggestions. That voice had told him that his participation in politics would be his early death. How far Socrates is from indifference between life and death is well proved by his unfailing attentiveness to this admonition of his singular god. He confirms his god's judgment on his own account by telling his judges to their face that they and any other multitude would murder any man who crossed them in their unjust and illegal courses. Only in a private station can a man fight for justice and save himself even for a little while. We may notice that his god did not warn him away from the life that he did indeed live, fraught though it proved with danger along the way and now about to end, if at a seasonable time. His god appears to have been a spirit of foresight, a Prometheus who declared what any man of experience and judgment, measuring risks and gains, might have concluded by natural means.

Now (32A) Socrates offers to prove to his judges by the record of his deeds that he would never be deflected from the right by fear of death, but it is impossible for him to make his demonstration without relating the occasions on which the democracy and then the oligarchy of Athens had threatened him, while he served in a public capacity, because he had withstood their injustice and illegality. He wants it known also that in living the life he had made private, he had avoided being a teacher as much as he had avoided activity in the city's government. He contracted with no one, spoke with those who wished to hear him, said openly to all alike what he had to say, and took no responsibility for how anyone who heard him evolved. It is Socrates' apparent understanding that if one contracts with another to confer a benefit, as to improve the state of the other's mind, and one seals the contract with the exchange of money, that minted token of high earnestness among men, one has performed an act for which one is accountable in the public jurisdiction. In this light, Socrates' familiar denunciations of the sophists' mercenary dealings acquire a point beyond mere disdain for their greed. As for himself, those who consort with him do so for the pleasure of hearing him deflate those who think themselves wise and are not. We must suppose that truthfulness rather than pride inspired Socrates' revelation of schadenfreude among his companions, but whatever might explain their listening, his talking is in obedience to the dictate of the god, delivered, as he says, in oracles, dreams, and in every way in which divine ordinance is delivered to man to direct his doings. The test that he proposes to confirm this remarkable claim depends upon a remarkable logic of corroboration: if his doings were not ordained by the god, then their outcome would have been wicked, namely, the corruption of the youth with which he is charged in the indictment; and if he had indeed corrupted the youth, they or their certainly uncorrupted relatives would stand forth to accuse him; but of all the large number of them who are present in court, including Plato by name, not one is joining in the accusation against him. On the contrary, they all support him. Therefore, none of his supposed victims nor their kin blaming him, he cannot be guilty of harming them; and his conduct toward them not having been harmful, it can be understood as laid upon him by the god, which is what was to be demonstrated. Surely the court cannot convict a man of obeying the ordinance of the god when the divine initiative is so apodictically proved.

Socrates has concluded the substance of his defense (34B) and will speak further only in order to justify the manner of his bearing

before the court. As his defense in what has gone before was the obverse of his indictment of the judges, so in what follows he shames
them with the contrast between his manly refusal to grovel and beg
before them and their own probable practice were they in his place, a
suggestion that he aggravates by presuming that as jurors they are so
base as to demand that same crawling as their due with which they
would disgrace themselves as defendants. Again he assures them
that he is not moved by any contumacy toward them. It is rather that,
his age and his reputation for distinction among men being as they
are, his shameful conduct would disgrace himself and the judges and
the whole city. Other men reputed for wisdom or courage have repeatedly given way to fear of death and have humiliated themselves
with their cringing behavior in court. That Socrates claims to have observed this himself gives reason to doubt that he is the stranger to
the parlance of the court that he began by pretending to be (17D)
when renouncing craft in favor of truth. Indefatigable in edification,
Socrates informs the jurors holding power over his life that they
ought never to allow the men whom the Athenians have distinguished in the city to benefit from contemptible behavior in the
courts, for thereby the city is diminished before the world.

The truthfulness of Socrates' speech is so confirmed by the jeop-
ardy in which it puts him that we cannot dismiss his expressions of
concern for honor and reputation, his own and the city's, as rhetorical
play. What are we to make of such a concern on the part of a man who
knows his superiority to the mass in which reputation has its usual
existence? As for himself, it might be answered that he has in mind a
select court of honor constituted across boundaries of time and place,
sitting in a city that has its territory beyond experience. But such a
spirit, if evincing disrespect for the decent opinion of mankind, not
only would mark the outlaw mind that is unfit to pronounce on the
affairs of gregarious humanity but would have lost sight of the part
played by opinion generally and not to be played by anything
thought capable of replacing it. So was the matter seen by the Eleatic
Stranger, so apparently by law-abiding Socrates, and so presumably
by any Enlightenment of prudent expectations.

Socrates concludes his oration by showing the judges that their
duty to their office, to the laws, to the city, to justice, and to the gods
requires them to resist the importunities of defendants who would
play on their sentiments. His immediate purpose is to solicit their un-

derstanding of his unbending conduct before them. He would have them know that if he had acted in the common way, he would have suborned them, officers of the city, to the impiety of forswearing their oath to judge by the law. He and they would both be guilty of the impiety of which he stands accused, and indeed he would have been guilty of corrupting them. Thus he manages with consummate skill to consolidate his care for them, his respect for the city, his devotion to justice and honor, his answer to the charges, and, above all, his reverence for the gods. Ending as he began, he declares that he believes as none of his accusers do (35D), which we may accept as the literal truth, for we have reason to think that the piety of Socrates consists in his immovability from the place of wisdom and virtue in which he has stationed himself. Comprised in his piety is a respect for the civil authority that he expects soon to extinguish his life. As the *Statesman* has foretold and *Crito* will confirm, Socrates is under the influence of an unfeigned if subdued patriotism that is born of the understanding, silently subscribed by him in company with the Eleatic Stranger, that the human authority erected in political society is our nearest guarantee of prosperity in an uncaring milieu. It is our enduring misfortune that both the subjects and the agents of civil life are inferior in wisdom and goodness to the beings they would have to be if they were to replace the gods.

When Socrates speaks next, it is in response to his having been convicted. He has been more successful in winning over his fellow citizens than he had expected, but he has not persuaded the majority. Now he must tell the judges what he thinks would be a proper sentence instead of the capital punishment demanded by the accusers. He recites the benefits he has conferred on them all, the decency of his having eschewed as beneath him the ways of life followed hungrily by all the rest of them, and asks what such a one as he deserves in return for a lifetime of caring. He deserves to be fed at the public expense, so that he may continue without caring for himself to care for them. He will propose no harmful thing for himself, for he has done no harm. Clearly he believes that justice and desert go hand in hand, certainly that for good only good should be returned, with the strong implication that if he had knowingly done wickedness he would deserve something of the nature of punishment in return, although it might be difficult to find a punishment that would operate as such on the singular human being who claims that he is not daunted by the prospect of death itself. While it is true that in *Crito* (49C) he will reiterate that evil should never be returned for evil, it is also true that the law-bound forum in which he was speaking was not the place for a lecture drawn on the high-minded premises of the *Republic,* wherein an aversion of the eyes from the plight of self-governing humanity was useful for the purposes of that discourse.

Among the penalties that he would not accept to save his life are exile and enforced silence at home. Exile would mean only an expatriate repetition of his Athenian troubles, and silence would be insubordination to the god. He does not expect his hearers to take him seriously, but he tells them nevertheless that discoursing every day about virtue and the other things that they hear him discuss, and examining himself and others, happen to be the greatest good for man; and the unexamined life is not a livable life for man. Nothing could be clearer than that his notion of what the god commands is indistinguishable from what the goodness of a human life comprises, or let us say from justice in its widest scope and as caring for oneself.

Granting that Socrates is thoroughly intransigent in the piety of his submission to the god's behest for justice, how does he differ from Euthyphro, who was intransigent in the piety of his submission to the god's behest for justice? Euthyphro was outrageous in invoking the gods against his very father; Socrates has invoked the god against the whole people and the city, which he will soon call his civil progenitor (*Crito* 50D). Euthyphro thought that he understood the gods better than the city did, and the people thought him absurd. Socrates too thought that he understood the gods better than the city did, and the city thought him absurd and worse. But what distinguishes Socrates from Euthyphro is what distinguished him from all the others he had interrogated: Socrates knew where his knowledge ended. Not only did he not know whether death is an evil or a good, he did not know to be true or, as we might say, accept on faith what "the god" told him. When divinity proclaimed him the wisest of men, he took that encomium as a charge not only to see what it meant but indeed to see whether or how or in what sense it was true. When he persisted in his exasperating beneficences, he was complying with his own meliorating impulse against which his saving daimon did not counsel him, fatal though it would prove to be, because his nature would have overruled his prudence; thus "the god" was silent. When "the god" warned him away from political life, Socrates could and did confirm the admonition with observations and reasonings that could as well have come from his reason alone as from any daimonic source, and he honored them. Euthyphro, a believer, is the type of the headstrong in piety who afflict even their nearest with the arguable maxims of their morality, attributed to god with as much sanctimony as assurance. Perhaps Socrates' vaunting himself on knowing what he does not know, and his peculiar corroborating way of hearkening to his familiar, and his utter rejection of an unexamining life are, taken together, the clue to his theology in which faith had no place. His piety supplied what his theology lacked.

Socrates must propose to the court a penalty that he would consider appropriate to his conviction. A small fine is all that he could afford to pay, but Plato, by name, and a few others advise him to suggest a larger fine, for which they promise to be responsible. The court imposes a sentence of death.

Socrates responds by shaming his killers, not only for their impatience in hastening the death of an old man but at greater length, recurring to an earlier theme, for punishing his refusal to abase himself before them by begging for his life. His passing reference to the conduct that would have saved him as being unfit for a free man (38E) can be understood as a reproach to the assembled democracy, whose boasted principle was freedom in the sense he tacitly rebuked as ignoble, and whose manifest behavior was as vindictive as any tyrant's. He warns those who voted to condemn him that when he is gone they will be afflicted by a host of youth who, no longer held back by himself, will attack the shortcomings of their elders with vigor. It must surprise his hearers to learn that, far from inciting his young companions to insubordinate blame of the prevailing ways, he had done the opposite. The plausible reason for his doing so is already clear enough to us in his solicitude for the civil institution, and will be clearer still in the discourse of *Crito*. Perhaps to admonish the parents on whose heads will fall the reproofs of their children, he recommends to the citizens that, rather than silence their critics, they amend their ways, and with this charitable counsel he leaves them and turns to those who voted to acquit him.

He greets these as friends with whom he would like to talk a while about what has befallen. First of all, what has happened must be for the best, for the divine sign did not warn him to desist in his speech or deeds at any time during the day. Therefore death cannot be an evil. On the contrary, it must be good. He professes to find this convincing, flagrantly though it ignores the demonstrated truth that a "not-evil" need not be "good" but might be irrelevant to both good and evil. To this reasoning he will add arguments favoring the *hope* that death is a good (40C). Death is either the end or it is succeeded by further life. If it is the end, then it is dreamless sleep without end, and we all know dreamless sleep to be delightful. That it can be delightful only in retrospect is a point not mentioned though it bears on the present matter through being ruled out by hypothesis. That death as the end might be anticipated with something like pleasure can be supposed if conscious life is an insupportable burden; but even if life were considered so unmitigated an evil that escape from it would resemble the good we achieve in the relief from pain, Socrates could not call the absence of pain pleasure without contradicting his own rejection of that identity at *Philebus* 51A.

But Socrates is in the course of pursuing an alternative, one branch of which is that death is good as dreamless sleep is good. The other branch of the alternative is that death is not the end but is the continuation of life. He begins his discourse on this subject with a conditional: *if* what is said is true, and all the dead are in the place to which we go, what greater good might there be? Perfect justice will be rendered, and the good and the great will be together, available to be interrogated in heaven as they were not on earth with a view to discovering who among them thought themselves wise and were not. Among those whom he likes to imagine himself testing are Orpheus, Musaeus, Hesiod, and Homer, the poet-teachers of Greece on the nature of the gods. How satisfying to improve them as he had improved Euthyphro in the same area! Socrates savors the fantasy of stinging the departed eminences as he stung the living ones, with no need to consider death as a consequence of his temerity, for "if what is said is true," all there are immortal (41C). The appeal of death is much enhanced by the fact that death is the passage to life everlasting. Thus, whether death is the unending oblivion or the portal to unending life, it cannot be bad and might be good—if what is said is true. Since his present purpose is to remove the sting from death, he touches only lightly on the punishment of the wicked, but the fate of those with a bad record on earth deserves much consideration. If it is in any sense true that evildoing redounds to the harm of the guilty and virtue is dependably rewarded with benefit to its agent, then virtue is wisdom and vice is folly. If the world is so superintended that guilty cunning and innocent simplicity are inverted and requited in heaven, which they are if what is said by the yet-to-be-questioned poets is true, then the Socratic equation of wisdom with virtue and folly with vice is confirmed hereafter. To argue that the confirmation occurs within nature here on earth is to maintain that vice begets manifest misfortune and virtue is patently rewarded. In the course of his speech (30B), Socrates had actually had the boldness to tell the judges that virtue does not come from wealth but wealth and all other good things come to the human beings, to the individual and the populace, from virtue. He had left it to them to reconcile this with his own vaunted poverty, but his statement was so evidently rendered dubitable by his own immediate circumstances that it can be regarded by us the readers as a sign that, within nature, although every act is indeed a cause that produces its inevitable effect, the justice of the connection between cause and effect is uncertain. The unclarity would be dispelled by a moral tautology that would save the Socratic equation of wisdom and virtue, and of vice and folly: virtue is defined by the good it confers on the doer, and vice by its attendant penalty. But what is good? The question whether whatever the gods love is virtue or virtue must be loved by the gods has a remarkable parallel if the gods are replaced by nature in the formulation of the question. For the preservation of the Socratic formula from the gross or popular consequentialism, a definition of virtue and good would be needed that transcends the conjunction of causes and their natural effects, a definition that would be confirmed and would operate hereafter, if what is said is true. The question of man's task if god and nature are alike distracted from the care of mankind is brought to attention again, this time by the bearing of Socrates' reflections on the course of his life and on his impending death.

His last words to his popular friends are in the vein of edifying admonition gently delivered. They must be of good hope regarding death, and must keep in mind the one truth that no evil is to be the lot of a good man, neither in life nor in death; nor in all these things is such a one ever uncared for by the gods. Nor has his own fate befallen him in some mindless, undirected, or "automatic" way (*apo tou automatou*) (41D); rather, it is better for him to die now and be rid of it all. He asks his hearers to care for his sons as he himself would do, as if his prayer for this sovereign favor were better directed to well-disposed men than to the god toward whom he had directed their hopes and trust. At the last, his own care for the Athenians seems to reveal itself in his effort to conceal from them their human loneliness and to make up for it, as far as possible, with a simple theology of the nameless god. If Socrates is doing what he can to impose a fable on their minds, the grandeur and beneficence of the invention raise it above mendacity to the dignity of a higher truth. What could better illuminate the paradox of the human condition than this act of human caring for man on the part of one who teaches that the oblivious deity is diligent in righteousness. All things in the world being as they have been described, the natural human suspicion of human superiority gives rise to the urgent need for a presence and a judgment above suspicion. The so-called noble lie is a product and a fact of the human situation in the cosmos.

Socrates says in parting that he goes to die and they to live, but which of them to better things is unclear except to the god.

VII

CRITO

CRITO ILLUMINATES A THEME THAT IS PERHAPS BEST KNOWN IN the Aristotelean formulation that sets side by side the human being as such and the human being as denizen of a civil society—man and citizen. Though he may claim that man is by nature a political animal, Aristotle knows that man is not by nature a citizen, for he goes on to report the conventional or simply legal qualifications for citizenship of the several regimes. Hobbes, Rousseau, and others will distinguish between natural and civil man. We may deplore that the human being is not born to comity with his fellows as the bee and the ant appear to be, but the fact seems embedded in nature, as thinkers since the Eleatic Stranger have maintained. *Crito* is set in the space we are prone to put between our duty as citizens on the one side and, on the other, our calculated interest together with those inclinations into whose service we choose to press our reason. The action of the dialogue occurs in the extreme situation in which the state is about to take the life of its worthiest citizen, who argues as if the good of the human being, his interest, rightly understood, corresponds to his duty as a citizen. Hobbes will maintain that it is right by sovereign nature for a condemned man on the way to the place of execution to use every means available to him to escape death. Socrates will argue that even for such a one as himself who has been condemned unjustly, it is right that he submit to the laws in apparent conquest of his nature. But Socrates has already made the argument that death is not likely to be the greatest evil, which, if believed, subtracts something from the weight of sacrifice entailed in submitting patriotically to capital punishment. There is no reason to think that Crito is or can be persuaded out of his purely natural fear of death. It is for the benefit of Crito the natural man that the philosopher must argue the duty of the human being as citizen to submit to the laws and to the city even in the face of death. This reasoning might seem strange coming from the Socrates who had argued to his good citizenship from his own disobedience in the matters of the ten generals and Leon of Salamis; but the present dialogue is addressed to the man whose citizenship is conditioned not by his superiority to the law but by his natural resistance to it. The tension between the demands of our civic salvation and the impulses of our natural constitution are grave and enduring. That the dialogue is named after the man in whom that tension is personified should serve to indicate sufficiently the preoccupation of the discourse.

Crito speaks for the man of natural impulses who first and above all regards death as awful, fears it, and hates it as the lot of his friend. He is loyal, affectionate, and devoted to a superior person as well as calculating and aware of money although openhanded in a good cause. He is mindful of the opinions of others without loitering to weigh the respectability of the others or their opinions. In the face of danger he naturally thinks of escape. He can propose to suborn the corruptible to bribery without a trace of mortification, because the life of his dear friend is at stake. He is, in brief, an everyman, not a paragon, not a hero, not a philosopher, not better than he ought to be and not much worse than many whom we meet with daily. Before we dismiss him as ordinary and beneath high-minded approbation, we should notice how gently and affectionately Socrates deals with this friend of many years, the first whom he calls to witness his innocence of any wrongdoing against the youth of Athens (*Apology* 33D) and one of the four whom he names as guarantors of his proposed fine (*Apology* 38B). Crito is the expectable human being, natural not in the way of a forest nomad looking over his shoulder but as a human being responsive to the unreflected sentiments that come spontaneously to the heart. His proposed defiance of the law and the city is rooted in his friendship for a man whom he loved and admired but whose wisdom he could never share. His partiality for Socrates seems as fortuitous as is the dislike on the part of those who had their opinion of Socrates from Aristophanes. Before many of those others like Crito, Socrates had argued that the duty of citizenship called upon them to let him live. Now he must argue that the duty of citizenship calls upon Crito to let him die. Apparently, where ignorance leaves a void, nature will fill it indifferently as well with antipathy as with solicitude, in one case with a confused sense of what is owing to gods and in another with a confused sense of what is owing to the laws.

The action of the dialogue begins before sunrise a day or two before the execution of Socrates, who has just awakened to the silent presence of Crito at his bedside in prison. Crito is there to beseech his friend to spare him and many others the grief of losing such a one as Socrates; and if Socrates will not be moved by a concern for himself, let him consider his friends, who will suffer the obloquy of appearing to have been close with their money when they could have saved him by spending it. To this Socrates replies by dismissing the judgment of the vulgar, which leads Crito to remind him of the effective bearing those vulgar opinions have had on his immediate plight. Crito's language is noteworthy: the many can work not the least but almost the greatest of evils if someone is of bad repute among them. Socrates replies that the many can no more work the greatest evil than the greatest good, the former being folly and the latter wisdom (44D). Crito, unwilling to be deflected from his purpose by an investigation into the summum bonum, presses on with his appeal to Socrates on behalf of the friends: they will not be incriminated in his flight, they will not be impoverished by the paltry bribes they will pay, and if Socrates has scruples about using Crito's money, the foreigners Simmias and Kebes are ready with theirs. The latter two will of course have much to say in the final discourse.

Crito deploys all manner of blandishment, reassurance, exculpation, and affectionate recrimination, including the prophecy that they will all appear cowards, in his effort to move Socrates to flight. Socrates replies equably that he must think over whether this ought to be done or not, "for not only now but always I am such a one as am persuaded by my reason to what by reasoning seems best" (46B). From this categorical declaration regarding his principle of decision the so-called daimon is thoroughly absent. At no point does Socrates say that he is refusing to escape on the advice of his no-saying ghost.

Socrates begins his response to the pleadings of Crito by depreciating the vulgar opinion which Crito desires not to offend. Socrates' demonstration that an opinion is no better than the mind in which it resides is striking in one compelling particular. In seven places within a single page (47B–48A), Socrates contrasts the judgment of the "one" who understands and the "many" who do not. The circumstances of the end of his life apparently confirm to him that his lifelong disjunction of One and Many is as significant for politics as it could ever be for metaphysics. The weight of public opinion is thus quickly disposed of. Not what people will say but the verities of right and wrong, of justice and injustice, should govern one's doings, as he had always affirmed and therefore must not now deny. Wrongdoing is so categorically wicked that it is wrong even to return wrong for wrong.

Thus the only question to be considered is whether it would be wrong for Socrates to escape.

From the beginning of his disquisition on the evil of evil, Socrates has made a particular point of soliciting Crito's agreement to the conclusions of the argument as they emerge. He has at the same time dwelt on the proposed flight as being done without the agreement or consent of the Athenians (48E–50A). His reason for cautioning Crito about consenting to the steps of the argument is made explicit: "There are few who believe or ever will believe" that wrong must not be requited with wrong. That verity is a paradox, literally *para doxa*, contrary to opinion. Socrates thus signals his awareness that his argument for submission to the city and the laws, depending as it does on the assimilation of citizen virtue to human virtue (every wrong, and especially the requital of wrong with wrong, is to be shunned), is contrary to human nature and is therefore doomed to failure in practice. As a corollary to his caution against unconsidered consent to the paradoxical moral precept, Socrates tells Crito that the few who accept it and the multitude who do not will never be of a common mind but must always despise one another's understanding. Apparently, the few will look down on the others as low-minded, crudely selfish, and the many will contemn the few as unworldly fools, ridiculously self-denying. We are reminded of the Eleatic Stranger's portrait of conflict between the aggressive and the accommodating human types, the animate warp and woof whose productive coexistence was said to be the statesman's decisive object, conceivably attainable by plausible means. Socrates too divides the civil population, but into enormously unequal fractions, a numerically insignificant few who live by a moral principle that the overwhelming remainder can never respect. Plato's Socrates is the archetype of that minority whose submissiveness must be understood as the civil veneer of an iron-spiritedness, unyielding without obstinacy, satisfying at the same time the private imperatives of the man and the politic requirements of the city. At work in the great majority is the restlessness that masquerades as vigor and prudence in the good causes of ambition and profit. Socrates offers no suggestion for overcoming the mutual contempt of the few and the many so seen, presumably because none occur to him, perhaps because none exist. The present situation is different from the one conjured by the Eleatic Stranger. The Stranger saw two human types, each of which was incomplete and in need of the truth that the other bore and protected. Thus it was their matrimony or fruitful conjunction or interweaving that had to be accomplished, measures that operated through the natural instrumentalities of procreation and gratified passion. In the case of Socrates' few and many, the essence of successful civility resides in the obscure minority where power is naturally absent, while the natural immunity to self-denying virtue pervades the relatively immense mass. Socrates' entire life of gadfly caring as he described it in his Apology illustrates the failure of a project for applying the wisdom of the few to the nature of the many. Where the *Statesman* teaches the conflict in equivocal nature between the aggressive and the accommodating virtues without reference to the proportions in which they are distributed among mankind, the *Apology* and *Crito* teach the preponderance of numbers and force on the side of those many who must by nature reject the moral premise of civility in its literal sense. Socrates appears resigned to a conclusion that follows from seeing his lifelong project for meliorating his fellows construed as a conspiracy for corrupting them.

Socrates now (49E) obtains Crito's agreement that one should abide by one's rightful engagements. Socrates would have it that each citizen has tacitly agreed to accept as binding all of the city's judgments, while Crito is still of the opinion that if the city has wronged someone, that man is free to do what he can to get back his own. Socrates' conception of the citizen's obligation to accept the ruling judgments as his own bears an obvious resemblance to that of Hobbes; yet Hobbes affirms and Socrates denies that the condemned citizen is justified in escaping if he can. Crito agrees with Hobbes that the convict does no wrong when he defies the city in trying to save his life, but then Crito has not yet (50C) agreed that the citizen has bound himself by agreement to submit to every judgment of the city as if it were his own. What is the source of the difference between the ancient and the modern doctrine, in both of which the civil life of man seems compounded of similar elements? It seems to lie in this, that Socrates finds nature on the side of Crito and exactly for that reason makes the claim of civil authority indefeasible, while Hobbes rejects as quixotic any plan to subvert the profound promptings of nature and must therefore try to make the claims of both civil authority and nature indefeasible at the same time. Socrates' developing discourse with Crito indicates how far the obstacle in the way to the good society is the human being's natural resistance to the justice that is indispensable to his social existence. The ancient writers, the Christian writers, and the modern writers seem with striking accord bent on prescribing the instruments for the human contest with that nature that is our inescapable matrix and which, whatever else it does, inclines us both toward and against righteousness. How much less troubled and ambivalent our situation in nature and society would be if we did not have to fear and make provision against death can be inferred as well from Socrates as from Scripture and Thomas Hobbes.

Beginning at 50A, Socrates enacts a conversation between himself and the city and its laws, in which the civil institutions assert their absolute claim to his loyalty and obedience. They go so far as to represent themselves as his progenitors because he was born in wedlock, hence under the law. Never was natural place more outrageously usurped by convention than in this astonishing civic assertion of parenthood. Socrates would put the laws where the tales that make men the offspring or artifacts of gods place divinity. He would have it also that the civil institutions can claim to have ordered his perfect education in music and gymnastic. Considering everything, he and his ancestors are the "progeny and slave" (*ekgonos kai doulos*) (50E) of the laws. It is no more right for him to strike back at the city than to strike back at his father; indeed much less so, for the city is more to be esteemed and honored and submitted to than mother and father. This is the demand of piety across the grain of nature. And if one should have something adverse to say to the city, let him try persuasion and then abide by the city's willingness to be persuaded. Mingled with the reasonable call for civil deference is a demand for self-abnegation so egregious as to explain why few will ever consent to it. Its flamboyant denial of the most obvious facts of life testifies to the potency of the indoctrination that would have to be deployed in the desperate project of subduing the human nature to undivided devotion to civil life. Something of the gravity of the human condition is revealed when we regard together the profound imperfection of indispensable law or convention as described in the *Statesman* and the unnatural state of the human being who must be hammered with implausible means into submission to that flawed but saving legal instrument of civilization.

The laws tell Socrates (51DE) that in not having removed himself from Athens, though always free to have done so, he showed in deed his agreement to obey the laws or, if he thought them wrong, to try to persuade them of their error. We know that Socrates thought the laws of Athens to be wrong in allowing capital cases to be concluded in one day, and we know also that he resisted the city on the few occasions when he had official duties and thought the city to be neglecting its laws, but we know of no occasions on which he tried to convince the city to correct its legislation. Endlessly busy admonishing the citizens to be better, he refrained from the project of improving the *polis*, for it would have meant his death before he was ready to die. In brief, the city's invitation to reason with it or to obey it or to be gone would be just if the city were open to persuasion by philosophy. That it is subject to persuasion by poets, rhetors, sophists, and comic playwrights has been shown. The *nomoi* on whose behalf Socrates is soliciting pious devotion are deaf to the one voice that might reason with them out of a full sense of their import for the life of man, or the one voice that speaks from a knowledge of the true science of the law.

Although Socrates failed to reason with the laws, the laws succeed in reasoning with him in the discourse that he is contriving in their name. Pursuing the theme that remaining in the city signifies consent to the city's laws, the laws remind him that, of all men, he stayed within Athens the most, refusing even to consider exile instead of death; therefore he must have been most in agreement with the laws and most engaged to submit to them. Were he to flee, would he not be ashamed so flagrantly to be contradicting himself by acting contrary to his agreement and to all of his former professions of fearlessness in the face of death? Consistently with his lifelong teaching, Socrates assimilates a practical or moral offense to a violation of reason, a contradiction, a folly as he said to Protagoras, or an "absurdity" as Hobbes too would call the breach of a covenant made.

To their arguments from right the laws add arguments from advantage. If he accedes to his friends' conspiracy, all will be incriminated, they at home and he abroad. In whatever decent country receives him, he will be forever barred from his life's preoccupation by the certainty of ridicule if he presumes to cry up virtue and justice and law-abidingness. If he runs away to the kind of city where his cunning frustration of the law will be thought amusing, will he not even there be thought a coward? There is no place to which he might flee and be safe from opprobrium on one account or another. In his repeated resort to argument from reputation, Socrates might be thought to contradict his own dismissal of the common opinion as an arbiter of conduct. When he appeals to opinion, he is in fact holding up to Crito a mirror in which Crito's own decent if uninvestigated, spontaneous, and in that sense natural opinions can be read. That those opinions can harmonize with the conclusions of settled reason only illustrates Socrates' agreement with the Eleatic Stranger's doctrine that nature is an equivocal teacher of morality.

The laws convince Socrates that flight would be wrong—wrong as unjust and wrong as miscalculated. They admonish him not to set children or life itself above justice lest the laws in Hades make common cause with their earthly brethren and demonstrate the folly of wickedness in the reception they accord him. It does not occur to Crito, and we may say that it is fortunate that it does not, to protest to Socrates that if wickedness is punished by the judges in Hades, then the judges in Hades must do justice by requiting evil with evil. Are human beings condemned to believe in divinity that torments them when it is too late for them to mend their ways? Were it better to believe in the god's injustice or in his neglect? A doctrine of forgiveness would perhaps avoid this dilemma but at the risk of putting temptation in the way of the unconscientious. Most seemly would be an evocation of Hades as school of moral melioration, where the errant would be taken aside and, by provocative questioning, would be enabled to look into their soul, to see at last their defects, and to be helped by the one who cares for them to regain the straight path. Hades would be what Athens was not and could not be on earth, provided that the disembodied souls were corrigible as the incarnate ones had proved utterly impervious. Piety shrinks from the conclusion that Socrates had attempted here what the god neglects to resolve hereafter; and that Socrates was permitted to reap death as the earthly reward for his pains.

The theology of the inertness of Zeus must be assisted by a doctrine that makes the god of judgment an agent of injustice who requites evil with evil. It seems impossible for human beings to think about their life and the cosmos within which they spend it without thinking about their death. In his final hour, Socrates will go so far as to say that the philosopher's lifelong preoccupation is with dying and death (*Phaedo* 64A). The last conversation of his life will argue that our life, our knowing, and our death, in brief our fate, are implicated in one another. As he will say that philosophy turns to death, so he will say that philosophy is the making of the greatest music (*Phaedo* 61A), which now seems to him to include writing hymns and fables in verse. How the two aspects of philosophy might prove to be one is what we may expect to learn in the sequel.

VIII

PHAEDO

*P*HAEDO, SO IMPORTANT BY REASON OF ITS SUBSTANCE AND OCCA-sion, receives its name from a historical figure about whom little can now be said to be known. Little enough was remembered of him in later antiquity when Diogenes Laertius wrote his paragraph on Phaedo's life: Socrates was helpful to Phaedo and Phaedo was a follower of Socrates. More to the purpose, Diogenes reports that Phaedo is said to have written two dialogues, one called *Simon* and another called *Zopyrus*. Perhaps *Simon* concerned the Athenian cobbler of that name who heard Socrates and wrote dialogues, and perhaps the "Cobbler's Tales" uncertainly attributed to Phaedo refer to that Simon. We would hardly know what to make of this even if it were true. What bears more plausibly on the naming of *Phaedo* is what comes down to us concerning the historical Zopyrus for whom the historical Phaedo named his own dialogue. Cicero, in *de Fato* (*On Fate*), relates that Zopyrus was called the Physiognomist because he held the view that the character and nature, eventually the very fate itself, of a man can be read in his body and the features of his face. It is as if Zopyrus had discovered an alternative to the divination of au-guries and oracles, a divination within the order of visible nature alone. The premise of this form of prophecy, as Cicero understood well, is that a man's character and fate are determined by natural causes that have the force of necessity and that disclose themselves in the physical conformations of his body and face. Cicero tells that Zopyrus pronounced Socrates stupid and affected to women. Cicero's brief comment is to the effect that whatever may be the natu-ral causes that shape our character, those causes can be overcome by the will with effort and discipline (*On Fate* 5.12–23). More on Zopyrus and Socrates is found in Cicero's *Tusculan Disputations* (4.37.80), where Socrates admits to the defects detected in him by Zopyrus's method but declares that he overcame them by the force of reason.[1] If Phaedo's *Zopyrus* addressed what appears to have been the signature

---

1. Cf. *Phaedrus* 230A: Socrates says, "I investigate not these [mythical] things, but myself, to know whether I am a monster more complicated and more furious than Typhon or a gentler and simpler creature who shares in some godly and tranquil fate by nature."

thesis of Zopyrus's thought, then, as a follower of Socrates, Phaedo, and his dialogue, would have argued for the moral conquest of nature by mind. Had he done so, his argument would comport with the teaching of *Phaedo,* where the account of the human *agōn* in the natural world reaches its climax with the struggle of philosophy against nature. On such terms, one might understand how this last dialogue received its name.

Phaedo is Socrates' testament of retreat from this world. His withdrawal from the world takes shape as a depreciation of body so intense that it becomes the disparagement of our corporeal existence itself, to the point that the line between living and death is blurred, earthly life at its purest and best being likened to a killing of the body and death idealized as the good life of unencumbered soul. The depreciation of body is complemented by a systematic appreciation of soul that comprises a psychology, epistemology, and morality—an integrated doctrine of immortality, of recollected truth, and of asceticism. The course of the dialogue will reveal a tension between that doctrine as myth and as verity.

Socrates' withdrawal from the world did not take the form of Heraclitus's egregious and embittered reclusiveness, which was literal and corporeal. Socrates rather had found means to live within the world while keeping himself from it. He was the scrutinizing critic and monitor of his fellow citizens but not from a distance, in the city but not of it, contemplating its politics while abstaining from them as the bringer of untimely death. His encomium on death and detachment from life have been seen as the morbid progeny of rationalism in misalliance with archaeo-evangelical spirituality, but it would be a grave mistake to characterize the Socratism of *Phaedo* without giving full weight to the Platonic conception of the cosmic setting of human existence, and thus of the high courage needed by mankind to confront its condition—at least as evident to the ancients as it could be to Nietzsche. *Phaedo* compels the reader to speculate on the end or good that is served by Socrates' insistent flight from body, a movement whose deficit in plausibility requires to be overcome by strenuous reasonings, as its alienation from experience demands an extraordinary showing of supreme good for man. The good that Socrates appears to achieve is manifold—a protected enclave for philosophy, a solution at last of the problem of knowledge and of the knowable, and a firm foundation for moral virtue in the facts of our coming into being and passing away. The putative goodness of the whole and the good of man within the whole are linked to the depreciation of body, a doctrine whose credibility must bear an immense burden, which is to say that it must be insinuated in the mind of broad mankind as opinion—perhaps as an aspect of that opinion that the true statesman must seek to cultivate. In *Phaedo*, Socrates declares the affiliation of music and philosophy, thus preparing for the dialogue's course and for its end, at which juncture his dying will awaken us to the fact that we have witnessed the birth of a new religion without theophany. As will be seen, in Socrates' theology the will of god is done in heaven, not on earth. There are no miracles; and even the reincarnation of the immortal souls is given a rational explanation in terms of the mutual generation of opposite states within nature. It is a religion of reason and justice rather than faith and charity. Its central figure might return to life as philosopher, never as king, a reincarnation guided by limited ambition.

    Phaedo is the discourse of Socrates in the hours before his death, as related long after the fact by Phaedo, who was present, to a certain Echecrates, who is eager to know what had transpired on that day. Phaedo must explain first why an exceptionally long time had elapsed between the conviction of Socrates and his execution. The reason is that his execution could not take place during a certain period in which the city had, out of perceived duty to the god, forbidden itself to defile itself by putting its criminals to death. This is to say that, at least according to the piety of the Athenians, the taking of a human life even for capital crime, in conformity with law and by the gentlest means known, was in some way an abomination. At the end of the tale, the executioner himself will touch Socrates' heart by the regret with which he hands him the cup that Socrates does not wish might pass from him. Whatever success Socrates will achieve in persuading men out of their abhorrence of death, he ought not attain it by persuading them at the same time out of their civilized and humane reluctance to inflict death, necessary as that might be in peace and war. Socrates himself, it will be remembered, blamed the Athenian law for hurrying a convicted man to his capital sentence rather than meditating it for a day or two. It becomes a task for the reader of the dialogue to judge the meaning of Socrates' persistent recommendation of death and his rebuke to intemperance in causing it.

    Phaedo prepares to give his account of the hours before Socrates'

177

death by remarking on something in his own feelings that astonished him. Unable to grieve for his friend who was triumphing over death, and unable to savor the joy of the philosophic discourse, he found himself in the grip of a strange combination of pleasure and pain. And, he goes on, the whole gathering was overhung with laughing and weeping—an observation that will be confirmed by the extraordinary number of times that a participant will be said to laugh. Later, Socrates will present a universal theory of the mutual and alternate generation of opposite states, especially life and death, in support of his argument for immortality. At that time (70D), and when Socrates will assert that pleasure and pain produce each other in series (60B), the simultaneous presence of the two opposite states of pleasure and pain, neither having been generated out of the other, should be recalled as standing against the reasoning there to be proposed.

Phaedo now satisfies Echecrates' desire to know who was present at Socrates' last discourse and death. Various Athenians were there and sundry foreigners, including Simmias and Kebes in the tradition of Pythagoras, and the Megarans Eucleides and Terpsion among others. Plato was absent, thought by Phaedo to have been sick. We have no way of knowing whether he was sick in body, that ongoing nuisance, or sick at heart, as he would have been if his grief were not to be mitigated by any ode to death and immortality.

After saying who was present and who was not, Phaedo tells Echecrates when the discourse and execution took place. It was on the day immediately following the return of the fatal ship from Delos, as the law prescribed; but we do not know whether the day of execution was the day immediately following that of the *Crito* dialogue or the second day after it. The ship seems to have arrived at Sunium on the day before *Crito*, for Crito knew of it as a reported fact before dawn on the day of *Crito*. Thus he reasoned that the ship would arrive at the port of Athens on the day of *Crito*, and that Socrates would die on the day following. But Socrates dreamed that he would die on "the third day," which would be the second day after *Crito*. It is vexing to the reader to be without an indication from Plato that would decide whether Crito's information or Socrates' prophecy was confirmed in the event. The point is of interest only with a view to the light it might shed on Plato's intention in presenting Socrates' casual oneiromancy as a basis for projections of the hereafter.

Phaedo and the others arrive early on the last day and find that

they have been preceded by Socrates' wife, Xanthippe, who is holding the couple's small son in her arms. Socrates has the grieving
woman removed as he goes on to reflect on pleasure, and how odd is
the relation between it and its opposite, pain. How strange that the
pursuit of the one should entail the consequence of the other. The
reader is left to wonder whether this rumination is enclitic or pro-
clitic, referring back to the generation of the child in his wife's arms or
forward to the imminent reflection on the pleasure of release that accompanies the removal of the painful shackles from Socrates' legs. In
the former case, Socrates' etiology of pleasure and pain is a tacit comment on a cosmos in which the human pleasures of family life, like all
pleasures, eventuate by some necessity in pain. In the latter case, humanity is compensated in some manner for the decay of every pleasure into pain by the inevitable succession of every pain by a relieving
pleasure. If life itself could be caricatured as a pain, then death might
be represented as the compensating and inevitable pleasure. But
since it is obvious—and would be so even without Socrates' argument (*Philebus* 43)—that the mere absence of pain is not pleasure, it
becomes necessary to show that death is more than the absence of the
pain of life but supports positive pleasure, in the interest of the position that the cycle of reciprocal pleasure and pain does not end with
death but rules beyond the terrestrial existence of man. Gone are the
subtlety and depth of Socrates on pleasure and pain in *Philebus*,
where the complex comminglings of the two "in all the tragedy and
comedy of life" (50B) are shown in their relation to the good, replaced
in *Phaedo* by the dogmatics of incorporeal existence.

When Socrates ruminates on the reciprocating genesis of pleasure and pain (*Phaedo* 60C), he projects a fable in which Aesop would
have told of their mutual antipathy and the god's inability to compose
it. Instead, the god joins them somehow by or at the head, so that
whenever one member of this gruesome construction appears, the
other cannot be far behind. Aesop having been mentioned, Kebes
is reminded that people have been asking him about poems that
Socrates is reported to have been writing, renditions of Aesop's fables
in verse as well as a hymn to the god. Why is he writing poetry now
for the first time in his life? The answer is that he has had a recurrent
dream during his life in which he was admonished to busy himself
with music. Hitherto, he had thought that he was being obedient to
the dream by philosophizing, for philosophy is the greatest music

(61A); but with death imminent, he thought it would be safer to leave no duty unfulfilled, and thus to make music in the common meaning of the word that the sender of the dreams might have had in mind. First, he writes his hymn to the god of the current festival, a deity who, as we know, happens to be responsible for prolonging Socrates' life. Then, in as coy an irony as he has perpetrated in a career long notorious for such modesties, he disclaims a capacity for mythmaking, explaining thus his mining the fables of Aesop for themes of his own poetizing—for a proper poet must be a mythmaker. It strikes us that old Socrates facing death assumes a posture resembling that of old Kephalos facing death, each of them doing what is necessary in order to appear at the judgment seat with a balanced account. Kephalos would like to make restitution of what he had gained unjustly on earth and, thus clad in justice, to arrive unspotted in heaven. Socrates puts himself in the position of one who owes something by way of restitution, so that he, like Kephalos, might embark on the fateful voyage in hopes of a prosperous landfall. Perhaps what he owes to poetry after a life of depreciating it is the spoken admission that philosophy, if it is the greatest form of poetry, cannot escape participating in the highest act of poetry, which is mythmaking. This would be an admission that he owed to truth without reference to anything that might or might not be required hereafter.

The question about Socrates' writing of poetry was conveyed to him by Kebes from one Evenus, who was curious not about Socrates' writing in general but about his writing of poetry. Having supplied the answer to the limited question, Socrates goes on to suggest quite gratuitously that Evenus do what he can, short of suicide, to die quickly. Taken aback, Kebes thinks it doubtful that Evenus will like the advice. The way is now open to Socrates to elaborate his thanatophilia, to which he is deeply committed just before his death in his seventieth year but which seems to have been only latent during the rest of his life while he took pains to avoid politics as life-threatening. Before Socrates can get to the heart of his message, he must explain why we are not all free to hasten to our final bliss by the direct route. The reason furtively put about is that we are the property of the gods, who of course care for us but who are also the keepers of the jail in which we must lie at their pleasure. Socrates claims to believe at least so much of this doctrine as maintains that the gods are our caretakers and we are their property (62B).

Kebes detects a difficulty. Who, claiming to be wise, could wish to depart this life in which we are under the care of the dear gods? Socrates is impressed. Simmias would like to know why Socrates in particular is so eager to be off. Socrates can satisfy both of them at once: he believes that he will be going to other wise and good gods, and to departed men who are better than the ones to be met with here. It is true that he is not quite sure of all this, but he is in good hopes that there is a future in store which is, according to ancient rumor (*palai legetai*), much better for the good than for the wicked (63C).

Simmias would like Socrates to provide some support for these edifications, which do indeed have a tentative ring, but before Socrates can begin he must notice that Crito has been trying to attract his attention. Crito has a message for Socrates from the executioner: too much talking heats the body, and that in turn impedes the working of the lethal drug, making a double or triple infusion of it necessary. Heat, which is an attribute of body, is life-giving, and its absence, as we shall learn when the dying Socrates becomes progressively cold, is death. The executioner's knowledge that life and death are other words for the temperature of body is empirical, superficial, but reliable so far as it goes, reflecting an innocent conception of mechanical nature at work. We who read are permitted to wonder why Plato saw fit to interject this consideration at the present point. The question would disappear if we were reading an authentic report of the original conversation, but Plato was absent from that conversation and there is no reason to believe that he learned of it from Phaedo's "report." We are left with uncertainty about the bearing, if any, of this small episode on ensuing arguments that declare soul, not heat, to be the vivifier of body. As bystanders, we will bear in mind that heat is a condition of or is somehow within body, while soul is a separate being that comes and goes independently but occasionally consorts with body and remains for a while joined to it by inexplicable bonds before traveling to another place.

At any rate, Socrates waves aside the well-meant advice that he restrain his talking. In his Apology he had already rejected such a measure as a means of saving his life, and now he rejects it although it would help to quicken his death. He is unstoppable in philosophizing. Now he sets out to explain to Simmias and Kebes why it seems likely to him that a man who has worn away his entire life in philosophy can face death bravely and be of good hope that he will possess the greatest good hereafter. To this piece of optimism Socrates adds a remark that is exceptional in its apparent bleakness: those who philosophize rightly have left the others unaware that they, the philosophers, attend to nothing but dying and death (64A). How odd would it be, then, if, faced with what they had hailed so urgently all their lives, they balked at it when it became imminent. Simmias excuses himself for laughing but laughs nonetheless,[2] saying that most men would agree that philosophers desire death, and that same multitude are not at all unmindful that the philosophers are worthy of what they desire. Socrates disagrees with "most men" only so far as to deny that they are not unmindful. They are indeed unmindful of how the true philosophers desire and deserve death, and what kind of death it is. This is not surprising, since Socrates has just declared that those who philosophize rightly have left all the others in ignorance of these sovereign matters. Now, facing death before nightfall, Socrates will make known what has hitherto been a mystery of those who philosophize rightly. That what will be disclosed will be intelligible or credible to most men, after it has been said to them, must be in doubt.

We for our part have been made privy by Socrates to two unexpected truths about philosophy. First, philosophizing is music-making. Second, philosophizing is preoccupation with death. Philosophizing seems to be the art of Apollonian threnody, of lucid response to the tragedy and comedy of life. But what if death is not the everlasting stuff of tragedy after all? Perhaps philosophy and poetry in union can draw the sting of death by giving it bright and promising features. If this could be made part of a teaching that the cosmos is a single realm of justice and clarity, a great boon would be offered to humanity, who need only reject the easily disparaged testimony of the senses in order to accept it. All good things will devolve from the immortality of the soul. It is to this supreme article of belief that Socrates now turns, with the suggestion that the company ignore the uninstructed many.

We think there is such a thing as death (64C). Is that anything other than the separation of the soul from the body? And is death not the existence of the body by itself apart from the soul and the exis-

---

2. For all the solemnity and weeping of this towering dialogue, laughter and smiling occur in it with extraordinary frequency. See 62A, 64B, 77E, 86D, 101B, 102D, 115C. Cf. 67D, 67E.

tence of the soul by itself apart from the body? Simmias answers in the affirmative without a pause, thereby granting as the premise of the demonstration what should emerge as its conclusion.

Next follows the defamation of body. Of course, every philosopher despises the so-called pleasures of the body—food, drink, and aphrodisia. We may perhaps believe that Socrates' children were generated out of a sense of civic duty or in a contemplative state of mind. Likewise despicable is the decoration of the body. Thus the wisdom of the philosopher: to live by the greatest possible abstraction of the soul from the body. Although he had recommended ignoring the crowd, he mentions now that most people regard such a life as death. If they do so, then the common herd have by themselves penetrated in some wise to the mystery of philosophic life, which Socrates himself had praised as a kind of death. If Socrates could ever bring the herd around to conceive of the literal death as good, he might then find it possible to persuade them to regard the figurative quotidian death also as good. Then they would scorn the goods of the body as the genuine philosopher does, and would live under the sun as if the good of the soul were the thing altogether needful. The human condition would be reconstituted and mankind prepared for the seventh regime. In spite of the long and wide dispersion of the belief that the soul ascends in freedom to a place of merited bliss, or settles into condign punishment, nature has baffled every hope that men would live on earth as if the pleasures and pains and satisfactions of their body were the merest epiphenomena of their existence. Perhaps it is because simple human beings know in some inarticulate way that what they are called upon to think of as pleasures and pains of the body must be facts of what they are taught is the soul, for who has seen weeping or smiling in the mere flesh of the visibly dead?[3]

Passing from the moral to the intellectual bearing of his psychology, Socrates maintains (65A) that the body is a hindrance to our learning wisdom. Body means the organs of perception, the eyes and ears that blur the truth, as the poets are forever droning to us. It is noteworthy that the verb predicate of "the poets" (*thrulousin*) is used only twice in the entire authentic Platonic corpus, in the present passage at 65B in reference to the poets and once again at 76D, where

---

3. At 83D, Socrates takes it for granted that it is the soul that experiences pleasure and pain.

Socrates will apply it to his own longtime going on about the existence of the good and the beautiful. The reiteration is given the overtone of a mantra, in keeping with Socrates' avowal that philosophy is a high form of music. At any rate, body deceives, and truth belongs to the soul alone. Eventually, Socrates will explain how the soul exposes itself to the alleged blandishments of the body and thus procures its own seduction; but until we can be persuaded that the flesh in and of itself and by itself can know pleasure and pain—as if a corpse might suffer—we will suppose that assertions of action or passion on the part of body alone must be edifying and, in the high sense in which philosophy is musical, poetic.

The conclusion drawn by Socrates is as well supported by common experience as by speculation: we—he means our soul—think better when our soul is less impeded by the burden of body, which we may take to mean when we are undistracted by itchings and uproar. Thus we may understand the yearning of the philosopher, i.e., of his soul, for his singular solitude, which is the abstraction of his soul from all consciousness that arises in the body. The purest concentration of the mind is the nearest approximation to death that we can enjoy on earth. His soul having simulated flight, the philosopher is dead to the world. His figurative death is the condition for his approach, which is to say his soul's approach, to the truths. The incorporeal truth admits the approach only of the incorporeal soul. From this it will follow easily that the perfect union of the mind with the truth can occur only when the abstraction of the soul from the body is accomplished perfectly in literal death.

Now (66B) Socrates begins a summary diatribe against the body in the interest of wisdom. It is in the form of a speech that conveys the opinion (*doxa*) of genuine philosophers as they address one another. The burden of it is that the body in its neediness and disorders is the source not only of our intellectual failure but of wars, rebellions, and fights. All wars grow out of the desire to acquire wealth at the prompting of the body (66C). The body is the ground of that love of money which is the root of all evil. It strikes us in passing that the most ancient revulsions against acquisitiveness and its polemic offspring teach the primacy of soul while the most modern ones teach its nonexistence. The former look for relief in death, the latter in history. The end of the matter is not in sight.

The "philosophers'" diatribe against the body is inseparable from the panegyric on death the purifier. This life-denying manifesto might be thought to collapse under the weight of a gross self-contradiction if it pronounced dogmatically on a subject that must be obscure to every human being while still encumbered by his body. The more true it is that the body clouds man's vision of truth, the more guarded will we be in receiving the ruminations of the still fleshly philosophers as they tell our postmortem fortune. This is a trap into which Socrates does not fall. Not only does he have his philosophers speak of their "opinion" on the subject, but in the entire passage from 66B to 67B, Socrates has his hypothetical philosophers speak of the "likelihood" (*hōs eoiken*) (66E) that wisdom will come with death; the "likelihood" (*hōs eoiken*) (67A) that in life we are closest to knowing when we are furthest from the body; the "likelihood" (*hos to eikos*) (67A) that in death we shall be purified and know what is "perhaps" (*isos*) (67B) the truth. These are the things that all rightly denominated lovers of knowledge must necessarily say to one another, and they must opine (*doxazein*) (67B) along these lines. The passage as a whole has the remarkable character of appearing to be a pattern of confident dogmatism while incorporating the most insistent marks of tentativeness.

In what follows immediately, Socrates reiterates his belief that there is a living purification that, as we might say in the vocabulary of imitation to which Plato has accustomed us, mimics the authentic purification of death as an image imitates the original. The terrestrial purification is philosophy, which is the act of the human being who withdraws his soul from every part of his body in the interest of thought. Philosophizing is thus the conquest of nature, an unnatural act with a numenous intention, like faith or priestly celibacy. That the human being must contend against necessity in the form of nature in order to approach the highest that his nature can display to him is at the same time the pleasure and the pain of life in the age of Zeus, or perhaps its comedy and tragedy. It may go without saying that on these terms the perfect conquest of his nature by man may be desirable but is unattainable, that history is no talisman against nature and thus there will always be war, revolution, and fighting, and that the prosperity of mankind on the plane of politics, where nature asserts itself with utmost force, will necessarily and always be only a weak imitation of human success on the level of thought, where nature is most resolutely put on the defensive. In general, if it were to be argued that the classical ancients conceived nature as the criterion and incentive of human excellence, while certain moderns invented nature as indifferent or unfriendly to our well-being until we learn to exploit it, the argument would not receive unqualified support from Plato.

Socrates believes himself to have explained sufficiently what he meant when he said that a philosophizing man spends his life simulating death (67E). The same account serves to explain the proper philosopher's eagerness to proceed to the other world, where the body is not and the beloved wisdom is. Would the self-proclaimed philosopher not convict himself of base somatophilia, thus of love of money or honor or even both rather than wisdom, if he feared dying? The ground has been prepared for Socrates to claim that the proper philosopher is the true possessor of courage and temperance, that he is the truly moral man. The philosopher's bravery in the face of death is not tainted with fear of a punishment, as ordinary men's is, and his temperance is not the product of a calculation that prompts an abstinence as the price of a later larger gratification. Plato is aware of the simple fact that a virtue may be simulated, which is to say replaced, by a play of passions, although he is not quick to make this notion the principle of public and private existence. Courage, temperance, and justice itself are mere counterfeits of virtue when they are masks for calculation of bodily good, and they become true virtue only when they are combined with wisdom. Presumably, the decisive wisdom is the utter depreciation of body and the twin insight that our only true good, wisdom itself, lies beyond the grave. A life well lived in philosophizing, as Socrates has tried to live his own, is a purification and a preparation for entering the realm of wisdom and truth, surely a place of bliss. We are troubled by the thought that, in spite of all disclaimers of calculation, the world hereafter has the appearance of a reward dutifully sought for a life well lived in the here and now. If Socrates were at this point to be confronted by Glaucon and Adeimantus, would he not have to convince them that a life well lived should be so lived even if it eventuated in the tortures of hell? Perhaps he would argue that a life well spent here is only preliminary to life proper, by which argument he would avow his contempt not only for body but for what it projects in microcosm, namely, all of human existence.

Not Glaucon and Adeimantus but Simmias and Kebes will desire further explanations. Before we proceed to them, it should be noticed very clearly that the spiritualism elaborated by Socrates has philosophers in its scope. In that character, it is not an instrument for the discipline of society. On the contrary, so far as it disparages as calculating the common morality of mankind, it seems to put before humanity the fruitless alternative of turning true philosopher or abjuring as mean imitations the courage, temperance, and justice that are within reach in order to embrace their ignoble antitheses. It seems further to be afflicted with the hope of converting philosophers, those who of all human beings have proved most skeptical, to what even the generality credit grudgingly if at all. It is a question whether the most implausible can be imposed on the untheoretical people in the form of opinion whose implausibility grows out of falseness, or can be proved to the philosophic few only by strenuous demonstration because its implausibility grows out of profound truth.

Kebes now intervenes (70A). He is in full agreement with everything said, but he would like to know what answer can be given to those many men who simply do not believe that the individual soul is an entity that survives death, real as the soul may be in accounting for life during life. In brief, show that the soul is immortal and that when it is alone by itself without the body it possesses a faculty to act and has intelligence. Socrates prepares the audience for a long discussion, remarking wryly that, under the circumstances, he could not be accused, even by a comic poet, of babbling about irrelevancies if he goes into the fate of the soul after death. We may infer that, for all his efforts to rise above the body, he was stung more than passingly by the ridicule of Aristophanes.

Socrates takes as the premise of his argument for the immortality of the active and intelligent soul "some old saying" (*palaios men oun esti tis logos*) (70C) to the effect that the souls of the dead go to Hades and return to be born again. If the living are born from the dead, the existence of souls follows easily. Everything must now turn on whether the living can be born only from the dead. Socrates proposes to prove the point by taking into view everything that comes into being, all plants and animals that are subject to the opposite states of life and death, and indeed everything in the world that shows opposition, including noble and base, just and unjust, to prove that each member of the pair must arise only out of the opposite other. The proof is forthcoming: a thing that becomes larger must have been smaller, the shrunken was larger, the weaker grows out of the stronger and the slower from the quicker, is it not so? Not only that, but the worse comes from the better and the more just from the more unjust, does it not? How could it not be so. The thing is proved. There is sequential and reciprocal generation between contraries, including cooling and heating, just in passing (71B). So it is between being alive and being dead. The living human beings are generated from the dead as certainly as the dead are born of the living; therefore the soul exists in Hades, which is what was to be proved. The transition from life to death is visible to us all; we must therefore concede the other half of the process or deny the symmetry of nature (71E).

In the context of Socrates' argument, nature surely means the world of body, a realm wherein the human and other animate beings are generated out of the motion of body. If for the present purpose he will enfold the comings and goings of souls within the order of nature, his larger structure, which has resisted or defied mere nature, will be threatened. In support of his increasingly doubtful position, he now (72B) speculates that everything would eventually be dead if death did not become life according to his spiritual formula. There would be a universal subsidence of all things into a single state without this reversal from opposite to opposite; and the dictum of Anaxagoras, "everything together," would be confirmed—that is, there would be no distinguishable things. Socrates concludes with a strong summary (72D), insisting that, as it seems to him (*hōs emoi dokei*), all is very much as he has said it is, return to life is a reality, the living come to be out of the dead, the souls of the dead exist, and things yonder are better for the good and worse for the bad.

Doubts gather darkly. Life may come from death and death from life, but there is no maintaining that in the entire order of nature, like comes from anything but its like, else there would be no species. And in the transition from this world to the next, good yonder is the sequel to good here. If one abstracts for simplicity's sake from considerations of reward and punishment, the general argument of cyclical life and death applies as well to every other living being as to man himself, for the ants and bees are animate too. We are invited to imagine a spirit world that is inhabited by the souls of all the two-, four-, six-, and eight-footed beings with which we share the earth.

It is clear by now that Socrates is proposing a decisive description of life, not what it is in itself but what it is in its attribute. His unstated postulate is that, in its sovereign attribute, life is inextinguishable and continuous and must therefore override death, which is a superficial or merely empirical epiphenomenon of earthly existence. This again is as much as to say that life proceeds only and necessarily from life, which ultimately contradicts his insistence that life and death are reciprocally generating contraries. He would more consistently have said that the unbroken tissue of life is occasionally marred by an excrescence of incarnation that soon drops off. It is easy to suppose that the argument has the form it has because without the attached doctrines of disparagement of body and reembodiment of the individual soul, and of reciprocal generation of opposites, the theorem of inextinguishable, uninterruptable life would have been natural science without the imperative moral bearing. In its problematic shape, the argument has indeed a moral bearing that extends far beyond the small community of real philosophers.

Kebes now (72E) turns the discussion toward what he takes to be a new line of support for the argument that the soul is immortal. He invokes Socrates' well-known doctrine of anamnesis, which, if true, must prove the immortality of the active intelligent soul. If our only means of knowing a certain thing known is by recollection of what we could not have apprehended first on earth, then we must have lived and learned elsewhere, which is what was to be proved. Kebes will eventually realize that anamnesis points to the prenatal existence of the soul without demonstrating the soul's indefinite existence postmortem. Now Simmias calls for help because of his faulty recollection of the proof of the doctrine of recollection. This small jest reminds us that we are being asked to believe that the soul is more apt to remember what it does not know it knew than what it is well aware of having known recently. Perhaps everything must be explained by the difference in the soul's powers when it is and when it is not encumbered by the body, although that explanation in turn raises unwelcome questions about the soul's flawed hegemony over the rebel flesh.

At any rate, Kebes obliges Simmias with a brief reminder of the argument for reminiscence: skillful questioning draws answers from us that betoken latent knowledge and right reason. This is eminently so in connection with such things as diagrams, a remark (73AB) that recalls to mind *Meno*, where the boy being questioned is steered tendentiously through one error after another until Socrates' knowledge is at last imparted to him. The entire corpus of Socratic dialogue illustrates Socrates' effectiveness in eliciting by interrogation conclusions that were foreseen by him and whose verity he effectually taught to his interlocutors by maintaining control over the examination. His claim that he never taught anyone anything might have been prompted by the foreseen need to confront accusations of impiety or sedition, and it might have served to distinguish him from the marginally acceptable sophists, self-professed teachers, but it rings false as a ground for such allegations as that one does not teach a child the alphabet but only reminds him of it. Whether souls destined for literacy in languages other than Greek have the benefit of the same prenatal instruction is not disclosed.

At this point (73B) Socrates offers to give Simmias a more persuasive account of reminiscence. He begins, as is to be expected, by asking a question that is a question in only the most literal sense: "Do we not agree that" our recollection of one thing that we knew by perception can cause us to recollect another thing that we knew by perception, as that one sees Simmias and is "reminded" of Kebes. This familiar experience is what we would now call the association of ideas. Socrates goes further: a picture of Simmias might be enough to remind one of Kebes as well as of Simmias himself. Since reminiscence works to associate like and unlike things (*homoion, anomoion*), are we not led necessarily to reflect on likeness, on unequal degrees of likeness, and thus of equality, thus of equality in, of, and by itself? Necessarily. But there is such a thing as equality itself, is there not, and we know it, do we not? Emphatically. Do we not distinguish between the equality in size of two objects of perception on the one hand and the equality of equality itself on the other? Emphatically. About the equality of perceptible things we can be mistaken, but about the equality of equality itself, never. Socrates elicits no explanation of the possible meaning of the equality of equality itself, leaving us to suppose that it means something like the equalness that makes equality be equality itself. This sounds like an explanation, and one might have to be satisfied with it, but it seems to generate an infinite regress of equalities that Parmenides, for example, would have recognized as a weakness in the support for the theory of Ideas. The conclusion that Socrates wants to reach is that we cannot derive the criterion of equality that we apply to the perceived things from our experience of those perceived things to which we apply the criterion of equality. Our knowledge of equality must precede our experience of it on earth. Thus the soul must have had prenatal learning opportunities in which it acquired knowledge not only of the equal but of the beautiful, the good, the just, the holy, and everything that we stamp with the seal of being (*hois episphragizometha to ho esti*) in our questionings and our answerings (75CD). It may be presumed that what Socrates means by the locution of stamping with the seal of being is certifying or confirming by discourse that the things themselves do exist. The alternative meaning is that we, in philosophizing, impress or impose their being on such things as the beautiful and the just in their abstraction from the perceived things. Regrettably, no one in the company questioned Socrates about the meaning of the arresting locution, and we are thus left in doubt.

Socrates sets forth two possibilities, both having as their premise that there is a decisive knowledge acquired before birth. One is that we possess the relevant knowledge from the moment of birth and throughout life. The other is that we forget the prenatal knowledge at birth but recover it piecemeal by recollection. Such recollection is prompted by sense perceptions which evoke the latent knowledge by association, that is, by their similarity or dissimilarity to the items of latent prenatal knowledge. Simmias cannot say which of the two accounts is the correct one (76B). Socrates will come to his aid.

If we human beings were born with and kept the knowledge in question, we would know that such is the case, and all of us could explain the presence of our innate knowledge; but, as Simmias says, the one man who could explain all these things will soon be dead. Far from human beings as such being able to testify to the presence in themselves of the relevant knowledge by consulting it, only one human being, at least among those known to the company, can do so. Plato puts no modest disclaimer in the mouth of Socrates. The supposition survives that if one man can do it, the thing is possible. But Socrates' purpose is not to maintain a case that is supported by the example of the extraordinary dialectician. Rather, he leads Simmias to the conclusion that we all forget our prenatal learning at birth and recover it by reminiscence, as has been said. Socrates claims to have proved that the souls existed with intelligence before being in a human form (76D). Simmias has conceded that we do not acquire the decisive knowledge after we are born, that is, in our incarnate state, and Socrates would like that concession to be equivalent to the admission that the knowledge must have been acquired before birth; but Simmias suggests the possibility that we acquire it precisely at birth.

Socrates demolishes this construction effortlessly: if we acquire it at birth and also forget it at birth, the supposed possibility does not exist. Simmias confesses his folly. Now (76D) Socrates makes a pregnant assertion disguised perfunctorily as a question: if it is as we are always droning on (*thruloumen*), namely, that the beautiful and good and all such really are, and are what we refer our perceptions to (rather than vice versa), then as those are, so must our souls have existed before our birth. If what he refrains from calling the Ideas do not exist, the argument fails. Socrates stakes everything on the existence and prenatal availability to the soul of the good, the beautiful, and all the rest: if these things are in the way described, then the soul also was before our birth, but if the things themselves were not, then our souls were not. Not so? Simmias is overwhelmingly convinced.

Simmias had remarked earlier that only one man knows the verity of our latent knowledge, an assertion that has the sound of a dirge for mankind at the same time that it resurrects the prominent questions of *Theaetetus,* namely, whether one can be said to know something if he does not know that he knows it, and how much of knowing altogether is inseparable from memory. If the actual knowledge of the mortal human beings is a prenatal acquisition that lies in latency until quickened into consciousness, then, in the imagery of *Theaetetus,* almost all men carry a fluttering aviary of knowledge that came to be they know not where, a manifold into which they reach on the haphazard stimulation of sense perceptions and without knowing properly what is in the cage. Socrates spent much of his life revealing to his fellows that they do not know what they do not know. Now he is about to leave them with the disclosure that they do not know what they do know. Our natural ignorance is vast, and it is best for us to know that it encompasses what we are told we somehow know as well as what we are shown we do not know. That we have even so tenuous an access to the truths of the world as is promised by our latent knowledge of the beautiful and the good is a reassurance to the human mariners who must navigate a very dark sea. Philosophy, the musical art, speaking with the voice of the poet Socrates singing his swan song, thus relieves the pains of profoundest ignorance and of the fear of death, at the price of belief in the immortality of the soul and of the existence of the intelligible things in themselves (76E).

Simmias is fully converted to the real being of the beautiful and the good and all such, as well as to the existence of the soul before its incarnation, but neither he nor Kebes is so sure about its survival after our death. What if the soul itself came into being as a composite, subject to dissolution when it is by itself after separation from the body? Socrates is being asked in effect to prove the eternal existence of the soul, presumably in parallel with the eternal existence of the beautiful and the good. His reply is that the question regarding the soul has already been answered: if it be granted that the soul precedes our birth, and that the opposites of life and death follow the universal rule of reciprocity in generation, then the unbroken alternation of life and death argues that there must always be soul. Plato forbore to make Simmias or Kebes ask whether this means that mankind is eternal; and whether the sempiternity of soul means that there must always have been life of some kind, "soul" being a locution for the life principle. Moreover, if "soul" is what we are to understand as the essentially living, and we are to mean consistently thereby that without it body in and of itself is simply dead, then we are to suppose that body cannot acquire life as its own predicate but can only have life added to it by an unexplained amalgamation of itself with a substance that is its own absolute opposite. Why do not life and death, soul and body, drive one another away in their absolute contrariety? We may suppose that Socrates would have disposed of such difficulties to the satisfaction at least of Simmias and Kebes if Plato had seen fit to make the two men introduce them.

Instead, Socrates addresses the more limited question of the soul's survival after the death of the man. Does it blow away and scatter in the wind? This is as much as to ask whether it has the nature of particulate matter. Are Simmias and Kebes afraid that their death will be their utter end and complete disappearance without a trace? Perhaps the "child" that resides within the man has some such fear. Then, says Socrates, you must dispel his fear with a daily incantation, exorcising it like an incubus. If the Socrates of the *Republic* could blame the poets for making the citizens fear the wrong things, the Socrates of *Phaedo* can appeal to the singers of songs, of course the philosophic poets, to relieve the human beings of their fear of what is not to be feared. Kebes now wonders where they will find such an enchanter after Socrates is dead. Socrates does not promise to sing the necessary songs from beyond the grave, whence he could do even better by offering the assurances of positive experience, but rather reminds them that Greece is well populated with natives and foreigners and advises them to spare no effort or money in the search, although they might find no one better able to lull them into tranquillity than their own selves (78A).

Socrates returns to the question whether the soul is dissipated upon death and vanishes. In what follows, he will do as he has often done and what he might be expected to do as the only man possessing the requisite wisdom, namely, to instruct by laying down a demonstration. The performance is no less didactic for the steps, sometimes assertions and sometimes avowed suppositions, being followed in all cases by the mandatory question mark. It is appropriate to call attention to this character of the discourse because Socrates himself makes a point of their need to question themselves on the subject (78B) and to "our questioning and answering" (78D) regarding the existence of changeless being itself.

The demonstration moves smoothly. Whatever comes into being by composition is subject to passing away by disintegration. The soul is not of that kind. Socrates might have stopped at this point, for the question has been in effect answered, but he goes on. The soul belongs among the simple, hence unchanging, hence eternal things, such as the equal, the beautiful and all the other things themselves, not called Ideas but discussed by reference to the terms of their being. The other objects are the corporeals, the composite, the changing. The former are invisible and intelligible, the latter visible and in other ways perceptible. The invisible is the unchanging, the visible always changing. But we human beings are nothing other than body and soul, of the visible and the invisible kinds, meaning by visible and invisible what are so to the human nature (79B). Kebes, whose reservation led Socrates to identify the invisible with the humanly invisible, does not pursue his question as he might have done by asking, for example, whether atoms and other such small things which are invisible to man are not in themselves corporeal and thus visible to a being of another nature. Perhaps a god can see a soul; and without any doubt a soul can see and even hear another soul, else how might their posthumous discourses be conducted? These considerations do not come to light, and perhaps they need not, for Socrates is content with the formulation that soul is more like the invisible than is body, and body is more like the visible than is soul. In each case, he resorts tacitly to the Visible and the Invisible as if they were in the class of the invisible entities like the beautiful and the good. We can see that he

194

might have wished to avoid a long explanation in the short time remaining of how the Visible must fail to be visible although the Equal
must itself be equal, and so on. We can understand how, for the same
reason, he would have hoped to be spared the task of explaining why
such opposites as visible and invisible do not participate in the universal scheme of reciprocal generation, by which not only would life
grow out of death and vice versa but body would grow out of soul
and soul out of body. We sense that the solidity of Socrates' conclusions is affected by the weight of the questions that are left unad-
dressed by the philosopher chanting his song.

Socrates gains Kebes' agreement that the soul's advance toward
wisdom depends on its emancipation from body, on its achieving the
liberated state in which it is by itself alone with the changeless immortal eternals. These are not gods but the verities whose being Socrates
has been at pains to maintain. With these, the soul, which is akin to
them, can consort only imperfectly while distracted by the body's im-
portunings. Now (80A) Socrates is in a position to raise the question
of ruling and being ruled as between body and soul. In brief, according to the natural order of things, the higher and divine is ordained to
rule and the lower and human to obey. The ostensible conclusion is
that soul resembles the divine because, although this is not said, it is
the natural ruler of body and the natural ruler is closer to the highest
than is the ruled. From its resemblance to the divine it follows that
soul is indissoluble, which is what was to be proved to Kebes. In fact it
is not quite indissoluble. It is altogether indissoluble or nearly so
(*parapan adialuto einai e eggus ti toutou*) (80B), the qualification owing
perhaps to the soul's being only "like" the divine. The subtraction
from the soul's perfect indissolubility is allowed to pass without notice.

While the greater or lesser resemblance of the soul to the divine
may stand out as the guiding conclusion of this part of the conversation, another matter deserves attention that it does not receive. We are
about to be told that the abstraction of the soul from the body is the
way of philosophy, the living death. Who requires to be told that philosophy is the exception to human existence, and that there might be a
large measure of truth in the remark that, when Socrates is gone, there
will be no one or very few who can enlighten Simmias and Kebes and
their friends, men who might have to search the world and spend
their fortune to find another such who lives by his solitary soul? The

rule of the better over the worse, of soul over body, is ordained by nature itself, yet we observe that it is scarcely ever to be seen. Socrates is not pressed to explain the imperfection of the rule of the soul over the body among mankind. Thus he is not pressed to explain the impotence of nature to give effect to its command that the higher rule the lower. Assuredly he is not pressed to explain why, in the natural order of things, such a one as himself is so rare a being that his friends must scour Greece to seek his like. For reasons that may be most accessible to the inspired zetetic of theology, what we know to be higher is weaker than what we know to be inferior. The soul's rule over the body is brought to its peak as the soul simulates withdrawal from the body, much as the philosopher practices on the city by withdrawing from it as well and as far as he is able. The power of the higher varies inversely with its proximity to its object. By this light, the rule that is effectual manifestly must be that which is imposed by like upon like or equal upon equal, the palpable rule of statesmen.

When the soul departs the body at death, it bears the effects of its degrading association in proportion to its involvement in the corruptions of its partner (81B). In consequence, so we are to believe (*oiesthai chrē*), the souls of the singularly hedonistic retain in some measure the heaviness and visibility of body, which accounts for the ghosts that are seen in graveyards. To this entertainment Kebes responds, "It is likely." Socrates replies with "Likely indeed" (*eikos mentoi*) and goes on to speak of the undesirable fate that awaits the gluttons and lechers whose souls are condemned to rebirth in lowly beasts while other evil types return as predators. There are rewards for those who have been habituated in the social and political virtues of temperance and justice without the benefit of philosophy: they are born again as the sociable bees, wasps, or ants, or even as decent human beings. Kebes thinks this is likely. Those departing with souls of perfect purity, emphatically the philosophers, are admitted to companionship with the gods. It is for the sake of this that the proper philosophers abstain from the indulgences of the flesh, not out of frugality or fear of disrepute as do the merely moral ones with civil habits. We recognize in the proper philosopher the disciplined calculator who possesses the wisdom to forgo trinkets for the sake of pearls. He is, on the other hand, also a gambler who bargains away the actual satisfactions for prospective ones which a proper philosopher must know that he does not know to be securely in his future. Finally, one might speculate on

the damage to public morality that would result from a general acceptance of Socrates' view of futurity: the many worthy people of ordinary moral virtue, of a race consigned by the god to need and thus to
toil, can look forward to the reward of a repetition of their industrious
life in the body of an ant, possibly of a human being. What Crito is
thinking as he hears this prophecy for the infraphilosophic we have
no way of knowing, but if Socrates is to be understood as meaning
what he is implying, then in his own reincarnation he will never wittingly tread on an ant lest in expiring it reproach him in the voice of
his loving but unphilosophic friend. As for the beneficiaries of the
gymnastic and music education that is prescribed in the *Republic* for
the moral habituation of the chosen citizens, that elite might look forward to returning to life as a swarm of wasps.

Socrates considers the time ripe (83) for a warning on the need to
arm the soul against the senses and their corruptions and deceptions,
of which the worst is the illusion that the things that cause pleasure
and pain truly *are*, for the soul must never falter in its certainty that
only the eternal incorporeals truly are. The consequence of error
along these lines is another transmigratory conundrum. If reincarnation is an instrument of retributory promotion and demotion, we
must conclude that whatever authority presides over the process either acts on a higher principle than justice or believes that justice is
served by visiting evil for evil and good for good. We abstract from
the fact that the evil are brought to wickedness by their surrender to
the blandishments of body, a tempter to which they were made irre-
sistibly vulnerable by the nature of things. Socrates is well known to
have taught that no man does evil voluntarily, a dictum to which he
appealed in the course of his Apology. In *Timaeus* (e.g., 86B), he listens
without objection to the explanation of his maxim by the explicit linking of the involuntariness of evildoing with the power of body over
soul. Apparently, humanity in its deeds is drawn without willing it
into the rebellion of body against soul. This fact of our natural condition requires that we be threatened with consequences in the same
cosmic venue whence came our turpitude.

Socrates concludes: the philosophic soul bred on the true and the
divine and eternal, eschewing passion and opinion and living accordingly, expects to pass from its hard-won tranquillity on earth to tranquil companionship with its congener; and it has no dreadful thing to
fear such as its dissipation by the wind.

A long silence falls on the assembly, broken by a murmuring between Kebes and Simmias that Socrates notices (84C). He asks whether more needs to be said, for, as he grants, many things are doubtful and open to objection. Simmias admits this on behalf of Kebes and himself, but neither of them has been willing to raise questions that might distress Socrates in his immediate predicament. Smiling gently, Socrates reassures them: like the swan, he has Apollo for his patron and sings his own death song in prophetic good cheer. He is, in effect, reminding those present, as he had avowed at the outset, that with his end in sight he has taken up fabulous poetry and the service of Apollo. Simmias is now free to proceed, which he does by pointing to the difficulty or even impossibility of knowing now what will befall hereafter, and our dependence therefore on the best of the human discourse, absent a divine one (85D). Starting with this considerate reminder to Socrates of his peculiar wisdom in acknowledging what he does not know, Simmias goes on to remind him also, if by implication, that he has not exhausted the question which we think of as peculiar to Socrates, namely, what is the thing in question—what is the soul? Simmias would like to be assured that the soul is not a harmonious (or as we might now say an organized) composite of such things of nature as heat and cold, dry and moist, which constitute the body, and is not, as such, subject, "in what is called death," to the same dissolution as the body, necessarily coeval with the animation of the body, that is, of the human being.

Socrates regards him intently and smiles once more, presumably in approbation, but reserves his response until Kebes too can voice his doubts. Kebes rejects Simmias's premise that the soul is no stronger or more durable than the body, but he persists in his original doubt that the soul is eternal in its existence after death, however incalculable its existence beforehand. Let it have been incarnated as often as one likes to suppose, and let it be indeed stronger and more durable than body, there may still be one incarnation that proves to be its last. We gather that Simmias and Kebes cannot clearly and distinctly conceive an incorporeal substance. Their difficulty with the concept expresses itself with regard to time rather than space. What is eternal must be indissoluble, and they cannot accept that something can fully and truly be and not be subject to dissolution. They cannot conceive of an existent thing that does not have the compositeness of body. Kebes overlooks the likelihood that what can disintegrate, as for example the soul on his present premise, must somehow have been assembled or have come into being at some definite time, so he does not hesitate to join anterior infinity with posterior finitude. Neither Simmias nor Kebes makes the argument that Socrates has projected an incorporeal that not only is capable of motion in space but also is presumably the initiator of motion while ruling over the body, thereby giving evidence of having properties and powers that presumably belong only to body. So far as their questions make an issue of the being of the incorporeal, they touch not only the soul, which is the intelligent, but the true, the good, the beautiful, and the equal, which are the intelligible. Very much will turn on Socrates' defense of his psychology.

Phaedo reports that at this point he and the others were thrown into confusion, no longer knowing what or how to think or whether the matter was beyond any determination at all (88C). Echecrates replies that he himself is at a loss, having found both the arguments of Socrates and the reasonings of Simmias and Kebes to be persuasive. How did Socrates and the discourse fare? Socrates fared so well that Phaedo has never ceased to admire the decency and skill with which he responded to the young men's skepticisms.

The entr'acte between Phaedo and Echecrates serves to introduce the theme of what follows. The speeches of Simmias and Kebes were so effective that the audience had been thrown into doubt about the power of reasoning to shed credible light on the crucial questions regarding man's life and death. By an apparent equilibrium of reasonings, all had indeed been made aware of what they did not know, but the force with which that salutary lesson had been brought home to them had made them wonder whether it was possible for them, through reasoning, to know at all. It will be necessary, one last time, for Socrates to teach the lesson of true philosophic courage, which is the determination to persevere in inquiry and not to turn against reason. Whether this is the true courage of philosophers or whether their fortitude in the face of death is what deserves the name is for consideration. We cannot fail to notice that when Socrates labored to inculcate diffidence in his unphilosophic fellow citizens who thought they knew, he had little enough success. Now, with his sympathetic and receptive friends to whom he hopes to impart an edifying vision, he is in danger of leaving them with the unwanted diffidence of misologism. As often enough during his life, he has again in his last days found himself elevating to a higher level the statesman's art of restraining the rash and emboldening the intimidated whether their fear be of the darkness of death or of confusion.

Socrates sets himself against misologism, which he compares with misanthropy (89D). Misanthropy is the hostility to mankind that results from the repeated disappointment of misplaced confidences. Misology is the hostility to reason harbored by those who incompetently accept and then renounce arguments with equal incontinence until they end vaunting as their wisdom that all is flux in reason and throughout all things. The spirit of Protagoras is abroad, and Socrates' advice at the end of *Theaetetus* needs to be renewed: if there really is some true and firm reasoning that can be grasped, it would be unfortunate were a man to blame reason rather than himself when he became frustrated by arguments that seemed to fluctuate between true and false (90CD). Let us then adopt as our premise that the fault lies not in reason but in ourselves, and that it behooves us to fit ourselves courageously and eagerly for it, you with a view to your living and I, Socrates, with a view to my dying. Now Socrates makes a surpassingly candid statement (91AB): the subject touches him too closely for discussion in a mood of philosophic detachment. He sees himself resembling those disputants whose only purpose is to persuade their hearers regardless of truth, except that he is more concerned to persuade himself of what he has been arguing than anyone else. If what he has been maintaining is true, then all the better for himself; and if it is not true but he can make himself believe it, at least he will die without distressing everyone around him with his wailing. At any rate, the pain of his ignorance will soon cease, for even or especially if death is the end, he will no longer be disconcerted by doubt. Having confessed to an urgent interest in the outcome of the discourse, he nevertheless admonishes his young interlocutors not to allow any concern for his peace of mind to influence their agreement or disagreement with what he will argue.

Socrates begins by reminding himself of the points at which Simmias and Kebes had reservations concerning the immortality of the soul. He is assured that whatever else they might have found doubtful, they subscribe fully to the doctrine of anamnesis: learning is recollection, and the soul must therefore necessarily have been elsewhere before its incarceration in the body. Thus Simmias's theory of harmony is effectively exploded by his acceptance of anamnesis. How might the soul be a mere harmony of the components of the body and still have existed by itself before its incarnation? Simmias is all apology for having entertained a doubt. His fault, he says, lay in his having adopted the harmony theory without due consideration of its implied disharmony with the anamnesis doctrine and the doctrine of the preexistence of the soul (92D). Simmias seems made in the mold of the man lacking the art of reasoning whom Socrates described (90B) as believing something to be true and then thinking it to be false, blown this way and that, concluding that all is in flux, which is his own mental state. Prompted by the condition of Simmias, Socrates had set to work against misologism and those infected with it. He succeeded so well that he ended by showing inferentially the shallowness of his interlocutors' concurrence in his reasonings. Plato in effect alerts the reader to the need for vigilance before falling in with the conclusions agreed to by the interlocutors: he has Simmias recall in so many words the young men's agreement to the proposition of the soul's preexistence, which in turn flowed from the bare and unsupported assertion of the substantive difference between soul and body.

Socrates is not satisfied with the state of the argument that refutes the harmony doctrine. He will pursue the matter at some length (92E). First he argues that if soul as such is a harmony, it is a state or condition of the components whose harmony it is, and thus cannot move or affect its host as if it were external to it, as the soul is by presumption external to the body. This settled rapidly, Socrates goes on to prove that if the soul is a harmony, then every soul is the same harmony; but souls differ in respect of their virtue and vice, which are themselves examples of harmony and discord respectively. Then harmony would have to be susceptible to discord as well to some second order harmony, which is absurd. We who read are sensitive to Socrates' proviso "if vice were discord and virtue harmony" (93E), for if this unsupported figure of speech were to prove misleading, the argument would dissolve immediately. Simmias, as might be expected, raises no objections.

More to the same purpose is to follow (94B). This time the premise is the familiar if troubled proposition that soul commands the body, as no harmony as such could do, and more specifically that it opposes the body in its appetites and angers and fears. The authority of Homer himself is brought in support of the reasoning. Thus soul is no consequent harmony but is a precedent governor of the body. That this demonstration depends absolutely on the power of body itself and as such to suffer and yearn, to have a sentient and rebellious life of its own, escapes Simmias. It could not have escaped either Socrates or Plato. As if to draw attention to this implication, Socrates makes the astonishing assertion that the soul commands the thirsty body not to drink and the hungry one not to eat, besides imposing a multitude of other denials that, in themselves and unsupported by medical authority, suggest that the soul would kill the body if it could.

Simmias and Harmonia, the Theban goddess, having been disposed of, it is now the turn of Kebes and Cadmus, the Theban god spouse of Harmonia. Cadmus is known for an anthropogony that depended not at all on any doctrine of the comings and goings of souls. He straightforwardly sowed the seeds of mankind on the surface of the earth and brought humanity forth as panoplied autochthons of the earth earthy. If there is a mystery in our having risen from the dust, it is no greater and no other than the mystery attending the genesis of every other living kind. The life of man is lived in and is perfectly absorbed in the medium of material nature. Thus, perhaps, Cadmus. Kebes, for his part, is full of confidence that Socrates will prevail over the argument of Cadmus. We do not know what the argument of Cadmus is, but we shall presently be shown a theory of natural or material causation attributable to Anaxagoras that might encompass the etiological principles of Cadmus.

Socrates now addresses directly the hypotheses of Kebes that, however eternal may be the career of the soul before its incarnation in birth, it is nevertheless subject to eventual dissolution. This must be refuted and the indestructibility of the soul must be proved lest the philosopher who dies in confident hope of living better for having lived well be proved a fool. Socrates' singular theological psychology has in view the infinitesimal fraction of mankind that can expect a reward for a life of distinguished intellectual, not moral, virtue. It appears also to be addressed to that numerically insignificant class of men who have never shown signs of being persuaded by it or of having any need for it as an inducement to live a philosophic life. In its gratuitousness it serves only as an inducement to believe that a providence that would rule benignly over the world would add to them that have most and take away from them that have less.

In the disquisition that begins at 95E, Socrates goes far beyond the immediate task of convincing Kebes, although it is the drift of the young men's arguments that provides the reason and the context of what now follows, namely the famous Socratic autobiography. Before proceeding, Socrates pauses at length to reflect, and decides that nothing less than a full account of the causation of generation and dissolution will serve. The reason for this is evident: the skepticisms of Simmias and Kebes rest on the premise that the natural whole of corporeal causation is the whole pure and simple. Their accession to the theory of anamnesis shows that they do not understand their own premise. Socrates' autobiography will recount the progress of his mind from the time when, as a young man, he too had an appetite, an astonishing appetite for what he calls not natural philosophy but natural history (*phuseos historia*), for knowledge of the causes of each thing—whereby it comes into being, and is dissolved, and exists. Are heat and cold the irreducible causes, and by what mechanism of material elements are we enabled to think and perceive and know and remember (rather, as we would note, than by some transcendental anamnesis)? He inquired into the dissolution of things and into matters of heaven and earth until, as he says, he fell into a kind of confusion and concluded that he was not of a nature (*aphuēs*) for such studies, from which he had gained no answers to his questions but which had nevertheless deprived him of his confidence in the simple knowledge of things that lies on their surface and is available to the naive prescientific understanding. To illustrate his abiding confusion, he reports that he used to think such things as that ten exceeded eight by the two that had been added, but now he is far from thinking that he knows the cause of any of these things. For example, consider the addition of one to one. What is the cause of the consequent two? Which of the ones has become two, the one that had been added or the one to which it was added, or is it both at once? And when one beside one can become two, how can one by itself be so divided as itself alone to become two? Two ones become two by some cause that he does not understand, and one becomes two by some other cause that he does not understand. He does not understand by these means the cause of the generation of one itself, nor of the generation or dissolution or being of anything at all. He had to renounce his method of inquiry as a failure in the investigation of causes.

Then he discovered Anaxagoras (97B), who propounded the grand and consummate doctrine of cause: it is mind that orders and causes all things. Socrates appreciated this explanation of cause, which he understood to mean that the cause of all generation, dissolution, and being is the good. We who read are left to suppose that this means that to each thing an end is appointed, and that end is its good or its reason; and so for the Whole altogether. We wonder whether there is a good that provident mind constrains itself to respect as it orders and causes all things, or are we rather obliged to understand as good whatever comes to sight as the dispensation of omnipotent *nous*? We are reminded as much of *Euthyphro* as of Job. Socrates does not stay to perplex the matter thus but goes on to relate what he had expected to learn from his new teacher. Anaxagoras would tell him whether the earth is flat or round and whether it is at the center, and most important he would tell Socrates why it is best for the earth to be whichever way it is. Henceforth, when Socrates would investigate the things in the sky, he would ask constantly how their acting and being acted upon as they do and are is for the best. Then he would be on the track of their cause—the true "why" of their being. He had only to discover what is best for each thing in its doings and sufferings and he would know its cause, how mind ordered it. If Socrates entertained the notion that mind is itself the efficient cause of all things, he would have made successful inquiry into the nature of things conditional on the power of the human intelligence to replicate the universal mind so far as to have authoritative knowledge of the Good. If mind is not the efficient cause, we have difficulty understanding how or through what medium it enforced its optimism on all things. Perhaps it is unnecessary to be clear about these matters, and Socrates therefore did not touch on them. Had he pursued the issue to its limit he would have found at its premise the axiom, and at its conclusion the proposition, that the essence of the natural whole is unambiguous good. It may be doubted that he would have given his mind to Anaxagoras on those terms.

What he does is to blame Anaxagoras for misunderstanding his own tenet that the cause is mind: Anaxagoras introduced the interactions of the corporeal elements—air, ether, water—as causes. Socrates makes his meaning clear by referring to his own immediate situation. Why is he sitting where he is? Because his mind directs him to do so, not because of some conjunction of his bones and joints in states of motion or rest. In the first place, he is in prison because of the act of the Athenians' mind, and then he remains there because of an act of his own mind, he having judged that it was more just and more noble not to flee. Socrates would have it that the mind of the legislator and the judge rather than the thickness of the wall is the cause of the prisoner's sitting in his cell. Bones and their motion and rest are not causes but are the material medium and the sign of the activity of cause rightly understood. The depreciation of body in relation to soul with regard to life is for the moment replaced or reinforced by the depreciation of body in relation to mind with regard to cause.

Socrates appeared to have found, in mind, the cause of the coming, going, and being of all things. In characterizing the cause as Power (*dunamis*) (99C1) and as something possessing a numenous (*daimonia*) strength, he appears to have discovered god the singular cause. But this Power is ruled by the end that it seeks or must seek so that the whole be good rather than that it simply endure as an articulation of material conjunctions and transmitted impulses, an object for natural history. Correspondingly, it was not Socrates' mind in its vagrant freedom that dictated his submission to the judgment of the Athenians but his mind in free subordination to the right. It goes without saying that the mind of the Athenians, divided though the vote of the dicasts showed it to be, was also subordinated to some good or goods, perhaps piety, perhaps patriotism, perhaps the gratification of a festering resentment. In his discovery that mind and the good are the cause, whatever that might prove to mean, Socrates had discovered also the error of those who look for the cause of the whole elsewhere than in good. They seek a supernal divinity, a power that rises above the good itself and keeps all together by force alone or, as might be said, by omnipotence. This is the thinking of "the many" (*hoi polloi*) (99B). The many do not construe their daily experience as testimony to the orientation of the whole on the good, but in this they do not differ from the natural historians, who profess the subject more proficiently and who, it is true, do so without personating the conjectured ultimate force as a god. Not surprisingly, and as will appear presently, Socrates was unable to find the good cause as long as he looked for it in the world of natural experience. Admittedly, it is a commonplace that the piety of the pagan vulgar consisted in the worship of what are conventionally called the forces of nature. Is it imaginable that Socrates might have sought to reform their religion by inspiring it with a higher piety? If so, he would have to have been prepared to exhibit a higher object, the Good, for popular veneration, and to make it credible against the authority of natural experience.

But even if he had entertained such an ambition, a great difficulty would stand in the way. It must be understood that in the foregoing, Socrates had been giving an account of his former thinking as well as of principles of his present conviction. Now he makes the admission that he had been unable to complete his investigation of the cause because he could not discover it through the examination of the natural world of entities. The world of experience does not testify to the good as its end, and thus does not disclose it. We who read must be troubled by this formulation, for how can the inquirer know that the good has not been disclosed before he knows, in whatsoever way, what the good is?

Socrates found himself unable to identify the cause of the whole by the means he was employing, nor could anyone he knew of teach it to him. He resolved to order his further inquiries on a different method. He appears to say simply that he started again, that he embarked on what he seems to call a second voyage or a second sailing (*deuteros plous*) (99D). His meaning is made clearer by reviewing the context of his statement. Socrates had been arguing that the soul is imperishable, thus implying that it is not of the nature of body, therefore not doing and suffering within the order of natural causes. His interlocutors then raised objections that showed they had not rid themselves of the belief that the soul could disintegrate, which is to say that it might act and be acted upon like any other thing within the order of natural causes. Socrates then recounted how he too had begun as a natural historian, seeking the universal cause within the natural order of things. He found himself confused and frustrated. Then he discovered Anaxagoras, who seemed to elevate cause to the level of *nous*, we might say to the plane of freedom above the plane of body. But Anaxagoras proved to be a disappointment, for he made causes of air, ether and water. Socrates could find no one to help him understand how the good of all things, that is to say the end that would be the only intelligible end promoted by *nous*, prevails as sovereign cause. With no one to turn to, he resolved to proceed by himself, by the different way that he calls *deuteros plous*. Scholarship (e.g., Liddell and Scott, s.v. *plous*)[4] notes three uses of this proverbial locution by Plato (*Phaedo* 99D, *Philebus* 19C, *Statesman* 300C) and two by Aristotle

4. *A Greek-English Lexicon,* 9th ed. (Oxford: at the Clarendon Press, 1940; reprinted 1961).

(*Politics* 1284b19, *Nicomachean Ethics* 1109a35), in all cases the expression having the meaning "second best way of going." The sense of it is: if the sail fails, use the oar. Socrates' second way of sailing is a method that he will have to content himself with, faute de mieux, because the first had failed him—as he has just said. Now he will describe his method. He would no longer make his inquiries among the entities (*ta onta*)—which apparently include such objects as the numbers, or quantities—that puzzled him in the world of natural history. Nor would he try to ascend to the realm of the things in themselves, for he feared being blinded by them as are those who look directly at the sun. We do not know what would correspond to the blinding of the incorporeal soul's eye, and are left to speculate that there is a confusion or folly that threatens those who would seek their wisdom in the realm of the things in themselves. Instead, Socrates would rely on a certain method of reasonings (*logoi*), which he owns to be his general method of inquiry to this day. In the employment of that method, he posits the proposition (*logos*) that he judges to be the strongest and then considers whatever agrees with it to be true, whether concerning cause or anything else; what does not agree with it he considers not true (100A). If the word of Socrates is to be trusted, this rather than argument by interrogation is the authentic Socratic method. And it is this method that he will apply forthwith to the investigation of the form of cause by *positing*, that is to say merely positing the being of beauty itself, of good, of great, and of all such things. Do but allow him this premise, which well fulfills the condition of remoteness from perceptible experience, and he will go on to demonstrate cause and, which is his explicit purpose, the perfect immortality of the soul. Kebes consents where a less complaisant interlocutor might demur at an apparent begging of the question.

Socrates reveals directly his reason for invoking, that is, positing, the things themselves—the beautiful, the good, the great—for his explanation of cause. The cause of each thing's beauty is its participation (*metechein*) (100C) in the beautiful, in beauty itself. On this basis we might look forward to a demonstration, or at least an explanation, of Socrates' conviction, already in place, that the cause of the whole is its "participation" in Mind and Good. In the meantime we notice that the language of "participation" has been familiar in the vocabulary of Socrates since his youth as portrayed in *Parmenides*, when he had to defend his theory of the Ideas. At that time he used the word "Idea" freely although he was not clear about its meaning: he did not know whether there were Ideas only of the noble things or of all things, or even whether there was an Idea of man. Was he at the time of his youthful conversation with old Parmenides still embarked on his first voyage in search of cause? Whether Socrates acquired the germ of his method of hypothesis during the same conversation with Parmenides is for consideration (*Parmenides* 136). On what terms did his immature idealism accord with his immature inquiry into cause, the former imbued with appeal beyond body and the latter seemingly unoffended by the limitations of a corporeal physics? Perhaps the arrival of Anaxagoras in his life with the doctrine of the sovereignty of mind struck him as the beginning of the end of his perplexities: the whole is the theater of body obedient to what transcends it. That immense conception has presented itself to other minds than that of Socrates, and to other dispensations than those of philosophy. In the present context, where the immediate purpose is to argue the transcendency of cause, Socrates will seek to deploy—which is not to demonstrate—at the end of his life what he strove to demonstrate at its beginning, namely, the doctrine of the being of the things in themselves such as beauty and good. In the present discourse, Socrates uses the word "Idea" very sparingly. He himself speaks of the *eidos* of cause (100B), but it is only Phaedo in a remark to Echecrates (102B1) who speaks of the "*eidos*" of the things themselves, such as beauty, good, and greatness. This accords with the practice of Socrates earlier in the dialogue when he was demonstrating the preexistence of the soul by means of the theory of anamnesis. Cause appears to be the only concept that he is willing at last to stamp and distinguish as "Form," so hard to distinguish from Idea. He does not denote it as god.

Now Socrates will elucidate the *eidos* of cause on the hypothesis that beauty, good, and the great as such and in themselves exist (100B). He cannot understand any other cause of the beauty of a beautiful thing than either the existent presence or the association (*eite parousia eite koinōnia*) of beauty itself. He admits that he does not "yet" understand how it comes about, but he is of the opinion that this line of reasoning is the safest one (*asphalestaton*) (100D) for him: it is by beauty that beautiful things are beautiful. At first glance, this proposition, which suggests a fatuous tautology, seems anything but safe. The immediately succeeding portion of Socrates' discourse, unlike what follows thereafter, will be devoted to strengthening it, or disclosing its strength, by taking up the alternatives to it and disposing of them. As he cannot understand how the cause of a thing's beauty could be its color or shape, so he cannot understand how a thing can be large or larger except by "the large," or small or smaller except by "the small." To clarify this notion, Socrates offers examples to the following effect. If one man is taller than another by twelve inches, he is not taller by virtue of a foot but by virtue of largeness, as the shorter man is shorter by virtue of smallness. Certainly the same foot cannot be the cause of a being larger and a being smaller. Even more to the point, how could the six-footer be larger by virtue of a foot, which is smaller than six feet? Socrates asks, for the second time, whether Kebes would not be afraid of being wrong about all this. Kebes laughs, as well he might, before giving the agreeable answer. Moving on, ten is more than eight not by virtue of two but by virtue of numerousness (*plethos*), and so forth. Socrates tells Kebes twice more that the young man would be in fear of being wrong on these points, and then goes so far as to lay it down that whatever comes to be does so by virtue of, or because of, its participation in the thing-itself of what it becomes. The cause of one and one becoming two is a participation in twoness. The reader should be perplexed by the manner of the two ones' marching into duality in order to lose their identity while each is still a full participant in unity. Socrates makes no attempt to be as precise here as he was when, for example, what was in doubt was the exact moment at which the human being gains and loses the knowledge of the eternal things themselves (76D). Help of a kind will be forthcoming soon when the doctrine of generation out of contraries is revived as an issue, with stunning consequences. (As will be seen, "one" must participate in both "unity" and "duality" at the same time.) For the present, Socrates reminds Kebes yet again that the young man would be afraid to depart from the assumptions that Socrates has laid down and has called the safest. We may recall the many occasions on which reference has been made to the fear of error or ignorance without reproof of the kind applied to the fear of death (cf. 95D). The fear of error is understandable and might even be thought productive of wisdom; but if it promotes an inordinate desire for the reassurance of belief, or assuages itself by favoring a hypothesis that has little to be said for it except its safety, it carries a danger of its own. In this connection it is necessary to emphasize the "safeness" of the premises of Socrates' present line of argument because of the forcefulness of his later denunciation of the safe but stupid account he blames himself for having given, after he discovers one that is safer yet (105B).

Socrates now concludes this phase of his discourse on cause, a sustained argument to the effect that the coming into being of each thing is consummated in the participation of that thing in the cause of its being, that is, in the transcendent entity in which it participates in order to be the precise thing that it is (101C). Put otherwise, the *becoming* of each thing is governed by the *being* of the unchanging transempirical essence in which the thing "participates" at last, toward which it is so to speak drawn in the course of the process that we call becoming. That transempirical which resembles a final cause is what Socrates calls the cause of the thing whose becoming has been perfected. Everything that is, is and is what it is by reason of its cause, which is its end. It comes into being and becomes what it becomes in order to be what it comes to be. Its end is at its beginning and its beginning is of its end, alpha and omega, world without god.

That there are difficulties cannot be denied. If cause and good are to be identified with each other, we cannot see how any process of becoming can be considered to eventuate in anything but good when the thing in question has come to rest in its terminal state of participation in its cause. On such terms, "good" bears a definition that perfectly reconciles the "goodness" of the whole with the god's abandonment of the whole to its natural disposition. We might see this as the replacement of theodicy by physiodicy. If cause defines good rather than good governing cause, we can do no better than to be resigned to what is as "good." Such a physiodicy or optimism offers the bittersweet consolation of seeing "the good" in the infinite chain of causes that brings bloodshed, wickedness, and calamity as well as genius, serenity, charity, and sacrifice. With little effort, the moral neutrality of nature can be converted into a benediction, perhaps as an invisible hand, a principle of population, a process of evolution, or an object of contemplation.

Further, if beauty, good, and justice have an ideal being that qualifies them as causes, then the ugly, wicked, and unjust may be supposed also to have an ideal being that qualifies them as causes of the things that end as ugly, wicked, or unjust, for does not the not-being also exist? Is it conceivable that the surrender of a thing to the ugly as its cause could be represented as good except by the most abandoned of optimists? In a surprising way, such a vision of the whole goes well with another apparent implication of Socrates' formulation of cause as the being in which becoming eventuates. If we suppose that the cause of the acorn's perfection in the oak is the good that exists as the oak itself, then we must suppose that the oak's eventual decomposition into earth as its destination is intelligible in the same terms, as is the transformation of the resultant earth into grass, which in turn seeks the good of becoming flesh, and so on ad infinitum. If there is an eternity that rules in Socrates' definition of cause, it appears to be the eternity of universal natural flux, of all things emergent from their opposite. But Socrates has not said his last word. He interrupts his argument in order to explain his method of inquiry once again (at 101D), this time at greater length than before (at 100A) and with the evident intention of accounting for his recent speeches, all of which had turned on what he had postulated as being safe and safest.

Socrates recapitulates his method in the form of an address to Kebes. If the question is How do one and one become two? insist very loudly (*mega an booēs*) (101C) that the cause is the participation of the ones in duality, and that is the only way you can understand it. Leave other sorts of answers to the clever talkers. Fearful of blundering, you would cleave to the safe hypothesis that the cause is in the being of the thing. Then if the hypothesis itself is attacked or questioned, do not reply until you have had time to consider its implications, and whether they agree with one another. Then, if you must, you would support it by hypothesizing another hypothesis, which would appear to be the best of the higher ones, and so on until you reached something that satisfied. Do not become entangled in discussion of the first hypothesis and its implications, which is what the irresponsible wranglers do who produce confusion. If Kebes is one of the philosophers, he will do as Socrates has just said. Most true, say Simmias and Kebes at the same time, the two as one (102A).

We have of course done the forbidden thing in speculating about the ground of the original hypothesis and in so doing were led into doubt, as he foretold. It is unthinkable that Socrates would stifle discussion in order to suppress the truth, or would lie to avoid defeat in argument, but it is not unthinkable that he would have in mind philosophy's affiliation with music. He says nothing here to indicate what higher hypothesis he would generate in order to support his actual one were it to be called in question. We may suppose that his inventiveness in ascending the scale of hypotheses would be guided by his understanding of the good for the humanity he has insisted was an object of his caring. Without any doubt, the good as it appeared to his wisdom would be the cause that metamorphosed a darkling natural truth into a poem of lambent beauty.

At this point once again, Phaedo's retelling of the discourse in prison is interrupted by a brief exchange between himself and Echecrates (102A). Echecrates cannot refrain from breaking in to join the remote Simmias and Kebes in approving Socrates' description of the philosophic method. In his opinion, earnestly entertained as the oath by god testifies, Socrates had made these things amazingly manifest to anyone with a little intelligence. Phaedo assures him that everyone who was there at the time was of the same opinion. Echecrates, whose qualifications are not disclosed in any detail, replies to the effect that hearing the report is by itself sufficient for those who were not present. It is for the reader to judge whether Echecrates speaks for the credulity or for the diffidence of those who subscribe to what must be profoundly unclear to them because it is unclear in itself, as Socrates will admit in his eventual palinode.

Phaedo resumes his report. Having gained agreement to his doctrine of the being of each distinct *eidos* or Idea, Socrates moves on to a proof that individual things can participate in opposite Ideas although no Idea can participate in its own opposite Idea. Simmias can be bigger than Socrates and at the same time smaller than Phaedo, which proves that Simmias can be bigger and smaller at the same time, which proves in turn that Simmias participates simultaneously in large and small. Socrates has to laugh (102D) as he says these things. He explains his way of speaking as caused by his desire that Kebes share his opinion, which is not necessarily flattering to Kebes. As Socrates continues, he makes the point that the greatness in us is in a state of repulsion from the smallness in us, so that although they are somehow both present in us, they cannot abide one another. If smallness advances on greatness, the latter either simply takes itself off or, at least, retreats. We may speak of the members of this territorial pair as dilating and contracting "within" us while we ourselves remain constant in size, although what exactly we mean when we speak so is at least uncertain and at worst reduces "the Idea of small" to a mere comparative, "smaller than something else." Oddly, it is exactly the corporeal "we" who remain unchanged in magnitude while the incorporeal big-itself and small-itself not only change place and size but do so in the perverse way that sees the small becoming larger and the large shrinking into evanescence. Socrates gives the impression of having resumed his pre-Anaxagorean voyage.

Someone in the company—Plato has it that Phaedo was unable to remember who it was—spoke up with some energy (103A) to observe that the doctrine of the mutual repulsion of opposites seemed opposite to the earlier doctrine that everything comes into being out of its opposite, especially death out of life and life necessarily out of death, hence the immortality of the soul. Opposition had been represented as the source of generation, and now is made a condition of destruction. Socrates easily explains the difference between the state of things that bear the names of their incorporeal forms, as a thing of beauty does, and the form itself, which is beauty or the beautiful. Beautiful objects, as generated, must have become beautiful and therefore must have been opposite to beautiful before beauty caused them to be beautiful. Nothing of the kind can be said about beauty itself, which never becomes, always is, and never having been produced cannot have been produced out of its opposite, with which it absolutely cannot mingle.

Kebes cannot deny that some things still disturb him (103C), though he does not say what they are. Perhaps what troubled Kebes is that, by the rule of opposite arising from opposite, not only must a truth grow from an untruth, but an untruth, perhaps a beautiful lie, grows out of a caring truth. Uninterrupted by any demand for clarification, Socrates extends his previous doctrine that the opposing Forms retreat and advance on one another, as the great and small maneuver within a human being like mutually repellent magnetic poles or propositions placed in tension by the principle of contradiction. Socrates argues now that the force of mutual repulsion or contradiction operates not only in the realm of the Forms but also in some instances in the world of the concrete objects that take their names from their incorporeal causes. He illustrates his thought by showing that snow, or, we might add, some cold-bearing thing like a poisonous drug, which is cold but certainly is not "the Cold," must retreat from fire, which is hot but equally certainly is not "the Hot" or heat itself; or, we might further add, the heat-bearing must keep its distance from the cold-bearing. The penalty for failure of the concrete to avoid the opposite abstract which is present in something concrete is destruction. To us who read, this appears like a premonitory description of the onset of death, of Socrates' death, without reference to the departure of a soul. Moreover, there are things that are so closely identified with their governing cause that they are called by its very name, as the number three is always to be called odd after "the Odd" and the number four to be called even after "the Even." All of the odd numbers are as eternally odd as is the Odd itself, and so with the even numbers. The Odd and the Even contradict each other by virtue of their being and their definition: they are immiscible and irreconcilable, so that where one is present in a thing the other must be absent. However, two things can be imbued respectively with contrary Ideas without themselves being contrary to one another, as three and four cannot be called "contrary." Socrates is now (104B) in a position to make clear what he has been aiming to prove, and he does so by the repeated use of the word "Idea": things that are not themselves contrary to each other but always contain contrary Ideas must repel the Idea contrary to their own or be destroyed. Three would perish before becoming even. He repeats himself: it is not only Ideas that repel their opposites; some other things do so as well. He would like to know what those things are. His inquiry produces a striking turn in his discourse. As we shall see, his emphatic introduction of the Ideas by name is the prelude to an argument that replaces them with their surrogates, as an odd thing might replace the Odd, in the course of the ongoing demonstration that the soul is imperishable after death. The descent from the plane of the Ideas to the plane of the things that carry the Ideas is necessary for the progress of his argument.

Beginning at 105A, Socrates repeats his image of the bearers of the Ideas, such as five as the bearer of the Odd, fending away the opposite Idea as it approaches in the persona of a concrete even number. As his example of an even repelling the Odd he gives ten, which he happens to mention is "the double," presumably the double of five. Whether the odd five and the even two should be said to have "admitted" each other as multipliers in this fanciful logistic we cannot say, but what they have not done is to admit the opposite Idea. Now Socrates proposes to start over from the beginning. He makes clear immediately that the recommencement he has in mind is far-reaching, for he admonishes Kebes that he should answer questions not out of Socrates' vocabulary but according to what he Socrates will do. What Socrates does first is to retreat from the doctrine that he had earlier (at 100D) called the safest, which was to the effect that the cause of the beauty of a beautiful thing is Beauty or the Beautiful. Now he has become able to see a better and no less safe explanation. If the question is What in a hot body makes it hot? he will no longer give the simpleminded (*amathē*) (105C) answer that is safe, namely, Heat, but the more polished answer, namely, fire, which is a material element, as Anaxagoras knew. Likewise, what is present in the sick body that makes it sick is not Sickness but fever-fire (*puretos*). An odd number is odd not because of Oddness but because of the unit (*monas*), by which unit he seems to mean not the number one but some alternative to the two that is a factor of every even number.[5]

Socrates has now prepared the ground for his conclusion regarding the posthumous imperishability of the soul. What, if it be in the body, makes the body be alive? The soul, always. A thing is alive by virtue of the presence in it of soul, not of "Life," according to the recent revision. As one might say, the soul is to Life as fire is to Heat. At this point, the reader might know more than he thinks he knows, as the human being in general possesses knowledge of which he is unaware before it is drawn from him by fruitful questioning. We have been told that a hyperactivity of the soul in speech heats the body, fortifying the life within it to such a degree that the body fends off the cooling, or death, that the poison drug brings with it. We have been told also that sickness is the state of a body in which the hot fever-fire is present in excess. We will know soon enough that Socrates perishes when the cold brought by the drug expels the retreating fire in his body. We know that health, which is the state of unthreatened vitality, is a balance or equipoise or measure within the body, which dies when the life-fire sinks or flares out of some proportion. Socrates' repudiation of his safe but simplistic doctrine of the Ideas as causes has put him in a position strikingly reminiscent of Anaxagoras's, wherein the action of the natural elements, say Cause, was seen by Socrates to replace Mind, meaning good, as the sovereign principle of all things.

Socrates' interrogatory demonstration moves forward rapidly. The soul bears life to whatever it seizes on. The opposite to life is death. The soul cannot admit death. Now Socrates relies on a parallel

---

5. Hobbes did not do justice to the Socrates of this remarkable revisionist statement when he declaimed against the "tudes," "ties," and "nesses" of the traditional philosophy.

that is affected by the peculiarities of a mere privative: he speaks of that which does not admit the Idea of the even by using for the first time the privative term "uneven" (*anartion*) (106C) rather than directly the very familiar "odd" (*perriton*). In the same mode, what does not admit the just or the musical are the unjust and amusic. Similarly, what does not admit death is the amortal (*athanatos*). This had been granted long since. In the present context it is supposed to serve as the premise for the demonstration that the soul is also indestructible. As the immediate sequel will show, Socrates is no closer to proving the imperishability of the soul now than he was before he embarked on the tortuous argument we have been compelled to follow. He proceeds by way of a series of conditionals (106A–C). If the Uneven (*anartion*) were indestructible, so also would be the number three; and if the heatless (*athermon*) were indestructible, so also would be snow, which would simply retreat from heat and not be dissolved by it. Likewise, the coldless thing, if it were indestructible, would survive the approach of a cold thing and would leave in indestructibility. Finally, if the amortal is indestructible, it cannot be destroyed when death approaches it. But the soul is amortal. Therefore the soul cannot be destroyed when death approaches it: it is indestructible.

Socrates is fully aware that his reasoning is subject to doubt. The unconvinced might ask why it is not possible that although the odd can indeed not become even when approached by an even, it can indeed be destroyed on the approach of an even and be replaced by that even? Why must it always go away unscathed? We would hardly know how to understand the metaphor of "approach" and "retreat" on the part of incorporeal things if Socrates himself had not referred to the five that became ten upon what we may suppose can be called the "approach" of two. Five did not become even, and nothing could possibly ever make it even, but neither did it "go away" to retreat into its sheltering oddness. It disappeared, swallowed up in ten, which is thoroughly even. This seems to be the thought implicit in the objection contemplated by the supposed skeptic, who is of course Socrates himself. Socrates allows the obvious truth that one could not refute this view of the matter by simply denying that the thing perished, for the uneven is not imperishable (*to gar anartion ouk anōlethron estin*) (106C). This concession appears to compromise the demonstration profoundly, as the sequel confirms. The crucial part of Socrates' argument lies in the speculation that the threatened thing retreats or "goes away" when the hostile opposite approaches, in that way avoiding destruction. What is to be proved is that the soul goes away, which is a locution for being at the same time topical and indestructible. Socrates offers no such proof, but says rather that if only it were granted that the immortal is imperishable, the soul would be imperishable by virtue of its immortality. Under such a stipulation, however, Socrates' ponderous argument would have been unnecessary from the beginning. Kebes, however, is quick to grant without further discussion that the immortal is indestructible, for how could anything repel destruction if the immortal, being eternal, admitted it? Socrates thinks that god and the idea (*eidos*)[6] of life and whatever else is immortal would be agreed by all never to be destroyed. We for our part can hardly doubt that the idea of life, which for all we have been told about it might be a law of thermal equipoise, does not admit what it contradicts in reason or logic, namely, death, but we may doubt whether the indestructibility of god or of the idea of life can be explained in terms of the retreat of either of those incorporeals from destruction by a "going away" of any description. The sustained metaphor of removal before a hostile approach transfers the issues to the realm of imagination, where Socrates would be the first to deny that they might be brought to a satisfactory conclusion. But Kebes stands by his concurrence in the proof, as he takes it to be, that the conditional is a demonstration, and the immortal is indestructible. Socrates declares the outcome: the soul is assuredly immortal and imperishable, and our souls will really exist in Hades (107A). It is left to Simmias to wonder if the whole matter is not beyond resolution by human weakness. In response, Socrates applauds Simmias and makes a decisive concession: the first hypotheses of the argument, however you may believe in them, should be investigated more carefully. When you have looked into them satisfactorily, I think you will follow the argument as much as it is within the power of a human being to follow it. If this is clear to you, you will not investigate further (107B).

Were any suspicion to arise that Socrates was unaware of the question-begging that supported his demonstrations, or that he did not know how far from apodeictic was his construction that made the

---

6. The translation of *eidos* as idea may be problematic but is more intelligible in the context than the usual form or species.

Ideas and immortality mutually dependent, that suspicion should now be replaced by the certainty that Socrates had never abandoned his assimilation of philosophy to music. To complete his project, Socrates, in what follows, will construct an immense geological myth that illustrates the caring deed of the man who knows what he and his fellow human beings cannot know at the same time that he knows what they need and yearn to know and what they incline, perhaps one should say incline naturally, to believe that they know. The geological myth that Socrates is about to generate is a story of the whole with a view to hereafter, a tale that will describe a landscape fit to encompass our existence while we live and then to contain the peregrinations of that absolute anomaly, the incorporeal that mimics body in locomotion. Such a paradoxical entity would be a standing demonstration that a thing can admit into itself a quality that is in direct contradiction to its constituting Idea. Socrates goes about to describe the scene of that entity's travels and of our own.

We must in the first place be mindful that there is a hereafter in which judgment is rendered on the soul for the life that was lived. There must be such a condition, and more concretely there must be a place to accommodate it, for if death were the end it would be a relief and a discharge for the wicked (107C). Then the murderers and the ones who commit outrage against their parents would suffer only such punishment as the laws of cities can prescribe, and all justice would be sublunary; but in the world of Socrates' myth there is a rendering of evil for evil and good for good in the venue of justice postmortem. But the soul appears (*phainetai*) to be immortal, and could in no way at all escape from evils or be saved except by becoming as good and as wise as possible. About this hint of rehabilitation nothing further is said, no word about taking the soul aside and improving it with homilies and admonishments (who would administer them?). Socrates' proemium to his edifying geology dwells more on the fate of the wicked than of the good, although he portrays each as having befall it what should befall it (*tuchontas de ekei hōn dei tuchein*) (107E). The orderly and wise leave life willingly, each conducted by his lifelong *daimōn*, every human being (of course not only Socrates) having one such; but the other soul struggles against separation from its body, and flaps about the senseless ashes during some long period after these were committed to the earth. Eventually the deplorable souls are led off to judgment, to a distinct place where, if they were unusually atrocious, they are avoided as pariahs by the other transparencies. The good and pure have their own condign destinations. The time has arrived for Socrates to reveal the grand topography of these and all other happenings. He lets it be known directly that the earth in all its wonders is not as the usual geologists say it is, and of this he has been persuaded by someone. We know that he listened at length to Timaeus, who spun his tale of the earth and the whole with a view to explaining the cosmos as the setting for the life of the human being and for the existence of the society of human beings on this earth in this life, at best in the good city. Socrates' myth will go further in aiming to describe a material world in which not only the incarnate but the disembodied can live and move and have their being. But we know too that Socrates had recently been reminded by the Eleatic Stranger of a feature of Parmenides' cosmology[7] that will soon come to the surface in Socrates' own myth. As his tale unfolds, we will be better able to judge whether the geogony of Timaeus's revisionist Pythagoreanism or the cosmology of Parmenides as invoked by the Eleatic Stranger could have informed the forthcoming Socratic myth.

In yet another testimony to his awareness that much of what we might need and yearn to know is beyond us, Socrates says that he does not expect to prove the truth of what he is about to propose, and even if he had the knowledge necessary to do so he would not have the necessary time. What he will do is to describe what he is persuaded is nothing less than the Idea of the earth (*tēn idean tēs gēs*) (108D). The Idea of the earth will prove to be composed of two things of which he says he has become persuaded—one a well-known speculation, expressed in the conditional mood, on what holds the earth up and the other an edifying vision presented as an article of belief. First, if the spherical earth with its matter uniform about its center is itself at the center of a homogeneous whole, it will be held in place by the equilibrium of pressure (*isorropia*) (109A) on all sides. This doctrine, well expressed much earlier by Parmenides, has the apparent effect in Socrates' scheme of implying a natural geology in which the earth is supported against falling neither by the air, which is dispar-

---

7. "On all sides like the mass of a well-rounded sphere, equally weighted in all directions from the middle; for neither greater nor less must needs be on this or that." *Sophist* 244E, Fowler trans. (Loeb Classical Library; Cambridge: Harvard Univ. Press, 1961).

aged in the sequel, nor by the god. The second element of the Idea is a long and intricate myth of the world that helps us to see ourselves as living in a valley of death and pollutions. This mélange is the Idea of the earth—a mythic construction that could imaginably pretend to rival Genesis but could in no way claim to be the eternal intelligible of Platonic orthodoxy.

Our portion of the immense earth is pockmarked by the corrosions of the water, mist, and air that have settled out of the pure surrounding ether onto the pure earth, lodging in hollows whose rims are the human habitation. To ask how the pure ether could have been the source of the precipitate that pollutes our earthly abode would be to quibble across the grain of the fabulous construction. The polluted hollows that are our home are very numerous and of very various Ideas and sizes (*pantodapa kai tas ideas kai ta megethē*) (109B). In this sentence, in which Socrates pronounces the word "idea" for the last time in his life, he is tacitly and in fact maintaining that there are many ideas of a single thing (the hollow) rather than the one idea of many things. No exposition of the Platonic Ideas is acceptable if it fails to measure the distance between the idealism of the youthful Socrates portrayed in *Parmenides* and echoed in the safe but stupid logistic, and that of the philosopher in the hour of his death. As will soon be seen, this departure from what is conventionally received as the orthodox Socratic idealism accompanies a parallel turn in Socrates' doctrine of Cause following his earlier rejection of the safe and simple linking of Idea and Cause that added nothing to understanding.

Socrates begins to elaborate the second element of the Idea of the earth (109B). The stratum of earth on which we live is to the true earth in its entirety as the bottom of the ocean is to the shore at the surface of the waters. If a sea creature could rise from the slime and darkness of the ocean bottom, it would see a brighter and more beautiful world than anything it could have known in its environment of corrosive brine. In the same way, if a human being could take wing and rise to the top of the sea of air and vapor that surrounds and corrodes our earth, he would see such light and beauty as could never come within his experience in our atmosphere. The earth that he saw there would be as (*hōs*) (110E) the true earth, the earth that is bathed in the true light under the true heaven. Socrates explains the cause (*to aition*) (110E) of the perfect beauty of the higher world: certainly not the presence in it of beauty itself but rather the absence from it of corrosive air and water, an explanation that might have been expected from the dismissed Anaxagoras, for it appeals to the action of the material elements rather than to *nous* as Cause. Socrates portrays an upper geography of precious stones and precious metals, an earth so effulgent that to behold it is to be blessed (*eudaimonon*) (111A), a place of islands in a sea of air under ethereal heaven, islands that he gives us reason to think of as islands of the blessed. The men who inhabit the upper region are free from disease and live to great age because of the mildness of the climate. Their senses of sight and hearing and even their wisdom greatly exceed ours because of the purity of the material medium in which they live. Men see and speak with the gods, and they see the sun, moon, and stars as they really are; and their other blessedness is consistent with these. This concludes Socrates' description of the upper region of the earth. It depicts a place in which the perceptible things and the senses of perception exist in a perfected condition, as do the living bodies of the inhabitants. The greatest good is the clear perception of the heavenly bodies. This upper region is the abode of incarnate human beings, not of ghosts; and the objects visible to them are not beauty but beautiful things which are visible literally, not metaphorically. Socrates has conjured an idyll of a corporeal world in which body is not a vehicle of corruption or the medium of distorted perception. He has sung a myth of earth in the age of Kronos, the world as it would be under the hand of god, not as it is in its rotation on the spindle of natural cause.

Now Socrates turns his musical attention to the world below our own. Various ducts lead from our world down into a vast system of streams flowing in fantastic convolutions of water, fire, and muddy earth in an endless flux accompanied by the blasts of a mighty wind. There is a ceaseless circulation of fluids between our world and the infernal region, the waters rising and falling again through our rivers, lakes, and oceans, with fiery mud and stone erupting into our landscape. It is to that region of flowing water, fire, earth, and air that the souls go for doom. Unnamed judges assign punishments and rewards to the ordinary run of mankind, who receive finite sentences that include credit earned for good behavior during life. The incorrigibly atrocious are thrown into Tartarus, where they remain forever. Corrigible, penitent murderers receive minimum sentences of a year in Tartarus, after which they may petition their victims for pardon and release. Those who had lived exemplary lives (*to hosiōs biōnai*)

(114B) are freed to ascend to a life in the pure upper earth, while those who had purified themselves with philosophy will live forever without bodies in places of a beauty that transcends description. The case for proper living appears to rest heavily on the principle of retributive justice, at least as Socrates makes the case before those who cannot be trusted to choose the best life as good in itself.

As Socrates says, a man in his right mind would not insist that everything is as the myth has it (114D), but since the soul appears to be immortal, such a man might well risk believing it, for it is a risk worth taking. A man should recite such things to himself like incantations, which is why Socrates says he has spun his myth at such length. In his early exchange with Kebes on exorcising the fear of death (77E), Socrates had already recommended the daily repetition of reassuring incantations as a remedy, and had not rejected the description of himself as a chanter of such epodes. Socrates all but declares that he has been giving an example of a philosopher, understood as a virtuous man who had deafened himself to the lyric of his body during life, on the point of death reciting to himself an encouraging tale. His reason for doing so cannot be to persuade himself to a belief in a story that he is fabricating. Nor does he persuade his hearers to such a belief, as will soon become apparent when they display all the grief that death inspires in natural humanity, and for which he will rebuke them only gently. This is not to say that multitudes might not be comforted and improved by an image like the one he had conjured; but in the context of the cosmology that has evolved in the discourses beginning with *Theaetetus* it is more reasonable to construe Socrates' myth as the completion of the account of humanity's existence in a world that does not favor humanity, and in which philosophy shows its care for mankind by subjugating their fears and hopes to retributive justice. In the world as Socrates discovers and reforms it, the duties that would be discharged by a self-revealing and legislating god are assumed by default by a philosophic poet, a singer of the highest music, and the evil that would be insinuated by a seducing satan is ascribed to corrupting body. As Socrates brings his myth to a close, he reverts to the theme that has dominated his discourse from the outset: man's good lies in living apart from his body and tending to the soul. This is his abiding formula for the exhortation to avoid disgracing the mind by preoccupying it with petty things. It is a counsel of perfection that philosophy has neither power nor hope to impose or enforce, only the power to commend and exemplify, for it belongs to philosophy to acknowledge that it is of the nature of the things of this world that reason consort with body, and that man compose his mind to the knowledge that his wisdom must forever be as well limited as guided by what lies beyond it in the regions of the uncertain. Taught the virtues of concessive serenity and indomitable courage, the philosopher becomes the paradigm of morality, joining in his soul the virtues that nature had put asunder. Socrates has propounded an enlightenment that is at the same time a new religion.

It is time for Socrates to die, and he declares himself ready to go. Crito, ever the natural Everyman, solicits Socrates' last instructions or wishes regarding the family he is about to leave fatherless. Socrates has no particular request, but admonishes them to attend diligently to themselves and then they will do well in all things, for him and for his family and for themselves. It can be supposed and must be hoped that Socrates did not mean by this gentle instruction that his friends should succor the widow and three orphans with homilies on rising above the pangs of hunger. Rather, from their proper care for themselves, from the goodness that must be learned yet cannot be taught, must emanate the righteous caring for others that is wise and firm and gentle.

Crito would like to know from Socrates how the friends should dispose of his body. Socrates tells the others, with a quiet smile, that Crito still believes that the real Socrates is the flesh and not the soul. All the talk to the effect that he is now about to go where he will enjoy an exquisite bliss seems to have been without effect on the others, who like Crito remain as they must, rooted in their natural humanity unless they learn from his example what his words can never teach them.

Preparations go forward. Socrates bathes what will soon be his corpse. He takes lengthy leave of the family of his body and rejoins his friends, the company in which he thinks it is better for him to die. The jailer arrives with an ominous announcement. He is full of the praise of Socrates and of apology for what he must do, and he weeps. Many times a bringer of death but still touched when it kills a dear one, he is another Crito in the natural humanity that will never give over mourning. Socrates in turn is touched by the good man's grace and by the generosity of his tears, but he wishes to proceed to what must be done and asks Crito to see to the poison. Crito would procrastinate, but he is sent on his errand by Socrates, who refuses to become ridiculous to himself by contriving a stay. The poison is brought, and Socrates would pour a libation of it to some being, but he may not, lest too little be left to kill him. He must pray to the gods for a prosperous voyage without sharing with them his lethal potion. Then he drinks, with the courage and resignation that generate one another and that his life has shown to be the twin virtue taught to itself by philosophy. The company breaks down in grief. Socrates rebukes their weakness and they compose themselves in shame. As the poison takes effect, the life or the soul or the heat begins to leave his body from the feet upwards. He has time to say, "Crito, we owe a cock to Asklepios, so give in return what is owed (*apodote*) and do not neglect it." Then the cold reached his heart, heat was expelled, and he was gone. His eyes and his mouth remained open in death, a blind and muted index to the manner of his living.

He seems to have died in the piety and justice of Kephalos, not only mindful of the gods but respectful of the rule that prescribes giving back for what one has received. Forgotten is his outlandish objection to this maxim as the definition of justice, on the ground that it would require restoring a weapon to a lunatic (*Republic* 1). That captious refutation, so unmindful of the legitimate rule of wisdom over justice, was hostile to the ordinary sense of rightness without which social life would disintegrate immediately. It is to this ordinary and recognizable notion of right that Socrates makes recommendation in his last moment. In the same act, he pays his respects to the popular piety by making his gesture of gratitude to the god of healing as if for a great cure. The disease of which Socrates is at last purged is of course life in the body. The god whom the multitude of natural humanity sees as patronizing the cure of ailing flesh for the prolonging of life is thanked by Socrates in symbolic gratitude for being rid of the body's ills by being rid of the body and life at once. In a single act of speech, his very last, Socrates has demonstrated the deference to the demands of common life that is required of every heedful human being; and he has in the same act of speech succeeded in defying the common understanding, from which he had always withdrawn himself, with earthly consequences now concluded. In dying as in living, he withdrew himself as an incommensurable, but unobtrusively and caringly, withal imperfectly.

Plato does not neglect to record the panegyric on Socrates as the best and the wisest and most just of the men of his time who were known to his companions.

SELECTIVE INDEX
OF NAMES

Achilles, 154
Adeimantus, 186
Aesop, 179
Alcibiades, 15, 80
Anaxagoras, 28, 153, 188, 203, 204, 206, 208, 213, 215, 221
Anytus, 151
Apollo, 198
Aristeides, 36
Aristophanes, 146, 167, 187
Aristotle, 10, 28nn2–4, 59, 166
Asklepios, 224
Atreus, 117

Bible, 126

Cadmus, 202
Callias, 4, 15
Chaerephon, 147
Cicero, 175
Cratylus, 29
Critias, 15

Diogenes Laertius, ix, 29, 175

Echecrates, 177, 178, 199, 208, 212
Eden, 130
Emile, 130
Empedocles, 37
Epicharmus, 37
Epimetheus, 7, 26
Eubulides, 29
Eucleides, 27, 29–31, 49, 178
Euphronius, 31, 45
Eurytos, 30
Evenus, 180

Glaucon, 186

Harmonia, 202
Hector, 154
Heraclitus, 37, 46, 48, 176
Hermes, 9, 117
Hermogenes, 29
Hesiod, 5, 163
Hippias, 15
Hippocrates, 4–6

Hobbes, 8, 34, 166, 170–72
Homer, 5, 37, 48, 163, 201

Isocrates, 30

Kephalos, 180, 224
Kronos, 117–19, 221

Lycurgus, 137
Lykon, 151

Machiavelli, 8, 35, 140
Meletus 61–64, 66, 67, 151–53
Melissus, 48, 49
Musaeus, 163

Nietzsche, 176

Orpheus, 163

Patroclus, 154
Pericles, 6, 79
Philolaos, 30
Pittacus, 16–19
Prodicus, 15, 17, 37
Prometheus, 7, 8, 26, 157
Pythagoras, 178

Rousseau, 166

Simon, 175
Simonides, 5, 16–20
Solon, 137
Spinoza, 34, 126

Terpsion, 27, 29–31, 178
Thales, 45
Thrasymachus, 47
Thyestes, 117
Timaeus, 219

Xanthippe, 179

Zeus, 8, 9, 104, 107n8, 117–20, 134, 153, 173, 185
Zopyrus, 175, 176

227